Ian. S

Gambling on Growth

Gambling on Growth

How to Manage the
Small High-Tech Firm

STUART SLATTER
London Business School

JOHN WILEY & SONS
Chichester · New York · Brisbane · Toronto · Singapore

Other Wiley Editorial Offices

John Wiley & Sons, Inc., 605 Third Avenue,
New York, NY 10158-0012, USA

Jacaranda Wiley Ltd, G.P.O. Box 859, Brisbane,
Queensland 4001, Australia

John Wiley & Sons (Canada) Ltd, 22 Worcester Road,
Rexdale, Ontario M9W 1L1, Canada

John Wiley & Sons (SEA) Pte Ltd, 37 Jalan Pemimpin #05-04,
Block B, Union Industrial Building, Singapore 2057

Library of Congress Cataloging-in-Publication Data

Slatter, Stuart St. P.
    Gambling on growth : how to manage the small high-tech firm
    Stuart Slatter.
        p. cm.
    Includes bibliographical references and index.
    ISBN 0-471-93558-1
    1. High technology industries—Management. 2. Small business—
    —Management. 3. New business enterprises—Management. I. Title.
    HD62.37.S57 1992
    658.02′2—dc20   92–11483
                                                                  CIP

British Library Cataloguing in Publication Data

A catalogue record for this book is available from the British Library

ISBN 0-471-93558-1

Typeset in 11/13pt Palatino by
Mathematical Composition Setters Ltd, Salisbury, Wiltshire
Printed and bound in Great Britain by
Biddles, Ltd, Guildford and King's Lynn

To
Alexis

Contents

Acknowledgements

This book would never have been possible without the generosity of the UK partners of Coopers & Lybrand, who sponsored the research project on which this book is based. Several partners were involved in making it happen, but I would like to pay particular thanks to Peter Allen and John Stuttard for their help and encouragement in getting the project off the ground.

Over 150 executives in small high-tech firms and several venture capitalists gave their time generously to this project. I hope they will feel the resulting book is useful in enhancing the performance of their businesses. While it maybe invidious to single out individuals, I would like to thank Richard Henshell, the Chairman of PAFEC Ltd and Peter Englander of APAX Partners for providing a sanity check on the manuscript from the practitioners' perspective.

While the responsibility for the context of the book clearly lies with me, I would like to acknowledge the ideas of the three researchers who worked on this project under my direction, Priya King, Peter Gist and Anna Maria Garden. Without their efforts, many of the ideas discussed in this book would never have been explored. The following MBA students at the London Business School helped with data collection: Michael Bunney, Dorothy Cassells, David Clarke, Julie Green, Jon Horton, Pam Robertson, David Ryan, Matt Thomas and John Vernon. To all of them I am extremely grateful.

As a researcher one depends on colleagues for constructive criticism. Various colleagues in the Strategic and International Management Department at the London Business School have provided useful comments, but I am particularly indebted to Dr Michael Hay for his comments on my first draft of this book. Various chapters have benefited from in-put from other colleagues in other departments most notably Chapter 5 from Dr Stuart Timperley and Chapter 7 from Professor Kenneth Simmonds.

The preparation of a manuscript is always a thankless task, but I have been most fortunate in having had expert secretarial help from both Yolande Smith and Hilda Silverman, who have made the task as painless as possible. To both of them, I am extremely grateful.

Finally, and most importantly, I would like to thank Clare Warburg for her creative genius in thinking up the title of the book, which I think captures the essence of small high-tech firms.

TRADEMARKS

Ethernet is a trademark of Xerox Corporation.
Acorn Computer is a trademark of Acorn Computers Group Plc, now owned by Olivetti.
Macintosh Computer is a trademark of Apple Computer Inc.
MS-DOS is a trademark of Microsoft Corporation.
*VisiCalc is a trademark of Visicorp.
Apple II is a trademark of Apple Computer Inc.
SPARC chip is a trademark of Sun Microsystems.
8800 processor is a trademark of Motorola Inc.
UNIX is a trademark, developed by Bell Labs, commercialized by AT&T.
Lotus and 1-2-3 is a trademark of Lotus Development Corporation.
VisiCalc is a trademark of Visicorp.

1
The Fragile Firm

Small high-tech firms require a different management approach from that commonly used in either large or small firms which are not technology based. This book explores the strategies and management practices used by the more successful small high-tech firms, and explains why successful growth is hard to achieve and then difficult to sustain.

Small high-tech firms are important to a nation's economy: many of them are innovators and developers of tomorrow's industrial technology on which future economic progress depends. When these firms grow fast they rapidly become glamour companies and the focus of attention for the press and the business community. However, among the large number of high-tech start-ups each year, very few become fast growth companies, and even fewer manage to retain fast growth for a sustained period of time. The few that grow fast for a sustained period become household names like Compaq and Apple Computer, although as shown later in the book these companies have all had hiccups on the way to where they are today. Each decade sees the birth of new glamour companies. In the 1980s we saw the birth of Sun Microsystems, Compaq, and Conner Peripherals. Compaq, which started up in 1982, became the fastest growing firm in US history, being the first to reach *Fortune* 500 status in less than four years. After five years sales revenues exceeded $1 billion, but Compaq was soon overtaken by Conner Peripherals, which exceeded the $1 billion sales level in its fourth year of operation. While these firms receive the media attention, there are an enormous number of small high-tech firms which grow at a slower pace or fail to grow at all.

DEFINING THE SMALL HIGH-TECH FIRM

There is no single definition of what constitutes a small firm or what constitutes a high-technology industry. How small is small? How advanced does technology have to be before it is classified as high tech? Answering these questions early in the book is important not only so that the reader can put the many management issues into context, but also because the characteristics which describe a firm as being a small high-tech firm have a considerable influence over the firm's strategy and the way in which it is implemented.

The Meaning of High Tech

High-tech industries are those built on exploiting new scientific advances that have been developed over the past 20 years. They are industries which are growing rather than declining, and above all they are industries where the firms within those industries are using product (or process) technology as a major source of competitive advantage.

High tech means different things to different people. The commonly used criteria to define high tech are product or process sophistication, research and development intensity, and the proportion of technical employees within the work force.

Product or process sophistication. Within industry, high tech is often used to refer to new, sophisticated products or manufacturing processes. The products and processes are often technologically complex and embody innovative advances in product design (product innovation) or in the manufacturing process (process innovation). Although products and processes do not have to be described as "leading edge" from a technological point of view to be "high tech", all high-tech industries use technology as a critical source of competitive advantage.

Research and development intensity. Research and development
(R & D) expenditure when expressed as a percentage of total
industry sales is often used as a criterion for selecting high-tech
industries. R & D activity is a reasonable proxy for technologically sophisticated output and is a good selection criterion
for industries in the early stages of product development.
Industries spending more than 5% of sales revenues on R & D
may qualify as high-tech industries using this criterion. However, most firms that regard themselves as high tech in the US
spend double this percentage. The US Semiconductor Industry
Association calculates its sector average as 11%, while a group
of nine successful chip makers, all of whom were start-ups
during the 1980s, invested 17% of sales in research and
development in 1988.[1]

Technical employees. Employees with a high degree of
technical/professional training play a critical role in high-tech
industries. Engineers, computer scientists, life scientists and
technicians of various types account for over 10% of the total
number of employees in most high-tech industries. Such
industries, therefore, tend to have a significant portion of
well-educated employees.

No single criterion is adequate by itself to define high tech
since some industries which rank high on one criterion rank
low on others. The petroleum refining industry, for example,
ranks high on per cent of technical employees but relatively
low on perceived product sophistication and the R & D intensity scales. The firms which are the subject of this book operate
in industries which meet all three of the criteria discussed
above. There are ten three-digit standard industrial classification (SIC) codes that meet all three criteria.[2] They are shown
in Table 1.1. Due to the broad definition of three- and even
some four-digit SIC categories, some product sectors that fall
outside these codes will have all the characteristics of high tech
so far described (e.g. some sectors of the medical instruments
and photographic industry). Definitions using SIC codes are
rarely perfect but give the reader a "feel" for the types of
industries covered under the "high tech" banner.

It is a common misunderstanding to equate high tech with
high growth since the popular press tends to focus on the high-
tech growth sectors of high-tech industries. While data from

Table 1.1 Principal high-tech sectors

SIC Code	Title	High-tech Employees as Percentage of Total (1)	R & D as Percentage of Sales (2)
376	Space Vehicles and Guided Missiles	41.2	12.2*
357	Office Computing Machines	26.7	11.6
381	Engineering, Laboratory and Scientific Instruments	26.4	5.3*
366	Communications Equipment	21.9	7.4
383	Optical Instruments and Lenses	19.8	6.3*
372	Aircraft and Parts	18.5	12.2*
283	Drugs	17.7	6.3
382	Measuring and Control Instruments	14.1	5.3*
367	Electronic Components and Assembly	12.8	7.4
737	Computer Programming Services	Not available	Not available

(1) High-tech employees include engineers, computer scientists, scientists and mathematicians; data is for 1980.
(2) 1979 data; 1990s percentages likely to be higher; asterisk (*) indicates percentage is average of more than one three-digit code.
Source: Adapted by permission from Markusen, A., Hall, P. and Glasmeier, A. *High Tech America*. Allen & Unwin, Boston (1986).

Inc. magazine shows that high-tech industries do indeed grow faster than most industries, this is *not always* true. In the 1987 *Inc.* 500 list of the fastest growing firms in the USA, 183 were classified as high technology related firms. Five of the top ten and 27 seven of the top 50 fastest growing firms in the list were high tech. [3] Firms on the 500 list averaged a 13-times increase in sales during the previous five-year period. In another listing—this time by *Venture* magazine—of the 50 fastest growing companies that broke the US$100m annual revenue barrier in ten years or less, half were computer related. [4] When compared to small firms in general, high-tech firms do tend to offer more opportunities for growth. However, rapid and sustained growth occurs in only a relatively small number of firms. There are many firms that can be classified as small high-tech firms which experience at best only modest growth, and at worst no growth and stagnation. The latter are sometimes referred to by venture capitalists as the "Living Dead".

How Small is Small?

Just as there is no one commonly used definition of high tech, so there is no wide agreement about how to define a small firm. Definitions of small firms typically revolve around the number of employees. The vast majority of the firms interviewed for the research underlying this book had less than 500 employees and the majority had between 50 and 150 employees. Using sales revenues to define small firms is more difficult, particularly in the service sector. Distribution businesses for example, may show comparatively high revenues but still have relatively few employees. Conversely, firms undertaking contract research or providing technical consulting services may have relatively low revenues and more employees. As a general guide, however, the majority of technology-based small firms are likely to have sales revenues of under US$100m, with the vast majority having sales revenues between US$5m and US$50m.

Quantitative measures alone, however, are not a good guide to defining a small firm. Small firms have a distinctive set of organizational characteristics, many of which continue long after the firm has exceeded the upper limits of size mentioned above. This is especially true for small high-tech firms which grow extremely fast, often at compound growth rates in excess of 100% per annum for five or more years. Such firms grow into "large" businesses, as defined by revenues and number of employees, but continue to exhibit the organizational characteristics of a small firm, even though on occasions revenues may be in excess of US$1 billion. The growth of Apple Computer and the management problems it faced in the mid 1980s provides a good example of such a company.[5] While these firms are no longer small, some of them have been included by way of examples throughout the book, where there are important lessons to be learned for firms yet to experience such explosive growth.

While size tends to define small, small firms also have other special characteristics which influence the way they are managed. Two characteristics stand out: the influence of the founder or founding team, and the firm's lack of resources. First a high proportion of small firms—particularly young firms which are predominant in high-tech sectors—are still managed by their founders or founding team. In some instances the founders may have relinquished management responsibility but will still exert influence through their equity control. Founders typically take executive roles in top management and exert a strong influence on the direction and success of the firm. With small firms the goals of the founder are usually the same as the corporate goals.

Besides the founder(s), the second characteristic of small firms is the firm's lack of resources—both financial and human. Small firms rarely have strong balance sheets. Many are undercapitalized, either because the founders do not wish to give up equity or because capital is difficult to obtain, particularly for very young firms who have yet to prove that they have a winning business. Resource constraints are not only financial. Human resources are also constrained. Managerial resources are generally thin and the firm's capabilities rather narrow. Resource constraints can show up in all areas of the business—both at the strategic level, where the firm drifts along not knowing how to control its own destiny, and at the operational level, where many technical, marketing, production and financial skills may be absent.

Types of Firm

However narrowly one defines small or high tech using the criteria discussed in the previous sections, there is still a wide range of business types that make up the small high-tech company sector. If we so wish, we can classify small high-tech firms into product and service firms, and then further classify the categories according to product or service characterization, such as the degree of product or service standardization, software versus hardware products, industrial products versus consumer products, capital goods versus consumable items, products for OEMs (original equipment manufacturers) versus end users, etc. In practice, however, any classification is usually arbitrary since the activities of many small firms span more than one classification. Few hardware firms can ignore software, and the distinction between what is standard and what is customized is blurred.

The main thrust of the research on which this book has been based has been towards product-based firms (see the Appendix for details of the research approach). Service firms have not, however, been ignored since they share many of the distinctive characteristics of the product-based firms. They are susceptible to rapidly changing technology and uncertain market conditions, and are likely to have a high proportion of technical staff which need managing in a special way just like product firms. Those firms providing manufacturing, distribution and service/maintenance for "third-party" products are not strictly "high tech" since they do not invest in research and development and they use technology as a source of competitive advantage. However, since their success is dependent on the success of the "third parties", who are high-tech firms, they are subject to all the uncertainties and risks which are characteristic of the high-tech sector. A few examples of such firms are therefore included later in the book in the chapters on crisis and recovery.

FORCES DRIVING FRAGILITY

The small high-tech firm is the most fragile of firms. Even those firms that are profitable and growing well in areas of strong market demand are vulnerable to major hiccups that can threaten the existence of the firm in a matter of weeks. Most small high-tech firms that have been regarded by the investment community as success stories have been in a severe crisis at some stage in their history. The nature of this vulnerability, or fragility as it will be called throughout the book, results directly from the characteristics that make small high-tech firms different from other small firms or from larger technology-based firms.

There are six groups of factors inherent to small high-tech firms that cause fragility:

1 the rate of technological change;
2 market volatility and uncertainty;
3 the nature of competition;
4 employee characteristics;

5 resource constraints;
6 the high-tech entrepreneur and the founding team.

These factors are summarized in Figure 1.1, and each is discussed in turn below.

The Rate of Technological Change

There is tremendous strategic uncertainty associated with the high-tech environment. Technological change is often difficult to predict, as are the time and costs required to develop and

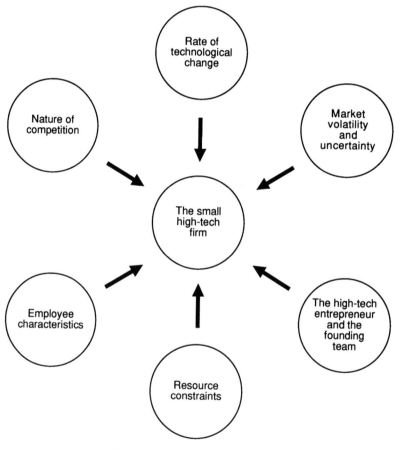

Figure 1.1 *Forces driving fragility*

commercialize new technology. [6] In many areas of technology, particularly leading-edge technologies, there are significant disagreements between the experts about which of several competing technologies will work. Small firms lack the resource to develop competing technologies and therefore usually have to bet on one. The problem is often exacerbated by uncertainty about the timing of the technological trends. Trends which are slower to materialize than originally forecast mean that the small high-tech firm may run out of money before it ever gets off the ground, while a more rapid rate of technological development may mean the small firm lacks the resources to keep up with its competitors.

The short product life cycle of many high-tech sectors means continued product competition and the need to avoid product obsolescence to ensure survival. As a general rule, the shorter the product life cycle the more fragile is the firm. While small high-tech firms are traditionally flexible and quick to respond to changing market needs, very short product life cycles do not give the small firm much opportunity to recoup their product and market development costs before the next generation of products has to be launched. Furthermore, since the typical small firm has a narrow product range it tends to "bet the firm" each time it launches a new generation of products. A single product failure therefore leads to a major crisis and sometimes insolvency.

Market Volatility and Uncertainty

The rapid and often discontinuous change in demand in high-tech markets, rapidly emerging new competitors (many of whom disappear equally quickly) and rapidly shifting competitive strategies produce a market-place in which it is difficult to plan. "Twelve months is a long-term plan in our business" is a comment one often hears in the personal computer market, for example. Again, generalizations are dangerous since there are some niche market sectors where competitive conditions are relatively stable, although the general trend is towards more new entrants into most markets when they reach a certain size. With market information usually inaccurate, obsolete or unavailable, there is likely to be a high degree of uncertainty about the market.

History shows that although high-tech markets can grow at phenomenal speeds they can also disappear almost overnight. The home computer market of the early 1980s provides the classic example. Inventories were built up ahead of demand and then demand evaporated almost overnight. The subsequent shakeout saw the demise of firms like Osborne in the USA and Acorn in the UK. Most new fast-growth markets are characterized by an enormous amount of hype and euphoria about growth potential. One US study in the mid 1980s showed that high-tech forecasts of market demand tended to be wildly optimistic: in five different sectors forecast demand five years ahead averaged 250% higher than actual demand. [7]

New technology can be applied to existing markets or can create whole new markets. Where new markets are being created, considerable uncertainty usually exists as the market emerges but has not yet shown signs that it will "take off". Even when a market need is apparent, the price of products using competing technologies may be dramatically reduced, thereby delaying or permanently putting an end to the prospects of market growth.

Apart from consumer electronic products, the buyers for high-tech products and services are industrial organizations. Thus, with a few exceptions the demand for high-tech products is a derived demand. Many of the customers are themselves competing in high-tech industries which are subject to all the uncertainties being described.

The Nature of Competition

Small high-tech firms rely on technology as their principal source of competitive advantage. The technology is usually embodied in a superior product (or service) offering that gives the customer greater satisfaction than competitors' products. A superior product offering means more features than competitors' products for the same price, or similar features at a lower price. The notion of a superior product implies not just the physical attributes of the product itself, but also includes those product dimensions which give the customer *confidence* that he or she is buying a superior product. In high-tech industries the confidence-building product dimensions are usually assured quality, reliability of supply and reliable after-sales service.

Customers for high-tech products tend to be demanding. Most are industrial customers who are themselves high-tech firms or are using technology to give them a competitive advantage in a more traditional industry. They are particularly unforgiving of poor quality, which impacts on the performance of their own products. Although there are exceptions, high-tech customers rarely show much loyalty to their suppliers unless significant switching costs are present.[8] They are often sophisticated buyers who are well aware of the alternative product offerings on the market. When a firm stops providing superior customer satisfaction—as perceived by the customer— the firm loses credibility with its customers extremely fast. Small firms are particularly vulnerable since customers, knowing they lack adequate resources, often adopt a dual sourcing strategy to protect themselves. Dual sourcing by customers inevitably increases the competitive risk for the small firm.

For as long as the small high-tech firm can provide superior customer satisfaction it has a competitive advantage. Where this advantage is based on the technological superiority of its product or service, the advantage is often short-lived. Technological advantages are more often than not easily imitated by competitors, and patent protection is weak or non-existent for small high-tech firms.[9] Thus any product superiority is unlikely to be sustainable unless the firm can find a way of *always* being one step ahead of the competition: not an easy task for the typical small high-tech firm.

The nature of competition is made more uncertain by the fact that industry structure is often ill-defined, particularly in emerging markets. The rules of competition, the degree of industry rivalry and the barriers to entry can all change extremely rapidly.

Employee Characteristics

Technical employees play a critical role in creating strategic advantage for the small high-tech firm. The motivational characteristics of these employees, often young, well-educated individuals with high job mobility, are a principal source of fragility. [10] Chapter 4 looks at the motivation problems of these employees in more detail, but normally they want challenging work, high pay and continued recognition for their work. They are the principal asset of small high-tech firms and their job mobility constantly threatens the existence of the firm. The rapidly changing technology and market conditions mean that the firm's speed of response is critical to its success, something which is endangered if the cumulative learning within the firm is dissipated. Not only do new recruits have to go down the learning curve all over again, but experienced technical employees may take their know-how to competitors. This problem is partially alleviated by the tendency for small high-tech firms to locate in proximity to one another—in Silicon Valley in California for example—where they, in turn, can recruit experienced employees from other firms.

The importance of technical employees as the firm's principal source of competitive advantage leads some small firms to develop a technology-led culture—which can be a great strength in a young and growing market but becomes a liability as competition increases and a more marketing-led culture is required. Changing corporate cultures is notoriously difficult and yet the need may occur very quickly as markets mature rapidly and new, often larger firms, enter the market. Some of the most successful high-tech firms develop extremely strong corporate cultures embodying the informality and flexibility which is necessary to cope with change. As long as the market is growing and the firm is doing well, such cultures can generate a high degree of excitement and be very motivating for those working within them. However, when the market and technology change, as inevitably they do, and radical changes are necessary to avert or deal with a crisis, there can be a rapid decline in morale which threatens the survival of the firm.

Resource Constraints

Limited resources is the one characteristic that is common to nearly all small firms. [11] Small high-tech firms even if well funded by venture capitalists are no exception, since money alone does not guarantee success. In fact, small high-tech firms are regarded as extremely risky investments by the financial community, and must usually rely on equity rather than debt financing in order to grow. One measure that venture capitalists often use to assess the short-term vulnerability of firms is how long the firm can survive (at its current level of expenditure) without obtaining any revenues. For most small high-tech firms this is only a matter of months, and acts as a potent reminder of the resource constraints facing such firms. If the small firm is not performing particularly well in terms of profitability, financial constraints may mean that the firm can never afford to invest in the number and calibre of people in the technical and marketing areas that are needed to break out of its current situation. If, on the other hand, sales and profits are increasing, and the firm is performing well financially, the small high-tech firm also finds itself people constrained, i.e. it is difficult to hire the number and calibre of technical employees the firm requires in order to manage the growth.

Most small high-tech firms tend to focus on one or a few specialized products often designed for specific customer segments. Consequently they are usually characterized by a narrow and highly specialized resource base. One central idea or technology constitutes the organization's distinctive competence. The origin of the firm is often a technological breakthrough on the part of an entrepreneur. The entrepreneur often lacks the management skills necessary to commercialize the product and develop the firm. Each time entrepreneurs come across new management tasks about which they have no experience, there are likely to be delays, mistakes and inefficiencies. [12] In an environment which is stable or moving considerably more slowly than the high-tech environment, the smaller firm entrepreneur and management team may be able to adapt to the changing situation. In a high-tech environment the need for speed to take advantage of the short windows of opportunity means that errors are more likely to lead to a crisis. Learning by making mistakes on the job is not a viable option.

The High-tech Entrepreneur and the Founding Team

Many small high-tech firms are created to achieve intellectual and professional goals as much as financial goals. [13] The founders of the more radically innovative, entrepreneurial organizations often value the opportunity to explore innovative technologies more than maximizing financial returns. Many such founders are more committed to a particular technology than to a market, and some will sacrifice significant growth opportunities in technology and markets they consider peripheral rather than risk losing their chosen technology focus. Studies have shown that growth-oriented entrepreneurs in both high- and low-tech firms are characterized by distinct psychological traits which give them a propensity towards growth. Such entrepreneurs have significantly higher levels of energy, risk taking and social adroitness than their low growth counterparts. They also have a greater desire for autonomy and adapt readily to change. [14]

Perhaps even more important than the goals of the founder (or the founding team) are the capabilities and commitment of the founder(s). The technical capabilities of the founding team are vital not only to the development of the first product but also to subsequent product development activities, as will be shown later. Leadership and management capabilities are also critical, but it is all too rare to find founders who combine strong technical capabilities with good leadership skills and sound management practice. Hambrick has noted that "the chief executives of high technology firms differ from their counterparts in low technology firms in ways that follow logically from the special requirements of the high-technology setting". [15] However, capability alone is not enough in a small high-tech firm. What is just as important, and sometimes more important, is total commitment by the founder(s) not just to the firm as a whole, but also to those key areas where fragility, if not correctly dealt with, will lead to the demise of the firm. Considerable academic research exists which links small firm performance to the abilities of the top-management team. [16]

The presence of founders as management, or even as shareholders if they have relinquished management responsibilities, has a profound effect on the management of small high-tech firms. On the one hand they often provide the entrepreneurial dynamism necessary for success, but at the same time their goals and shortcomings may be the root cause of crisis and failure. In particular, their management style may hinder effective decision making and implementation. The speed of change in high-tech sectors requires, for example, fast strategic decision making because delays and indecision will quickly erode any technical and market advantages the firm may have. Thus, the inability to make quick decisions under conditions of great uncertainty and other types of behaviour on the part of the founder of a small high-tech firm will hinder firm performance and increase fragility.

The degree of fragility bought about by the presence of the founder depends on how easy it is for the board of directors to remove the founder if the firm is under-performing. Where the founder has the majority shareholding and is unwilling to accept the fact that he or she cannot run the company, the situation is obviously more fragile. Even where the founder no longer has majority control, but is still a major shareholder, the founder's influence may still be very strong and removing him or her may be difficult. While the vast majority of small high-tech firms are still run by their founders, the introduction of new chief executives does not automatically reduce fragility and may well increase it if the "hired hand" is less capable than the entrepreneur of running the business.

In theory, the firm's chief executive, whether the founder or not, should provide the management capability to combat effectively the other five forces driving fragility. However, in reality, the chief executive of a small high-tech firm needs to be almost super-human to grow a business successfully over a long period of time; and will in practice have some personal failings which will contribute to the fragility of the firm.

MANAGING FRAGILITY

The combined effect of the six forces driving fragility is to make the small high-tech firm have a high propensity for crisis. Crises of one type or another are inevitable for the small high-tech firm and Chapter 8 shows how within weeks what appeared to be a healthy firm became a turnaround situation. A single event, such as a quality problem or a new product introduction by a competitor, can be enough to trigger a chain reaction which causes a severe crisis and puts the very survival of the firm in question.

There can be no simple panacea to the issue of fragility since the inherent characteristics of small high-tech firms are such that considerable risk is inevitable. The small high-tech firm is competing in a hostile environment where considerable technological, market and competitor risk exists with resources that themselves are scarce (money, management know-how, company reputation, etc.) or vulnerable (the technical employees).[17] Investing in and working in such companies can be exciting and rewarding but the risks will always be high until the firm has grown to such a size that some of the forces driving fragility have been negated.[18] The larger high-tech firm is still vulnerable to changing technology, and changing market conditions, but is better placed to develop sustainable competitive advantage to deal with the nature of competition; and has much greater resources to deal with any crisis that may develop. The typical small firm suffers from resource constraints and has to take account of the motivation of its employees and the influence of the entrepreneur or chief executive. What is different about the small high-tech firm is the particular combination of the six forces it must overcome in order to survive and prosper.

The aim of this book is to convey to the reader some of the lessons that emerge from research in the USA and Europe into the management practices of small high-tech firms. The research on which this book is based shows that the more successful small high-tech firms adopt appropriate strategies and actions for dealing with the forces driving fragility. The management practices of the most successful firms deal with the forces driving fragility in such a way as to avoid or minimize the problems that arise due to the characteristics of the firms and their environment. In the chapters that follow, the strategies and actions used by successful, small high-tech firms will be described. These firms have the following characteristics in common with each other:

- They seek ways of overcoming their resource constraints through innovative actions (e.g. designing foreign sourced components into a product for a foreign market for ease of service) or entrepreneurial behaviour (e.g. a deal with a major customer).

- They invest management time and effort in ensuring that key areas of potential crisis are constantly monitored and controlled (e.g. product quality, the morale of the technical staff).
- They avoid product-market options which are too risky given the firm's limited resource base (e.g. entering completely new technologies).
- They focus their resources on products, markets, technologies, projects etc., so as not to dissipate the firm's limited resources.
- They continually strive to build and maintain competitive advantage through differentiation, which permits them to earn high margins.
- They pay careful attention to the timing of product-market entry decisions.
- They remain flexible and responsive to their customers' needs.
- They keep costs variable and financial leverage (gearing) low.
- They manage their human resources in a way that recognizes the unique characteristics of high-tech employees.
- They introduce "professional" management in a selective way so as not to kill the innovative capabilities of the firm.
- They develop flexible, high performing organizational cultures.

In many instances managing fragility involves a delicate balancing act between the external forces driving fragility and the firm's internal resources. For example, the rate of technological change may mean there is a short window of opportunity to develop and launch a new product and that any delay will mean being leap-frogged by the competition. However, due to limited internal resources and capabilities the firm is unable to launch within the desired time frame a product that is fully tested and can meet customer delivery requirements. Does the firm take short cuts in product development and risk losing its customers' confidence? Diversification provides another example. Many small high-tech firms are heavily dependent on one product or one major customer—partly as a result of a need to overcome resource constraints. They then decide to diversify their product and/or customer base to reduce their dependence on a single source of revenues. In theory this is fine, but in practice the managerial and technical resource base of the firm is so narrow that diversification efforts are unsuccessful. The firm ends up being more fragile than it was before, and a full-blown crisis often ensues.

DECISION MAKING IN THE FRAGILE FIRM

Strategies and organizational practices that provide a good strategic fit with the environment and the firm's resources are the substance of this book; but unless they are accompanied by an appropriate decision-making style, success will be elusive. To cope with the forces driving fragility, management must adopt a decision-making style which is fast, analytical and bold.

Fast Decision Making

Fast decision making helps firms cope with the rapid pace of change in their environment. Windows of opportunity are short in high-tech industries and so a management that procrastinates and postpones making decisions until more information is available, or more analysis is due, tends to lose out. Late 1980s' research in the rapidly changing environment of the microcomputer industry indicates that the shorter the time frame in which strategic decisions are made, the better the performance of the firm. [19]

There are five principal characteristics of fast decision-making firms:

1 They use extensive information, particularly real-time information on the firm's operations and competitive environment. [20] Extensive use is made of qualitative tracking of operational indicators such as orders, inventory, cash flow, product returns and competitors' moves rather than reliance on accounting data. Real-time information permits managers to spot problems and opportunities sooner and may even help to develop their intuition. [21]

2 They consider multiple alternatives simultaneously. This speeds up decision making by building confidence that the most viable alternatives have been considered, reducing the psychological commitment to any one alternative (which permits shifting between options if necessary) and by providing a fall-back position if one alternative fails.

3 They use experienced counsellors. While the chief executive might obtain advice and information from all members of his or her management team, faster decision making appears to occur when the chief executive also has a "confidante" or special adviser. Counsellors provide a sounding-board for ideas, relate the issue in question to past experience and generally share the decision-making burdens. Counsellors are typically outsiders such as non-executive directors, consultants or venture capitalists, or senior (often older) executives who "have been around" for a long time.

4 They take active steps to resolve conflicts. Some degree of conflict is inevitable and healthy within a management team; but the decision makers themselves must take specific steps to resolve conflict if the speed of decision making is not to be affected. The leadership style of the chief executive is the key to this process and is discussed in more detail in Chapter 4.

5 They integrate key strategic decisions and action planning within the decision process. Decision integration helps executives see the broader picture: how the various decisions relate to each other and how they relate to action plans. If decisions are treated as discrete events, functional executives are often unable to build a mental map of what is happening, which in turn leads to ambiguity and lack of confidence in what they are doing.

Analytical Decision Making

The lack of accurate and complete information about the market-place, competitors and technological developments means that it is easy to make costly mistakes. Some management teams in small high-tech firms "muddle through" adapting to the changing environment in a reactive mode; but there is some evidence that effective teams attempt to structure the situations facing them using rational decision-making processes. [22] The better performing firms tend to use a more analytical approach and adopt a more thorough and continuous search for strategic alternatives. While rational decision making provides order to a rapidly changing environment, strategy must remain flexible. Some small high-tech firms have achieved this by building implementation triggers into their strategic plans. Trigger mechanisms such as the achievement of quarterly results or specified actions by a competitor allow management to keep options open and avoid major errors.

While the firm's strategy may remain flexible, it is important that management articulates clear and explicit goals to provide employees with a strong foundation on which to build their actions. The most successful firms appear to develop a simple statement of strategic intent and communicate this very clearly to all employees throughout the firm. [23]

Bold Decision Making

Rapid change, severe time pressures and crisis situations are classic causes of managerial stress. A common response to such situations—often found in failing companies—is to centralize authority and continue with known recipes for success. However, in environments undergoing radical change, new innovative approaches are often required. Chapters 2 and 3 show that product strategies which are imitative or involve at best incremental improvements to competitors' products are likely to fail. The small high-tech firm must be constantly differentiating itself and reasserting its niche position to deal with shifting technologies and changing competitor strategies. This requires experimentation and a willingness to take risks.

The use of rational high-quality decision-making approaches which involve structured discussion and careful analysis may seem to be in conflict with the need to move quickly and boldly. Conventional management thinking believes there is a trade-off between quality and speed of decision making and that innovation is brought about more by a series of incremental actions than by analysis. In the small high-tech firm, the dilemma facing management is that it is easy to make a mistake by acting too soon, but it can be equally disastrous to delay making a decision or to imitate competitors. The dilemma is made worse by the fact that it is often difficult to predict the significance of change as it is occurring, as was the case at Atari. [24] The signals indicating a need for change are often very weak. To be successful, management in the small high-tech firm must learn to live with the dilemma. They must make strategic decisions carefully but quickly and be bold, while at the same time remaining flexible by building in implementation triggers.

PLAN OF THE BOOK

The start-up phase of small high-tech firms is typically the time of greatest fragility. The new firm has few resources other than the capabilities and commitment of its founder or founding team. The success of the firm is critically dependent on developing a first product that provides superior customer satisfaction and on the timing of market entry. Chapter 2 identifies six factors which influence the success of first products, and shows how the timing of market entry affects risk. The new start-up can reduce the inherent risk involved by avoiding certain product-market options, by having a founding team which combines strong technical expertise with total commitment and by avoiding six typical start-up problems. However, choosing product-market options which reduce fragility, and hence risk, may also reduce the future growth potential of the business.

The development of a first product that provides superior customer satisfaction at the appropriate time in the market's development is a prerequisite for early success, but success will be ephemeral unless sustained efforts are made to develop the market, and continue new product development efforts. Chapter 3 explores how the most successful small high-tech firms build and maintain customer credibility by constantly differentiating their product/service offering in the market-place. At the same time as the firm is busy trying to establish its first product in the market-place before its "window of opportunity" disappears, the small high-tech firm must be working on improving and developing its product range. At this stage the high performing, small firm should have more feedback from the market-place than it did when developing its first product, which should improve its chance of success. However, strong technical superiority and the continuing involvement of the entrepreneur are also required if subsequent new products are not to be more "me too" products. A successful first product is no guarantee of subsequent success in new product development. Since the firm is still young and lacks resources, the small firm needs to take great care to focus its product development efforts and to access multiple sources of technology if it is going to keep up with the pace of technological development. Failure by the young firm to develop its limited resources appropriately to both product and market development will allow competition to dislodge the firm from its early market position. Either other small high-tech firms will use product- or time-based competition to win out, or alternatively larger firms will start to compete using price competition and their greater marketing power.

Chapter 4 describes a number of organizational issues that distinguish the management of small high-tech firms from other small firms. It discusses the motivation profile of employees, and what needs to be done to ensure that the employees—the critical competitive weapon of the small high-tech firm—are committed and motivated. All small high-tech firms have to learn to adapt to constant changes in technology, market demand and competition. Flexibility is vital for success. If the small firm is fortunate enough to be really successful and to grow very fast, the problem of adaptation is magnified many times. Managing rapid growth in an environment which itself is changing rapidly is one of the biggest challenges facing any manager. Chapter 5 outlines the typical problems encountered by small high-tech firms when they grow rapidly and how the better performing firms deal with these problems. The ability of the entrepreneur or the chief executive at the time to deal with growth is a key issue, as is the ability of the organization to adapt rapidly to significant change. The conventional recipe of introducing "professional management" is too simple a solution since, as shown in Chapter 5, the issue is how to add stability through adopting some "professional management" techniques but not to lose the flexibility which is the hallmark of the small high-tech firm's success.

Once the small high-tech firm has survived for about seven to eight years it has usually established enough credibility in the market-place and enough in-house capability to reduce its fragility. The exit rate—the rate at which new firms go out of business—starts to decline in high-tech industries at about this period. Figure 1.2 shows how the exit rate changes over time for high-tech start-ups in the USA. [25] After seven to eight years, resources are often less constrained and management starts to look for further growth, either to maintain or improve historical growth rates, or as a means of reducing risk. Chapter 6 looks at various types of small high-tech firms that survive into adulthood and at the typical strategies they use in search of further growth. Product diversification, acquisitions and international expansion are the major routes used by small high-tech firms when moving away from their initial product-market focus. Such moves are often fraught with danger since any one of

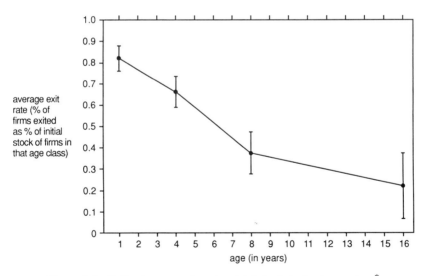

average exit rate (% of firms exited as % of initial stock of firms in that age class)

age (in years)

Figure 1.2 *Exit rate curve for nine high-tech industry sectors**
Source: P. Verdin, private correspondence, 30 May 1991

---

*Sectors identified in Table 1.1, excluding computer programming services; vertical bars denote one standard deviation.

these moves may highlight just how fragile the on-going, small high-tech firm remains.

While the firm is growing successfully it is able to add layers of resource to its initial fragile base. Retained earnings increase the capital base and may improve debt capacity. As more management and staff are added the firm's competence base increases. Market credibility improves and competitive advantages become embedded in the organization. A high-performing culture may have developed which also increases the chances of subsequent success. However, the extent to which fragility can be reduced is limited due to the inherent characteristics of some of the forces driving fragility. The characteristics of the entrepreneur and those of the technical employees make the small firm continue to be fragile.

Chapter 7 looks at the specific management problems of going international. The global nature of high-tech markets and the small domestic markets in many European countries, for example, forces many small high-tech firms to internationalize at a very early stage of their development. The chapter identifies the common problems small firms encounter and how the more successful firms have overcome them. Finally, Chapters 8 and 9 look at the inevitable crisis that hits nearly all small high-tech firms at some stage in their development, and what strategies and actions are necessary to get out of crisis. Chapter 8 highlights how a single problem can cause a major crisis very quickly; unlike the situation in non-high-tech firms where several factors usually need to be present simultaneously for a crisis to develop. The high propensity for crisis among small high-tech firms is matched, however, by an ability to stage a rapid sales-led recovery when the conditions are right—a much faster recovery than is possible in non-high-tech crisis situations. Chapter 9 discusses the major recovery strategies used by small high tech firms.

NOTES

(1) "Nine New Mavericks", *Electronic Business*, 4 September (1989).
(2) The ten sectors all ranked as "high tech" on the basis of a product sophistication analysis by the Massachusetts Division of

Employment Security as cited in Vinson, R. and Harrington, P. "Defining High Technology Industries in Massachusetts". Boston, MA: Commonwealth of Massachusetts, Department of Manpower Developments (1979).

(3) The 1987 "*Inc.* 500: America's Fastest Growing Companies", *Inc.*, December 9, No. 13, pp. 47–49 (1987).

(4) Garrett E. M., Henricks, M., Hosansky, A., Handley, A. and Mangan, D. "Venture's Decade: A Galaxy of Super Stars", *Venture*, Vol. 11, No. 5, May, pp. 29–44 (1989).

(5) Sculley, J. and Byrne, J. *Odyssey ... a Journey of Adventure. Ideas and the Future.* Harper & Row, New York (1987).

(6) Hamilton, W. F. "Corporate Strategies for Managing Emerging Technologies", *Technology in Society*, 7, pp. 192–212 (1985).

(7) Wheeler, D. R. and Shelley, C. J. "Toward More Realistic Forecasts for High Technology Products", *Journal of Business and Industrial Marketing*, Vol. 2, No. 3, pp. 55–63 (1987).

(8) The concept of switching costs is discussed in Porter, M. E. *Competitive Strategy.* Free Press, New York (1980).

(9) The lack of patent protection is discussed further in Chapter 3.

(10) See Chapter 4 for a discussion of the unique motivational characteristics of employees working in small high-tech firms.

(11) Stinchcombe, A. "Social Structure and Organization", James G. March (ed), *Handbook of Organizations*, pp. 142–193. Rand McNally, Chicago (1965).

(12) Stinchcombe, A., ibid.

(13) Corman, J., Perles, B. and Vancini, P. "Motivational Factors Influencing High Technology Entrepreneurship", *Journal of Small Business Management*, Vol. 26, No. 7, pp. 36–42 (1988).

(14) Ginn, G. W. and Sexton, D. L. "Comparative Psychological Preferences of High Tech and Low Tech *Inc.* 500 Founders", in M. W. Lawless and L. R. Gomez-Mejia (eds) *Proceedings, Second International Conference on Managing the High Technology Firm*, January (1990).

(15) Hambrick, D. C., Black, S. S. and Fredrickson, J. W. "Executive Leadership of the High Technology Firm: What's Special About It?", in M. W. Lawless and L. R. Gomez-Mejia (eds) *Proceedings, Second International Conference on Managing the High Technology Firm*, January (1990).

(16) For a discussion of how founding top-management teams influence the growth of new firms see, for example, Eisenhardt, K. M. and Schoonhoven, C. B. "Organizational Growth: Linking Founding Team, Strategy, Environment and Growth Among US

Semiconductor Ventures, 1978–1988", *Administrative Science Quarterly*, September, pp. 504–529, (1990).

(17) Covin, J. G. and Slevin, D. P. "Strategic Management of Small Firms In Hostile and Benign Environments", *Strategic Management Journal*, Vol. 10, pp. 75–87 (1989).

(18) There is a growing body of research on the "liability to newness" concept. See for example: Singh, J. V., Tucker, D. J. and House, R. J. "Organizational Legitimacy and the Liability of Newness", *Administrative Science Quarterly*, Vol. 31, pp. 171–193 (1986).

(19) Eisenhardt, K. M. "Making Fast Strategic Decisions in High Velocity Environments", *Academy of Management Journal*, Vol. 32, No. 3, pp. 543–576 (1989).

(20) Real-time information is defined by Eisenhardt as information about a firm's operations or environment for which there is little or no time-lag between occurrence and reporting.

(21) Intuition relies on patterns developed through continual exposure to actual situations, and is discussed in more detail in Simon, H. "Making Management Decisions: The Role of Intuition and Emotion", *Academy of Management Executive*, Vol. 1, pp. 57–64 (1987).

(22) Bourgeois, L. J. and Eisenhardt, K. M., "Strategic Decision Processes in High Velocity Environments: Four Cases in the Microcomputer Industry", *Management Science*, July, Vol. 34, No. 7, pp. 816–835 (1988).

(23) Hamel, G. "Strategic Intent", *Harvard Business Review*, May–June, pp. 63–76 (1989).

(24) Sutton, R., Eisenhardt, K. and Jucker, J., "Managing Organizational Decline: Lessons from Atari", *Organizational Dynamics*, Spring (1986).

(25) Verdin, P., private correspondence.

2
Successful Start-up Strategies

All new company start-ups are known to be extremely risky. Estimates of the failure rate of start-up firms vary from 65% failing in the first five years to 80% failing within the first three years.[1,2] New high-tech companies are no exception. The high failure rate of technology-based ventures soon after start-up results in part from the general characteristics of high-tech industries discussed in Chapter 1; but also from the inability of the founders to strike the right balance along a number of strategic and organizational dimensions which are unique to small high-tech companies.

Management decisions made at start-up or in the early months after start-up not only affect the chances of short-term survival, but can also have a profound long-term effect on the growth potential and eventual success of the business.[3] For example, technical decisions made during the development of the first product can drive the company unwittingly into market segments with limited growth potential. Similarly, the larger the size of the founding team and the wider the variety of its experiences, the greater the chance of building a high-growth company.[4,5]

This chapter will describe some of the major decisions which are critical in distinguishing between success and failure in the early years of a new high-tech company's life. First, it will look at how entrepreneurs survive in the period before they have developed their first product, called here the "experimentation" stage—where the fledgling company lacks both resources and product and is not at all sure of how the business will develop. Not all companies go through this stage, but most of the ones who manufacture products or produce software do. Then it looks at the six factors that determine the success of the firm's first product and how the timing of market entry influences success. It concludes by outlining six problems that are commonly found among high-tech start-ups.

EXPERIMENTATION

Most founders of high-tech start-ups have worked in larger technology-based firms before branching out by themselves. In most cases the new business is related to the founder's existing knowledge and experience in particular markets or technologies. Contrary to popular belief, not all of the founders of high-tech firms are "technical boffins". Many have a marketing background. In most cases they leave an existing high-tech firm, technical consultancy or university where they have gained considerable market or technical expertise, to start a new business in a related or very similar business area.

The background of the entrepreneur(s) is crucial because the know-how and enthusiasm for the project is the only resource the fledgling high-tech company has. On occasions, the entrepreneur may have considerable funds available—as in the case of the entrepreneur who has been successful once and is out to do it again—or where the entrepreneur has persuaded financial backers to invest in no more than a product idea. But this is rare, since in most cases financial backers do not like investing in start-up situations due to the risks involved. More typically, the entrepreneur starts out with a shoestring operation, working from a garage or a room in his or her own home. The stories of Bill Hewlett and David Packard starting their business in a garage in Palo Alto, and of Steve Jobs starting Apple Computer in his garage, are well-known examples of this approach. When these businesses start—often before incorporation of a legal corporate entity—the key issue is how do the entrepreneurs bring enough resources (in the form of time and money) to move the project forward? They often have little idea as to what their first product will look like or, in some cases, what it will be. They are in what can be called an experimentation mode. Mintzberg calls this "crafting strategy", using the analogy of a potter at his wheel. The potter has a general idea of the artefact he wants to create, but the finished product is the result of an evolutionary and creative process. [6] The founder of a computer-aided design company commented: "When we started we had no clear idea what our first product was likely to be. All that we knew was that it would be in technical computing and computer-aided design. We had no idea how the market was going to evolve."

The biggest problem facing the high-tech entrepreneur at this stage is a shortage of time and money. The two are obviously connected.

- Time is important because, if the experimentation stage takes too long, others may move faster and pre-empt the supposed business opportunity.
- Money is important not only because the entrepreneur needs to live during the experimentation stage, but may also have to buy equipment (e.g. testing machinery) and incur certain overheads such as travel costs.

The entrepreneurs in this research dealt with the problem in two ways—by "capturing resource" from their former employers, and by generating revenues from selling services—both of which are worth discussing in more detail.

Capturing Resource from Former Employers

Experimentation can and often does begin before actual start-up. The entrepreneur often obtains a business idea through being involved with a project at a former employer. This is common for non-high-tech start-ups where individuals may decide, for whatever reason, to set up on their own. However, more often than not such spin offs are clones of the former employer. While this is still true in some sectors of what has earlier been defined as high tech, the typical high-tech start-up is more likely to focus on a different product-market segment than that of the former employer. This usually arises because the former employer is reluctant to develop a product idea developed by, or worked on by, the employees; or because the employee recognizes a market opportunity in a product-market area related to, but different from that of the employer's business.

Domino Printing Sciences Limited, a successful UK start-up in the ink-jet printing industry, is a classic example of such a situation. When the company was founded by Graeme Minto in September 1978, Minto had been working for seven years on developing ink-jet technology for his employers, Cambridge Consultants Ltd (CCL). When CCL decided not to proceed with one of the projects, Minto left to start up by himself, largely as he says, "because I did not want to be associated with yet another stillborn project". He persuaded CCL management to give him a licence for the ink-jet technology and to produce the higher tech parts of the print head and electronics free of charge. CCL also took a small equity stake in Domino at a cost of £1000. CCL's support was critical to Domino's survival in its early months, something which was handsomely repaid less than six years later, when that equity stake was worth £1.5m. [7]

Besides capturing the necessary time and money needed to develop new products, the entrepreneur can also obtain other benefits from the former employer, such as:

- intellectual capital, [8] which is the knowledge about products, customers, technologies, etc., which an individual learns while working in a knowledge-based job;
- reputational capital, [9] which is the credibility an individual develops as his or her expertise begins to be recognized by customers, industry specialists, etc.;
- customer relationships/contacts which can be exploited;
- the right to exploit patents and intellectual property rights which the former employer does not wish to exploit;
- financial help.

While some spin offs are encouraged, there are many situations which are quite acrimonious. In fact, it has become increasingly common practice in the USA for high-tech firms to file lawsuits against former employees as soon as they leave to start up their own businesses, purely as a defensive measure just in case they attempt to use technology taken from their former employer. Thus, when Gordon Campbell and others left Intel in 1981 to form Seeq Technology with the aim of making EEPROMS (electrically erasable programmable read only memories, also known as E-squares), Intel immediately filed a lawsuit claiming they had taken valuable technology with them. The lawsuit was settled out of court. [10]

Generating Revenues from Services

The need for finance while generating the first product leads many high-tech start-ups to generate cash flow by undertaking technical consulting services. Besides meeting the obvious financial need at this stage in a new company's development, the provision of services can bring the entrepreneurial team close to the needs of a group of customers which, as shown later, is crucial to the success of new product development activities. It can also provide the new company with a set of reference customers which may be important later when the company is trying to establish its credibility with its first new product.

The benefits of starting off with a service business were put to me by the founder of a Boston-based software company, as follows:

> "We deliberately started on a service strategy. We knew we could make a living out of services, whether it was technical consultancy or bureau services ... Our company launch strategy was to build up a base load of service business and from that to finance product development. We did not want to spend more on product development than we could afford to write off immediately ... Consulting was good and bridged the gap between our academic background and commercial future. We learnt to work to tough time scales and we just had to deliver well-defined products."

High-tech start-ups which start with a period of technical consultancy to finance product development, are most likely to be found:

- in very young and uncertain markets;
- where the technology—first in the form of consultancy services and later in the form of a product—has a high value-added contribution to the customers' business;

- where there are extremely long lead times to develop and commercialize new products.

The early days of the CAD/CAM (computer-aided design/computer-aided manufacture) and LAN (local area network) markets, prior to the development of the personal computer, provide examples that meet the first two criteria. The establishment of Cambridge Interactive Systems Ltd in the UK (later bought by Computervision Inc.), relied on consultancy in the CAD/CAM market for years prior to moving into product development. In the LAN market, 3-COM, the Silicon Valley company founded by Bob Metcalfe who co-invented Ethernet—a technique for linking multiple computers together with a local area network—is another such example. Although Ethernet was invented in 1973, there was little or no market for computer networks until the end of the 1970s. In 1979, Metcalfe left Xerox Corporation and set up 3-COM with a partner as a consultancy firm since the market for Ethernet products did not yet exist. When Xerox, DEC and Intel drafted standard Ethernet specifications in 1980, 3-COM moved into developing its first hardware product which was launched in 1981.[11] Biotechnology start-ups, where the majority of companies survive by undertaking research contracts for the large pharmaceutical companies on a cost-plus basis, meet all three of the criteria set out above.

How successful entrepreneurs are in generating revenues in this experimentation phase depends on:

- Their own technical expertise. The greater the technical expertise the more likely they are to be successful (providing they can communicate clearly with, and relate to, the customer).
- The ability to identify opinion leaders as customers. Working with leading-edge customers who are likely to influence other customers is important for both generating new product ideas and for providing as reference customers when obtaining future orders (see Chapter 3).
- The ability to identify customers who can afford to pay for technical consulting services. Many organizations are willing to talk about technical problems, but far fewer are prepared to buy consulting from outsiders.

- Focusing on specific types of consulting problems so as to build the knowledge base in a way which is consistent with the desired product development objectives. Lack of focus may mean spreading resources too thin and constantly going down new, unrelated learning curves.
- Avoiding over-commitment to individual contracts which can not only divert the team from their product development goals, but also make the fledgling business overreliant on one source of revenue.

While the advantages of starting up with a consulting base are clear for all to see, there is a fine line beyond which consulting becomes detrimental to the original vision of what the new business was to be about. This was neatly summarized by a marketing manager of one of the early computer-aided design start-ups in the UK:

> "I think we got our first product late. If all the people who were involved ... had started work on it in the early 70s, the company would now be among the world leaders, because just when we focused [on our first product] in 1980 companies in the US, like Intergraph, entered the market. If we had come out with our product earlier and had become more commercially aware rather than dwell on consultancy, we would probably be among the world leaders in the computer-aided design industry."

One late 1980s study, albeit based on a fairly small sample, showed that the average length of time from receipt of start-up financing to the shipment of the first product is 15 months (with a range from 9 months to 24 months). [12,13] This gives some rough indication of how long the experimentation phase may need to be.

THE FIRST PRODUCT

The experimentation phase just described often provides the founding team with the source of their first product idea and product specifications. The customer orientation of experimentation ensures that what emerges has a chance of being what some customers want; however, experimentation via technical consulting may not indicate whether the product idea can be turned into a viable business venture. Technical consulting *per se* may not reveal a product's market potential, nor whether that product can be designed and manufactured at a price the customer is prepared to pay. Besides analyzing customers' needs, competitors' products are an important source of ideas. The entrepreneur will seek to improve competitors' products by either offering a more technically advanced product which has a superior performance compared to existing products on the market, or offering similar (or improved performance) at a lower price.

Where experimentation—at the expense of customers or existing employers—is not an option, the idea and specification for first products arises from either technological innovations, recognition of unfulfilled customers' needs, or existing competitors' products. It would be wrong, however, to give the impression that entrepreneurs conduct a reasonably broad search for new product ideas. This is not the case. What happens most often is that one of the founders comes across the idea while not really searching at all.

Technological innovation is a strong source of new product ideas, and many small high-tech firms have been established as the result of a technical entrepreneur searching for improved ways of "making things work". The danger of course in this approach is that one develops a product in search of a market. Clive Sinclair's C-5 electric-powered car was such a product, although the history of many small high-tech firms shows us that this approach can sometimes work if management is flexible enough to seek out alternative market opportunities and switch market priorities if the initial market potential is non-existent. The start up of Microvitec, the first UK company to manufacture high-density colour monitors for personal computers was a classic case in point. Anthony Martinez, the founder, developed a superior product, initially focusing on the market for videotex, but subsequently switched focus to video games and personal computers as better market opportunities emerged. [14]

The recognition of unfulfilled customer needs is the classic marketing approach to product development and has triggered off many new start-ups in both the high-tech and non-high-tech sectors. This approach has been particularly common in establishing software firms—particularly where a need for application software has been identified in a vertical market. Manac Systems International, the Canadian software company specializing in legal software, is just one of many examples. Lynn Verchere, the company's founder, talking of Manac's start-up, says:

> "In 1975, while serving as the (law) firm's business manager, I conducted a search for a computer system that would meet their needs. I wasn't able to find software that met my quality standards. As a result I founded Manac Systems to develop software products on IBM computers for law firms of all sizes."[15]

Competitors' products are a constant source of new product ideas to the innovative engineer. Taking apart competitors' products, and seeing how they can better be designed for greater performance is the process by which incremental product innovation typically occurs. Japanese companies have shown themselves to be masters at this process. New companies that adopt this approach, while in danger of developing only an "incremental" product as compared to a major innovation, can find themselves further down the learning curve at less cost than firms that established themselves at an earlier stage in the evolution of the industry. In the CAD/CAM industry, for example, the source of first product ideas for firms starting prior to 1980 was technical consulting, but for all firms starting after 1980, competitors' products were the principal source of ideas.[16]

The success of the firm's first product—and hence the early success of the firm depends on:

- the importance of the product to the customer;
- the degree of product innovation;
- the scope of product specifications;
- the technical expertise of the founder(s);
- neither underpricing nor overspecifying;
- top management commitment to the success of theproduct.

The Importance of the Product to the Customer

Many start-ups have developed innovative products—which have been recognized as such by their potential customers—but fail to be successful in penetrating the market. There may be marketing reasons for this which will be discussed later in the chapter, but there may also be a question of product type. Firms making products which play a strategic role in the customer's industry—strategic products—tend to perform better than those that do not. Strategic products are those that permit customers to lower the price of their own product significantly or differentiate their own product better in the eyes of the customer.

Domino Printing Sciences, a UK manufacturer of ink-jet printers, enabled customers to replace their traditional methods of labelling and coding with faster packaging lines. This had a significant impact on the customer's competitive position by lowering manufacturing costs. Similarly, fault-tolerant computer systems first introduced by Tandem and Stratus Computers allowed financial brokerage houses to operate their dealing systems with little or no down-time, improving efficiency and customer service in the process. These products are quite unlike computer peripherals and software packages for accounting systems, which are not perceived by customers as directly improving their competitive position in the market-place.

Firms choosing to sell strategic products tend to meet less customer resistance than those that do not. However, product value is not the only consideration in the purchase decision. Customers usually want to be sure their suppliers are reliable and are going to provide adequate after-sales service and support. The start-up company has a major problem in establishing credibility in these areas however good the proven performance of its first product. Thus developing a strategic product is important but does not by itself ensure the product will be quickly accepted in the market-place.

The Degree of Product Innovation

Chapter 1 showed that the small high-tech firm competes by using technology in its product (or process) as a major source of competitive advantage. Not surprisingly, therefore, we find that at start-up the founder or founding team aims to develop a new, innovative product—a product that is dissimilar to any product already on the market and would clearly be identified by customers as "new" and "advanced" compared to existing offerings. New products are typically developed from young, developing technologies. New products based on completely new technologies are rare among high-tech start-ups. Small firms rarely have the start-up capital to invest in completely new technologies, and venture capital firms rarely encourage it due to the risks involved. Exceptions are some biotechnology start-ups. Investors prefer to see a technology established and then invest in radical product innovations which build on the proven technology. Apple Computer, for example, exploited existing technology which had already been developed, but not exploited by, Xerox.

The small high-tech firms that established themselves as glamour companies and household names in the early days of their existence—Wang, Lotus, Microsoft, Apple, Compaq—all produced new innovative products which were clearly superior to existing products on the market. Developing innovative products is at the heart of what the small high-tech firm is all about, but not all start-ups are lucky enough to develop such products. Many start-ups introduce only incremental improvements to existing products, even in the developing phase of the technology. As the technology matures, new entrants develop at best incremental products and at worst, "me too" products.

The most common start-up strategy for high-tech firms involves developing a new product based on a young, developing technology. These companies can become the glamour companies referred to above, providing a competitor does not develop a superior product—which is often not too difficult as the technology is still developing and new applications are still emerging. These are the product innovators in Figure 2.1. Where the start-up company manages to develop only an incremental product, success usually requires a more focused application-oriented approach to the market (perhaps involving some degree of customization) or high degree of market (as opposed to product) innovation. A start-up whose first product is incremental or "me too", using a mature technology is almost certain to be a failure as it can rarely develop sufficient competitive advantage to dislodge existing products.

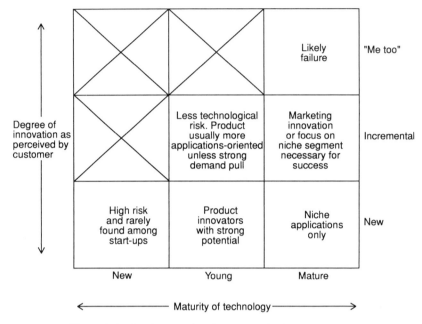

Figure 2.1   *Product technology positioning at start-up*

The Scope of Product Specifications

The key to the success of the new high-tech firm's first product is the scope of the product specification: is the product designed to be a robust, general purpose product which can be sold to a wide variety of market groups, or is it a specialist product designed for a specific user (vertical) market? The choice management makes is fundamental to the growth potential and future risk profile of the whole company. Here firms adopting the first approach, the general purpose product approach, are referred to as product specialists, and those adopting the second approach are referred to as market specialists.

The choice of which route to take is partly dependent on some of the other factors discussed below—particularly the capabilities and vision of the founding team, the nature of the technology and the stage of market development. Each product strategy requires different financial resources and different capabilities on the part of the management team. Since the only resources of a new company are really the technological and marketing know-how of the founders plus some funding (usually limited), the choice of product direction is driven largely by the characteristics of the founding team. The most important characteristics of the founding team appear to be their education and their experience base.

In many instances the founders do not have a choice, *per se*, since the nature of the technology drives the product strategy decision. In biotechnology firms, for example, defining product strategy is considered to be extremely difficult. James Grant, the Chairman and Chief Executive of T Cell Sciences Inc., explains the difficulty as follows:

> "The technology that the small company is working with is often evolving rapidly. You have to follow it where it leads. You can't really know the destination beforehand. So you may not have the choice of saying: 'Let's aim our strategy only at smaller market niches.' It may just happen that the technology doesn't give you a product that's applicable to a smaller market niche. You've got to take what you get."[17]

The stage of market development is also important because, as we shall see later in this chapter, it becomes increasingly difficult to develop a new general purpose product once the market has grown beyond a certain size. The later the market entry, the more likely the new venture will adopt a market specialist focus.

Product Specialization

The aim of those firms choosing the product specialist route is to design a general purpose product which is robust enough to be sold to a wide variety of market segments. The founder of a successful CAD/CAM company commented thus:

> "When we started, we were very keen to sell a standard piece of software, so we had only one major piece of software with a number of options. Everyone gets the same basic core software. There are options which makes this one product more specific to a customer group, but all options are linked to the basic core product."

The marketing manager in another company in the same

industry commented in a similar vein:

> "All our products have evolved from a core product. We can be called a single product company based on this core product. All our vertical products have come out of this core product. It is a matter of putting a different face on it, the art is to make them look like tailor-made vertical market products."

The principal advantage of adopting a product specialist approach is the access that it gives the firm to a large market potential. The future is not dependent on the vagaries of a particular market group. Product specialists rely on technological innovation as their principal source of competitive advantage. The product development effort is usually very focused and is the principal activity of the company in its early stages of development. The big disadvantage of this approach is that the firm becomes technology or product driven instead of market driven. At worst the firm produces a product that no one market segment really wants (because they have failed to segment the market) or, not much better, its product is perceived to be general purpose and unsuitable for specific market groups. This dilemma was highlighted by the founder of one software company who said:

> "The one particular weakness of anybody that takes the general purpose product strategy we have taken is that they could always be outmanoeuvred by somebody with a very narrow niche and, indeed, that is precisely the area where we tend to lose orders. Our main aim was to sell to multi-disciplinary users such as the large engineering firms who would find a powerful general purpose product more useful than a specialized vertical market product. In order to approach the vertical markets we have something called user programs, which allows a specialist user to write an application specific product. But this has not gone very well."

Heavier than expected marketing development costs are usually necessary to ensure the success of product specialist firms. The product is likely to be new and require substantial customer education and the company, being new, has a credibility problem with the customer. Successful implementation of a product specialist strategy requires:

● Strong technical skills among the founders. Above all they must be capable of designing powerful and robust general purpose products.

- Access to specific market groups often requiring the core product to be licensed out to third parties who have in-depth market knowledge and suitable distribution capabilities.
- The market to be a young (emerging) market because as markets grow the costs of product innovation start to rise quite sharply. Small firms then find it difficult, if not impossible, to make the type of product breakthrough necessary to develop a robust core product.
- The availability of adequate resources to invest in product development and market development too, if multiple vertical markets need to be attacked.

Market Specialization

Firms adopting the market specialist route aim to cater for the specialist needs of their markets. Firms following this approach are normally started by individuals with an in-depth knowledge of their chosen market segments. For example, in the UK CAD/CAM industry it was found that all the founders of market specialist companies had a background closely related to the markets on which they were focusing.[18] The strategy adopted by such founders is to be leaders in highly defined markets where they can develop an image for being specialists. Two comments from market focused CAD/CAM companies illustrate the typical strategies:

"Our strategy in a nutshell would be to provide comprehensive micro-computer based services for the house-building industry. Our strategy is to find a narrow market and find diverse packages to satisfy that market need."

"Our aim is to lead in the construction industry and to provide a complete design system for the construction industry. We want to be leaders in a tightly defined market. You have to limit the number of vertical markets you go after. Unless you are big, like Intergraph, you cannot address all the needs of different user groups and perform all of them well."

The advantages of market specialization relate to the obvious fact that the products are specifically suited to the unique needs of the market, and that market development costs are typically lower than for product specialists. The disadvantages are: dependence on a narrow market (with the danger of having "too many eggs in one basket", thereby making the firm vulnerable), limited growth potential, and a tendency towards too much customization as a result of customer pressure.

Building an attractive business—defined as one which can go public or is an attractive acquisition candidate for another firm—depends crucially on the selection of attractive market segments. The factors that determine attractiveness are: the size and growth rate of the segments, the extent to which sophisticated customers exist for the new small firms to learn from, and the profitability of the customers themselves (i.e. do they have the ability to pay?). Just as important as the market, however, is the ability to develop a robust core product for the chosen market, since even quite tightly defined markets have diverse needs to which the core product must cater.

As a general rule, product specialists have a greater potential for developing into large companies than do market specialists, although some target markets may be sufficiently large to build big businesses. The product specialist route, while offering more growth potential, is the riskier of the two product strategies. It is a strategy based almost purely on technological innovation and this requires both a significant breakthrough on the part of the product development team and no competitor to imitate or supersede the product before it is established in the market-place. This is an unlikely scenario for many founding teams. Market specialists, on the other hand, have limited growth potential but the risk is usually less. In those situations where the market specialist's target customer group is large, a high-tech start-up can grow into quite a large business with less fragility than a product specialist has at a similar size. Market specialists tend to build up a reputation and image with their customer base. This gives them an intangible source of competitive advantage which, unlike most technology, takes a long time for a competitor to imitate or supersede.

Companies that succeed as product specialists are the venture capitalists dream investment—Apple Computer, Intel, Lotus, etc.—but for every success story there are countless failures. The market specialists are usually less glamorous companies but tend to be safer investment bets than product specialists. Neither type of company is immune, however, to constant technological change. The introduction of UNIX-based software, for example, is currently making life difficult for innumerable application software firms that have adopted market specialization strategies over the past two decades. UNIX will take away any competitive advantage derived from the software application packages, leaving firms to compete on service rather than product.

The Technical Expertise of the Founders

Strong technical expertise within the founding group is necessary to develop a robust core product. The UK CAD/CAM study already referred to showed a very clear linkage between the technical expertise of the founders and subsequent success. This evidence is supported by several US studies. [19] The technical expertise of the founder(s) influences not only the nature of the first product, but is likely to have a long-term influence on the future success of the company. A successful first product from a technically expert team will in all probability establish a culture in which new product development is regarded as the driving force of the company. This in turn should lead to subsequent product development efforts (discussed in the next chapter) also being successful and the company maintaining a strong competitive advantage based on its technological capabilities. There are very few examples of successful high-tech start-ups where competitive advantage arising from technology was not established soon after start-up. Some start-ups have a false start in developing their first product but few survive unless a robust product is developed fairly quickly. Early product development efforts, therefore, have a profound effect on the long-term future of the start-up.

Technical expertise is particularly important in young markets where the technology is immature and industry standards are unclear. A high level of technical expertise among the founders is critical in product specialist companies but the potential of both product specialist and market specialist companies is brighter with technically competent founders. The

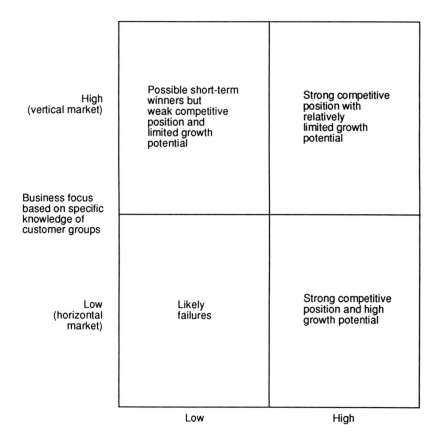

Figure 2.2   *Success potential matrix*

success potential matrix shown in Figure 2.2 provides a useful way of seeing how the potential success of the firm is influenced by the type of product approach and the technical expertise of the founding team.

Neither Underpricing nor Overspecifying

Two common and often interrelated characteristics of poor performance of start-up companies are underpricing and overspecifying. This is particularly acute in situations where the start-up is almost exclusively technology driven by technically-oriented founders. Unfortunately, it is not just a characteristic of the start-up phase, as shown later. Technically-driven companies, which many of our small high-tech companies are, have a tendency to want to design and engineer a technically superb product regardless of what the customer really wants and is prepared to pay for. Very often the majority of potential customers want a less sophisticated product at a reasonable price, as opposed to the very latest sophistication at a high price. There may be one or two potential customers for the sophisticated expensive product. Unfortunately it is often these customers who the founders know, since they are like-minded technical boffins. The end result is a product where the gross margin is insufficient to cover the high product and market development costs and the varying other risks that the small high-tech start-up faces.

Gross profit margins of 70% may be quite possible on strategic products in the same way that potential pharmaceutical products may have margins of over 90% because of the inherent added value of the product. Founding teams often shy away from such margins believing that the only way they can sell their innovative product is by "pricing below competition". This is usually the wrong pricing approach since if the product is truly innovative it will command a premium, and under-pricing may actually devalue the product in the eyes of customers.

Top Management Commitment to Success of the Product

Many successful first products appear to be characterized by a near messianic belief in the product itself and what it can do to improve society. This passion for the product often starts many years prior to actual company start-up. The founder of one CAD/CAM company whose product became the market leader in the domestic market commented:

> "I was totally committed to the project. I had been working on it for more than ten years. I was fanatic about it and obsessively interested in new methods and applying them to the whole of industry. The project to develop the product became the ruling thing in my life."

The need for such commitment and devotion by the founder or a senior member of the founding team is critical to the success of the first product. Some writers refer to this individual as the product champion—the individual who makes a decisive contribution to the innovation by actively and enthusiastically promoting its progress through critical stages. All small high-tech firms that develop an innovative first product have a clearly identifiable product champion—usually the entrepreneur himself or herself. [20,21,22,23]

TIMING OF MARKET ENTRY

The decision to start a new business in a high-technology industry has more to do with the entrepreneur's perception about market opportunities than any careful analysis of the market. Indeed, market analysis is often exceptionally difficult to do, particularly when new technology is involved and the market is at a very early stage of its development. Yet the stage of the market when the new firm launches its first product is a critical determinant of future success. Many successful venture capitalists invest in markets rather than products, because products have shorter life cycles than the firms that make them, and they want the maximum opportunity to reap the rewards of their investment. Don Valentine, founder of Sequoia Capital, a private venture capital partnership, says:

> "I prefer opportunities in business that are launched in an existing worldwide market, where the growth rate is rapid, where there is lots of competition and *not* patents and exclusions and market development problems. By rapid growth, I mean 100 per cent annually for four or five years. In a world of simple-minded alternatives: a market development risk, or a competitive risk in a fast growing market? We would clearly opt for the fast growth, lots of competition market ... Cash flow breakeven occurs when there is a demand pull marketplace and a product that fits adequately or slightly better into that marketplace, as contrasted to a situation with an unknown demand characteristic to it... [24]

Valentine, who invested in Apple Computer in 1978, and obtained a return for investors which exceeded 30 times the initial investment within three years, believes that the micro-computer market already showed clear demand-pull characteristics at the time of his investment. Where clear demand-pull characteristics are not yet in evidence, start-ups are undoubtedly riskier. Those start-ups at the leading edge of technology often aim to fill markets which will be created by the technology itself, or will exist by the time the product is developed. These situations are all characterized by market development risks—a risk which when added to all the other risks associated with high-tech start-ups makes the firm extremely fragile. Timing of market entry is, therefore, a critical variable that influences fragility.

Many writers have used the idea of the technology life cycle to explain how product innovation needs to change over time. As new product classes emerge based on new core technologies, new markets develop and old markets are revitalized. Just as we can talk about technology life cycles (and product life cycles), so we can also talk about market life cycles. Markets emerge, grow, mature and decline just like products. In high-tech industries there is often a marked similarity between the technology life cycle and the market life cycle. Each stage of the market life cycle is characterized by different competitive and market forces, with the result that the number of start-ups, the type of entry strategy and the longer-term potential of the new start-up company varies over the life cycle. Table 2.1 summarizes the differences that one can expect to find at each stage of the cycle.

Table 2.1 *Entry strategies and the market life cycle*

	Stage of market life cycle		
	Emerging	Growth	Maturity
New start-ups	likely	most likely	least likely
Typical entry strategy	product class	product segment	specialized niche
Growth potential of entry strategy	highest	average	least

Entry at the Emerging Stage

Firms entering emerging markets have the greatest potential for future growth because they can grow as the product class develops and have the opportunity to select which segments of that market offer them the best potential for future growth. They have a wide choice of marketing strategies open to them and can build learning curve advantages over later entrants. However, if entry occurs too early, there will be considerable uncertainties about whether the market will "take off", and the new firm may incur prolonged negative cash flows as it waits for this to occur. The markets for many biotechnology products, artificial intelligence and robotics are examples of young markets with a high degree of uncertainty in customer acceptance, which explains the prolonged negative cash flows in most of the participating firms. In many instances, emerging markets never become growth markets, or when they do, the early entrants are too weak to exploit the market effectively.

In some markets, new product classes based on young technology take much longer to take off than originally anticipated, because existing technologies manage to improve their price/performance characteristics enough to defer the acceptance of product classes based on newer technology, or existing competitors use their marketing muscle to preserve their existing technology. An example would be the UNIX operating system of AT & T, which has taken longer to gain market share in spite of its superior features, due to constant improvements from already well-established operating systems, and initial rejection of UNIX by the big players in the industry who wished to protect their proprietary systems.

However, being a late entry at the emerging stage can also be risky. Many successful start-ups not only pick young markets, but focus on a particular product or customer segment of the product class at an early stage of their development. This is a high risk/high reward strategy, but few small firms have the courage to focus early for fear of concentrating on an unattractive market segment. New firms are usually desperate for sales, and consequently experiment with a variety of products in diverse market segments. Such experimentation is a suitable strategy while there is a high degree of uncertainty as to which product or customer group will evolve as a potential market, but it leads to the dilution of the new firm's product and market development efforts.

Entry at the Growth Stage

The growth phase of the market for an individual product class is an extremely popular point of entry for new high-tech firms, but growth often attracts new firms with no significant competitive advantage. The microcomputer market shows ample evidence of start-ups which have had significant sales growth in their early years but have gone bankrupt in the following year. Such rapid and "temporary" super performance of technology-based start-ups can be seen in almost all high-growth markets such as computer peripherals, software, CAD/CAM, etc. However, there is some empirical evidence to show that entry at the growth stage of the market increased the chance of survival of firms in the US minicomputer industry; [25] and led to many young semiconductor firms becoming larger than those founded in emergent or mature markets. [26]

The key to successful entry at the growth stage of the market is selecting a particular segment of the product class on which to focus one's efforts. Even then the new firm may find itself competing against later entrants who have focused early on the same segment and derived learning curve advantages over the earlier start-up (which was early to start but late to focus). In some product classes such as microcomputers, major product innovation continues well into the growth phase, which means that new entrants have to cope with both the need to be innovative and the need to gain market share from earlier entrants—a difficult combination to achieve. The important thing to remember about entry into growth markets is that the existence of a market opportunity does not imply that there is a viable business opportunity for the long term. [27] The reverse is often the case. However, in the short term the new entrant might be successful because stronger, earlier entrants are too busy coping with demand to worry about the later entrants.

Entry at the Mature Stage

Few small firms enter the mature phase of a product class, but those who do should always attempt to avoid direct competition with established firms. New entrants need to have a specific competitive advantage if they are to succeed, and since substantial product innovation is unlikely to occur at this stage, successful entrants adopt specialized niche strategies. The niches are characterized by the need for "customer-specific" products and services, or highly specialized products which large firms following a standard product strategy find difficult to offer. The major problem facing entrants in this sector is lack of growth potential. Most specialized niches are small market segments, and so the firm has to enter new product classes and new markets soon after start-up, if it is to grow to a significant size. The advantage of niche businesses, however, is that they rarely encounter significant competition from large competitors, since the market segments are too small to be of interest to them.

The Market Opportunity Funnel

Each of the three identified types of product strategy—product class, product segment, specialized niche—tends to correspond to a particular stage of the market life cycle. As the market grows, the entry options narrow rapidly as barriers to entry rise and the market begins to segment. The "market opportunity funnel" (see Figure 2.3) helps us visualize the process.

The point of market entry determines both the scope for growth and the choice of strategy. Firms entering emerging markets nearly always have innovative products but as the market grows, many new entrants have only incrementally superior products, or worse still, me-too products. Those with me-too products who enter a mature market are almost certain to fail, while those with an incrementally superior product may succeed initially in a growing market but will have increasing difficulty as the market matures. Some later entrants may still be truly innovative—often leapfrogging the technology of the early entrants—but this becomes increasingly difficult to do

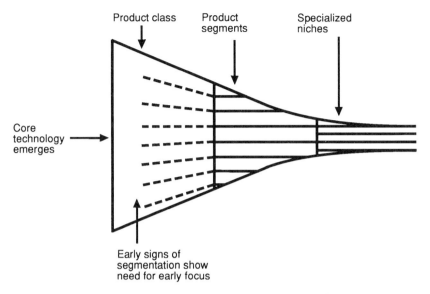

Figure 2.3   *The market opportunity funnel*

once large players are established in the market. The early entrants have by now grown large or the market has attracted big established companies to enter, both of whom can outgun the later entrant in terms of both product development and marketing expenditure. To succeed, the later entrant must find a specialized niche. Only rarely will a later entrant revolutionize the market to such a degree that the whole market goes through a further growth phase. This usually happens only when there is a breakthrough in the relevant core technology.

Failure to understand the implications of different product-market strategies at entry means that both managers and shareholders are often surprised when new high-tech firms fail to meet their growth targets or show a need to change their initial product-market strategy early in their history. A clearer understanding of the consequences of choosing different product-market strategies at start-up should help both managers and shareholders better assess the risks and rewards associated with high-tech start-ups.

Figure 2.4 shows the pattern of product market positions at start-up and the likely success of each position.

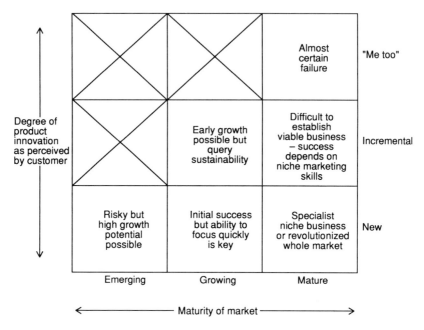

Figure 2.4 *Product-market position at start-up*

MARKETING INNOVATION

Not all small high-tech firms rely on technology to give them a source of competitive advantage. Product innovation tends to drive the development and subsequent growth of most small high-tech firms, but a few high-tech start-ups have been phenomenally successful by focusing on marketing innovations. After IBM moved into the personal computer (PC) industry and took a dominant market share position, experts declared the PC industry closed to newcomers. One industry analyst advised entrepreneurs in small computer companies "to go into the restaurant business". However, the second half of the 1980s saw the growth of several new companies that found ways of competing successfully against the giants—notably the Dell Computer Corporation of Austin, Texas, and Everex Systems Inc. of Fremont, California. These companies have discovered that innovative sales and marketing strategies which provide added value to their customers can be as successful as innovation in product design and technology. The start-up strategies adopted by these companies deserve closer attention.

Michael Dell founded his company as a 19-year old student at the University of Texas in 1984, selling microcomputer components to local computer enthusiasts. By 1985, when Dell started assembling his own line of PCs, it was already too late to challenge the technological standards set by IBM, or to challenge the strong dealer networks of Compaq (for its IBM clones). Dell chose a different strategy—one defined by a unique marketing and distribution approach. He side-stepped the dealers and sold direct to customers (both end users and major corporations), using telesales and a key account salesforce. Dell calls this a direct relationship marketing strategy, the advantage being that it:

- avoids the dealer channel dominated by IBM, Apple and Compaq;
- avoids channel conflict problems;
- provides more efficiency than maintaining a large field salesforce;
- maintains lower prices and higher profit margins by eliminating middlemen, dealers and distributors;
- fosters customer loyalty through a direct relationship with users;
- provides a channel for quick customer feedback about both the product and emerging market trends.

By cutting out the middlemen, Dell has been able to under-price major competitors by up to 40%. As important as price is the support given to customers by the company's service organization. Here too, Dell has been innovative by organizing cells consisting of three salespeople, three technical support people, and two customer support people. Customers are assigned to a cell and obtain personalized service. Dell's overall strategy is perhaps best summarized by a quote from its founder:

"There's no great mystery to building a PC. The parts all come from the same few suppliers. I simply identified a market segment that was having to pay too much for what they were getting, and found an efficient way to reach that segment."[28]

Dell Computer Corporation has been profitable from the start and went public in June 1988. For the year ending January 1992 sales reached $890m and profits before tax were $51m.

Dell claims that over 90% of user problems are resolved over the telephone, although it is backed up by a sub-contractor (Xerox Corp.) that provides field service. The phone calls also help Dell to maintain quality by allowing them to identify defects quickly. One of Dell's marketing managers said:

> "If we get more than a few complaints, I go about 130 feet to the people who design the thing. Within five or six hours engineering has fixed the design, and within two or three days, the factory's got that change incorporated on the line." [29]

Dell's close-to-the-customer approach is supported by its flexible manufacturing operation, which allows products to be custom built at low cost with short response times. Michael Dell describes the manufacturing process as "an assembly line to build one at a time". Unlike the large competitors whose products are configured to customer needs at the dealer level, Dell's plants undertake product customization.

Another company adopting a similar strategy is Everex Systems Inc., which manufactures PCs and peripheral equipment. The company was founded in 1983 by Steve Hui, who has built his entire strategy around fast response—a system he calls "zero response time", since most orders are translated into a product that is manufactured and shipped within 24 hours. The company also relies on telemarketing. Every two hours orders are collected and analyzed, and the production schedule changed as necessary. Everex grew from start-up in 1983 to sales of $266m in 1988.

For start-ups which lack proprietary technology in an already established market, marketing innovation is one route to building a successful company. Marketing innovation can take many forms, but it usually involves identifying segments of the market whose needs are not being properly met by current suppliers. The key to success in marketing innovation is speed of implementation. Once the start-up strategy is seen to be successful, it is important for the new firm to grow as fast as possible to dominate its chosen segment. Innovative marketing strategies can be imitated like innovative product strategies, particularly if the potential market is large—as with mail order personal computers. However, when the strategy involves providing a high level of customer service, marketing innovations are sometimes more durable, since firms who are left in the catch-up position do not usually find new marketing strategies easy to implement. Thus, direct marketing experiments by some of Dell's competitors have failed since attempting to switch from one distribution strategy to another resulted in channel conflicts and disruptions.

PRODUCT-MARKET RISK

The degree of risk inherent in technology-based start-ups can be seen as a spectrum from relatively low risk or "soft" start-ups, to high risk or "hard" start-ups.[30] Risk includes operational, managerial and financial risk, as well as marketing and technical risk.

The least risk start-up is one which involves experimentation through the provision of technical consulting and contract research and development. Risk increases for firms that have not developed their own products at start-up; the degree of risk increasing as the type of start-up focus shifts from consulting to customized products to semi-customized products, and eventually standard products. Risk is also increased if the firm adopts a wider market focus. Thus, market risk tends to be higher if the firm focuses on a wide mass market than if it focuses on a niche segment. If the firm decides to produce standard products for the mass market, risk can be further increased if the firm decides to try to capture additional added value by participating in additional stages of the supply chain (e.g. by manufacturing components instead of just assembling them). Figure 2.5 illustrates how risk increases as the start-up focus of the firm moves from "soft" to "hard".

Soft start-ups provide custom-made products and services (e.g. technical consulting) on a "contract" basis to specialist markets. A soft business's focus is on analysis and design work in its broadest sense. These firms are generally self financing , building sales step by step, and as a result only experience modest growth. The soft start brings numerous advantages to

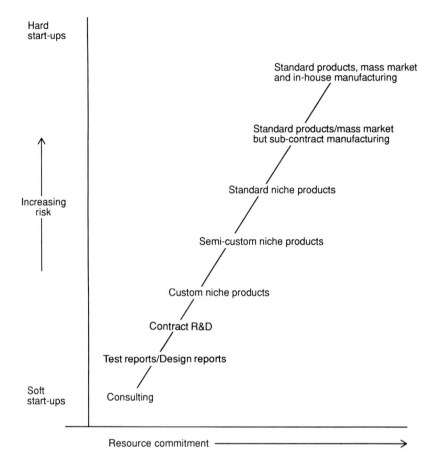

Figure 2.5   *Risk model of start-up activities*
Source: Adapted from Bullock, M. "Academic Enterprise, Industrial Inno-
vation and the Development of High Technology Financing in the United
States", by permission of Brand Bros & Co., London

the small technology-based firm, such as customer-financed
product development, minimum investments in fixed costs at
start-up (hence, low entry barriers), secure sales through contracts, and internally generated funds available for growth and
low downside risks.

At the opposite end of the spectrum are hard start-ups.
These firms start off with a standard product design, often with
investments in manufacturing and distribution. The model
postulates that the "hard" start-up involve higher downside

risks for small technology-based firms and hence should be avoided, particularly by bankers, although they may be favoured by venture capitalists who believe the higher risks may lead to higher returns.

If one assumes that at start-up most high-tech firms have a very limited resource base, one can postulate that in an ideal world firms would start soft and only increase the degree of risk as their resource base increases. In practice, product market decisions are based on a combination of "external" and "internal" features of the firm. While the "soft/hard" model addresses degrees of risk in different activities, it fails to highlight how the levels of return are determined by the external and internal features of the firm. External features include the nature of the underlying technology, the nature of the market, and competition. Internal features consist of ambitions of the founder, degree of product innovation, breadth of technical skills, and objective and focus of the firm.

The situation of a firm starting soft and then hardening step by step may be ideal from the point of view of reducing risk, but is rarely found in practice. The characteristics of the external and internal features of firms often means that a hard firm remains hard and a soft firm remains soft. Transition from soft to hard (or vice versa) has to be gradual and planned in order to be successful.

Features Affecting the Hard/Soft Choice

While there are a large number of factors that influence start-up success, the degree of product-market risk inherent in a new high-tech venture is determined by five principal factors:

1 *The ambitions and background of the founder(s):* An academic, risk-averse entrepreneur will prefer a "soft" start-up whatever the stage of market development, while an ambitious, risk-taking entrepreneur will prefer a hard start-up. Academic spin-outs started by technical entrepreneurs may choose a soft strategy, selling technical consulting and bespoke products, although opportunities may arise for later hardening.

2 *The technical base within the firm:* Small technology-based firms are often started by entrepreneurs with narrow skills. Such entrepreneurs may succeed in designing a "winning product" for a particular market (or segment), rather than have the skills to undertake bespoke products for a variety of customers. In such a situation, the soft start is not a choice available to the firm.

3 *The degree of product innovation:* A winning product and a large market are suitable conditions for a hard start. Examples of successful hard start firms which had these conditions are: Intel (which invented the microprocessor in 1971); Apple Inc. (first to introduce the microcomputer to a wide range of customers in 1977); Domino Printing Sciences (first British manufacturer of ink-jet printers); and Microvitec plc (first to introduce a highly innovative, high resolution colour monitor for microcomputers). All these firms adopted hard strategies as they all had excellent innovative, standard products with tremendous market potential.

4 *The nature of the product:* Some markets, such as industrial capital goods, are such that nearly all products are custom made and the volume of sales low. The superconducting magnets made by Oxford Instruments are examples of such products. In such markets, firms take a "custom" approach. However, the risk need not necessarily be lower (as in other soft starts), as investments in R & D and marketing can be higher.

5 *The stage of the market development:* A soft strategy is usually more suitable in very young and uncertain markets. Firms which harden in such highly uncertain markets experience high downside risks. Firms which aim to take a "central" position in their market grow and harden as the market matures. Those firms which pursue a soft strategy in mature markets experience limited potential for growth. Figure 2.6 helps to understand the need to link the soft/hard distinction of the firm's strategy to the stage of its market.

Soft start-ups are common when markets are very new and there is a high degree of uncertainty as to customer acceptance. Examples are the robotic and artificial intelligence markets.

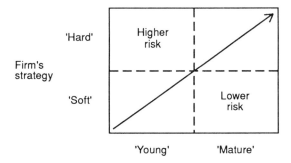

Figure 2.6 *Stage of the market*

Firms in these markets need to experiment to pick a winning product design and identify a lucrative customer group. Research shows that it is foolhardy to undertake speculative designing using one's own resources in such young and highly uncertain markets.

Soft start-ups are also common in mature markets where small firms often enter with a custom strategy. There is little chance for standardization of product designs, as large firms which entered early would be dominating most of the "standard" product segments. As such, these firms do not harden in their initial markets. Growth is via diversification into other markets based on a custom strategy.

Firms which are in rapidly growing markets and which are beyond the uncertainty period benefit from a standard product strategy. Adopting a custom strategy in such markets may mean losing a central position in the market and foregoing considerable growth potential.

Reducing the Inherent Risk in a Hard Start-up

Firms which, by the nature of their business, are forced to go for a standard product, reduce their risk in the following ways:

- By undertaking manufacturing, distribution or servicing for products designed or made by other manufacturers. Such activity complements their main activity and provides cash flow needed for growth.

- By designing highly innovative products in high-growth markets, hence compensating high risks with high rewards.
- By maintaining a portfolio of custom and standard products. The custom products assist the firm to keep pace with the changing needs of their target customer groups. This is especially important for firms adopting a strategy of selling products tailored to the unique needs of a particular customer group within a market. Additional benefits from the custom products are the challenge and motivation they give to technical staff and the assistance they give in identifying new products and their market opportunities.
- By obtaining large contracts which provide secure streams of cash flow to finance speculative product designing.
- By undertaking "private label" and OEM contracts.

Firms which start with a standard product without any of the above "softening" features are likely to experience financial problems. Examples of such firms are not difficult to find. There are many failures of firms which rush into committing resources in manufacturing and overseas distribution with a single product which is only incrementally innovative over competitive products. They are fooled by the initial rapid sales of the product, which are due to the rapid take-off of the market, and not to the firm's competitive advantage. As the new chief executive, Brian Moore of Dragon Data, exclaimed: "I think at the end of 1982, any product that we called a computer with a keyboard on would have sold." Dragon Data entered the booming UK home computer market in 1981 with a me-too product. It was the only microcomputer manufacturer with in-house manufacturing (other manufacturers concentrated on designing and subcontracted manufacturing), and was late in bringing out new products (which also turned out to be me-too products). Sales jumped from £2m to £15m between 1982 and 1983, but sales were down to £2m by 1984, when the company became insolvent. Dragon Data illustrates the case that is typical of many small technology-based firms which jump on the bandwagon of a rapidly growing market with little or no competitive advantage.

TYPICAL START-UP PROBLEMS

The high-tech start-up faces all the common problems characteristic of any start-up (see Table 2.2 for a list of typical problems). However, the following six problems appear to be the most common:

1 delays in product development;
2 premature market entry;
3 incorrect customer and market identification;
4 lack of credibility with potential customers;
5 unrealistic delivery promises;
6 lack of control over subcontractors.

Delays in Product Development

Problems in product development are prevalent in small high-tech companies, but particularly in those that have yet to achieve a sustained period of profitability. Since product development cycles are short and rates of innovation are fast, it is critical for success that initial product development should progress quickly. Even minor delays in development can bring a young company to the point of crisis. Seeq Technology, already referred to in this chapter, was a year late in shipping its first EEPROM products, although its initial start-up capital of $50m was sufficiently large to forestall an immediate crisis. [31]

A Japanese venture capitalist, specializing in high-technology companies in the USA commented:

> "I've seen more companies fail through not concentrating on their product than for any other reason. Product development always falls behind plan which obviously has serious repercussions on the viability of the investment. I always allow for this delay in assessing business plans. It is the most common reason that second and third round financing is needed."

A good example of what often happens is provided by a Silicon Valley company started by two British scientists who were developing a revolutionary semiconductor scanner. The

Table 2.2 *Typical start-up problems*

Difficulty in finding suitable premises
Finding the right people
   Do not know where to find them
   Poor at judging them
   Cannot pay enough to recruit top-quality people
Managing the people
   May have little or no experience in this area
   No established systems, procedures or standards exist
   New working relationships to be established
   Setting standards for both work and behaviour
   Need for intense supervision in the very early days
Suppliers
   Untried and untested so may be unreliable
   Unwilling to sign contracts
   New company lacks creditworthiness
Costs overruns
   Poor estimates in original business plan
   Cost of going down learning curve not taken into account
Market credibility
   Customers suspicious
   Underestimate marketing costs
   Underestimate time to get established
   Overestimate sales revenues
Lack of focus because desperate for sales volume
Technical problems
   Unforeseen product design difficulties
   Manufacturing equipment does not work to specification
Difficulties in scaling up production from pilot operation
Delays due to:
   Difficulty in recruiting
   Suppliers
   Customers
   Approval authorities, etc.
Overtrading—grow faster than cash resources permit
Accounting and control systems relegated to bottom of priority list
Financial leverage too high
Time pressures on entrepreneur
   To much to do
   24 hours/day not enough
   Stress and its effect on health and family
Entrepreneur's attitudes
   Lack of real commitment to the business
   Lack of urgency when no cash flow problems exist
   Poor leadership ability when the inevitable crisis arises
   Partnership problems or boardroom conflicts

Everything takes longer than planned because entrepreneurs consistently underestimate:
- The time necessary to implement even simple actions
- Speed of market acceptance
- The cost of going down the learning curve.

Hence most start-ups run into cash flow problems

company's first generation model was built according to schedule and was used on two blue chip beta sites (test sites) at IBM and Philips. The tests highlighted two significant problems with the design, which took a further two years to resolve. There were many reasons for this delay: not enough resources were channelled towards the development; too much of management's time was spent on demonstrating and gaining orders for the prototype model; offers of help were ignored by a team of engineers who were too proud to acknowledge that they needed assistance in development of "their" product. The length of time spent on product development enabled two multinational competitors to launch similar but more reliable products into the market.

Premature Market Entry

Entering the market with a less than acceptable product is clearly a recipe for failure, but it often happens in high-tech start-ups as management is usually eager to generate revenue to stem the cash outflow caused by product development. Financial pressures may not be the only reason influencing an early product launch. One venture capitalist commented:

> "Scientists and engineers are often so wrapped up in their products that they are too eager to bring its benefits to the public. This is usually a decision based on the need for recognition and satisfying egos rather than sound business reasons."

Seeq Technology also provides an example of premature market entry. In 1982/83, Seeq encountered much greater difficulty selling EEPROMS than had been expected. Commenting on the company's difficulties at that time, the new chief executive appointed in 1986, J. Daniel McCranie, said:

> "[Seeq] management would give all these occult reasons why the E-square market wasn't growing, like lack of standardization. That was baloney. The reason the market wasn't growing was that E-squares were on average five times more expensive than EEPROMS. It was felt that innovation would occur and the next thing you knew E-squares would cost no more than EEPROMS. That didn't happen."[32]

An early product launch where the product does not live up to quality and performance criteria has obvious cash flow implications, but it also leads to two additional problems for the high-tech firm: (1) larger competitors are able to examine the product, assess the apparent market potential from the reaction of the customers who have already bought the product and then focus their (larger) resources on its development; and (2) the marketing effort required to launch the product and subsequent engineering management effort needed to placate customers distracts from and delays the final development of the product.

A US vacuum technology start-up believed that the market was eagerly awaiting its product, and took the view that customers would be willing to put up with the flaws in order to gain the productivity advantages that the product provided. The decision backfired as customers were far from satisfied with the product's reliability, and competitors were able to get an early look at the new technology.

Incorrect Customer and Market Identification

The failure of high-tech start-ups to meet initial sales targets is often due to incorrect customer identification. Sometimes this is due to a failure on the part of management to segment the market, and to target their scarce marketing resources accordingly. This is not a problem unique to high-tech start-ups. A Chicago company produced an instrument that measured and recorded the performance of several critical parts of an aircraft and its engine. The product had a very good reputation in the aviation industry but the company suffered for a number of years with a sluggish sales record. The problem was one of customer identification. In the words of the present chief executive officer:

"In the first couple of years our company tried to sell to everyone who owned an aeroplane. This was in effect a world-wide marketing campaign. It involved a high number of salesmen and a high advertising budget that we just couldn't afford."

Segmentation of a potential customer base is not the only problem—that is relatively straightforward to solve. What is a bigger problem is the difficulty many high-tech start-ups have in identifying the customers for which their product technology is most suited. It seems that a certain amount of experimentation is necessary in the market-place, particularly where new technologies and/or new markets are emerging. Many successful high-tech start-ups had a number of false starts in their early days and had to switch market focus more than once.

British Vacuum Technology (BVT) Ltd, a British start-up in the vacuum technology equipment field was set up with the idea of focusing on those customers who would be manufacturing videotape for the emerging 8 mm video camera market. Contact with potential customers confirmed the market potential. As it happened, although the 8 mm videotape market did start to grow fast, existing chemical technology improved its performance characteristic, and the expected demand for BVT's technology never developed in that market area. Instead, the company started serving a completely different market, the hard disk manufacturing equipment market, albeit with the same technology. This market was not identified in the original business plan. The history of Microvitec's market development is similar. The company was established in 1979 with the aim of manufacturing screens for the videotex market. Sales to the market were small and the company was in danger of failing when suddenly the video-game market expanded rapidly and Microvitec took advantage of what was an unexpected opportunity. After very rapid growth in 1980 and 1981 that market stopped growing, only to be replaced immediately by a market opportunity to sell monitors to schools on the back of the very successful Acorn computer.[33]

Start-ups which stick rigidly to their original choice of customer base in the face of inadequate sales volume will find themselves in a financial crisis very quickly. While early focus is a characteristic of successful high-tech start-ups, innumerable case studies show that new markets are highly unpredictable and that the new company must be flexible about alternative market possibilities. The trick is to do this without spreading one's limited resources so thinly that there is no chance of penetrating any market.

Lack of Credibility with Potential Customers

Most start-ups, high tech or not, underestimate the marketing costs necessary to establish themselves in the market-place. The issue is one of lack of credibility. Customers—particularly industrial customers, who are the major customers for high-tech products—know that the failure rate of high-tech start-ups is high and that most small firms are under capitalized. How important these factors are depends on the nature of the start-up firm's product, and in particular whether the product is critical to the quality and performance of the purchaser's own product. If it is, the purchaser is going to want to be reasonably sure that the start-up firm is going to survive the life of the product. If the product is a capital purchase, such as a piece of production machinery, then the purchaser wants to ensure adequate after-sales service. If the product is a component or a subsystem, then the purchaser is particularly concerned with continuity of supply of a reliable quality product.

Establishing credibility is not, however, just a question of proving that the product and service is reliable. The start-up firm's financial backing—its capital base and the existence of quality investors (respected corporations, banks and venture capitalists)—can do a lot to establish credibility with major customers. More and more sophisticated customers are trying to off-load contractual risk onto their suppliers. When BVT Ltd obtained its first order from a Californian aerospace company in 1984, the customer asked BVT, whose start-up capital was £1m, for a £50m performance bond. The basis of the demand was the total value of the customer's own contract with the US Department of Defence. This was obviously impossible to arrange and eventually the customer settled for a performance bond to the value of £500,000. While the bond was arranged, albeit with great difficulty, any failure on the part of BVT to perform would have meant immediate insolvency.

Unrealistic Delivery Promises

Customer and competitor pressure in the high-tech sector often forces young companies to promise unrealistic delivery dates. A Chicago-based software firm provides a classic example. The company was started in 1982 by a software writer who, having worked in the insurance industry, designed application software to make the administration of insurance companies quicker, more accurate and less labour-intensive. The product was good and the company received an immediate and positive response from the market-place. Insurance companies were desperate to install the systems, costing about $200 000 each, as quickly as possible. Under pressure from customers, the Vice President of Marketing promised delivery dates that could not be met. The chief executive commented:

> "Yes the marketing guy would consult with the other two [software engineers] on feasible deadlines but he resorted to putting tremendous pressure on them to deliver. At first they said that the product could be delivered at best in three months. The marketing guy would shout at them saying it had to be ready in two. After a while they simply agreed to whatever he said, knowing that there was no chance of meeting the imposed deadlines."

This self-created problem was compounded by a change in the market-place. More software houses decided to enter the market, forcing prices down, which put pressure on the marketing VP to promise even more unrealistic delivery dates.

Lack of Control over Subcontractors

It is common practice for small high-tech firms, particularly at start-up, to contract out certain activities. On the surface this can make a lot of sense since it can enable the founder(s) to concentrate on product development and to avoid the high fixed costs associated with undertaking the activities in-house. Companies may contract out any part of the value chain (the sequence of activities from purchase of raw materials through to delivery of finished product), although small high-tech firms most commonly contract out manufacturing/assembly, engineering and distribution. The theory is to keep the higher value added activities such as research and development and service in-house; and subcontract the more commodity-like functions. [34] The theory is fine but in practice can cause major problems—particularly since in the period immediately after start up:

- management may not have any experience in working with subcontractors and hence does not know which ones are reliable;
- management is desperately short of time to institute proper controls over sub-contractors;
- the company is not (yet) a big enough customer of the sub-contractor to have much bargaining power with the sub-contractor.

A manufacturer that used CD-ROM (compact disc read only memory) technology to provide in-flight information to pilots sub-contracted out all three of the activities mentioned above—engineering, assembly and distribution. The company encountered problems in all three areas, as the following comments from the chief executive suggests: on contract engineering—"We had virtually no control over the contractor. He did not share our timetable or our sense of urgency"; on contract assembly—"We were trying to persuade pilots, whose lives depended to some extent on our equipment, to relinquish the tried and tested form of information in favour of our technology. And yet our equipment was proving unreliable"; on contract distribution—"There was lots of interest in our product but it was not top of our distributor's priority list."

SUMMARY

Most new high-tech firms fail to meet the forecasts made at the time of start-up—usually by a large factor. A few—very few—exceed the forecast. While there are many factors contributing to the success and failure of new high-tech start-ups, the initial choice of product-market strategy is crucial in determining how far the firm can grow without a major change of product-market direction. Many high-tech start-ups are doomed from the start because their initial product-market strategy has insufficient long-term potential to meet the objectives of both the entrepreneur and the shareholders. Consequently, many firms change product-market direction soon after start-up, often with disastrous effect.

This chapter started by looking at how high-tech start-ups begin with a period of experimentation, and then looked at how early success is dependent on both the success of the firm's first product and the timing of its market entry. Six factors were highlighted as being critical to the success of the first product: (1) the importance of the product to the customer; (2) the degree of product innovation; (3) the scope of product specifications; (4) the technical expertise of the founders; (5) neither underpricing nor overspecifying; and (6) top management commitment to the success of the product.

After discussing how different strategies are required for different phases of the market, the concept of the market opportunity funnel was introduced to illustrate how the entry options narrow as barriers to entry rise and markets begin to segment. The way in which marketing innovation as opposed to product innovation may be important for high-tech start-ups was also discussed.

The issue of product-market risk among high-tech start-ups was discussed, using the concept of "hard;" and "soft" start-ups, and several suggestions were made for reducing risk among the hard start-ups. Finally, six common problems that occur with high-tech start-ups in particular were highlighted. These are: (1) delays in product development; (2) premature market entry; (3) incorrect customer and market identification; (4) lack of credibility with potential customers; (5) unrealistic delivery promises, and (6) lack of control over subcontractors.

NOTES

(1) Bracker, J. S. and Pearson, J. N. "Planning and Financial Performance of Small Mature Firms", *Strategic Management Journal*, Vol. 7, pp. 503–522 (1986).
(2) Vesper, K. H. *New Venture Strategies*, Chapter 1. Prentice Hall, Englewood Cliffs, NJ (1980).

(3) Boeker, W. "Strategic Change: The Effects of Founding and History", *Academy of Management Journal*, Vol. 32, pp. 489–515 (1989).

(4) Feeser, H. R. and Willard, G. E. "Founding Strategy and Performance: A Comparison of High and Low Growth High Tech Firms", *Strategic Management Journal*, Vol. 11, No. 2, February, pp. 87–98 (1990).

(5) Eisenhardt, K. M. and Schoonhoven, C. B., "Organizational Growth: Linking Founding Teams, Strategy and Environment and Growth among US Semiconductor Ventures 1978–1988", *Administrative Science Quarterly*, September, pp. 504–528 (1990).

(6) Mintzberg, H. "Crafting Strategy", *Harvard Business Review*, Vol. 65, No. 4, July–August (1987).

(7) Slatter, S. St. P. *Cases in Strategic Management for the Smaller Business*, pp. 346–372, Basil Blackwell, Oxford (1988).

(8) Handy, C. *The Age of Unreason*. Business Books, London (1989).

(9) Handy, C. *The Age of Unreason*. Business Books, London (1989).

(10) Weigner, K. K. "You Can't Keep a Good Technology Down', *Forbes*, 18 April (1988).

(11) Rickman, T. "Who's in Charge Here?" *Inc.*, June, pp. 36–46 (1989).

(12) Keeley, R. H. and Roure, Juan B., "The Management Team Element in Technological Start-ups", in M. W. Lawless and L. R. Gomez-Mejia (eds) *Proceedings of Second International Conference on Managing the High Technology Firm*, University of Colorado, January (1990).

(13) Schoonhoven, C. B., Eisenhardt, K. M. and Lyman, K. "Speeding Products to Market: Waiting Time to First Product Introduction in New Firms", *Administrative Science Quarterly*, Vol. 35, pp. 177–207 (1990).

(14) Slatter, S. St. P. *Cases in Strategic Management for the Smaller Business*. pp. 329–345, Basil Blackwell, Oxford (1988).

(15) Manac Systems International Limited. Harvard Business School Case Study, 9-587-076 (1986).

(16) Slatter, S. St P. and King, P. "Stages of Business Development of Small Firrns in the Computer Aided Design Industry". London Business School Working Paper, June (1986).

(17) "Technology Alliances: An Interview with James Grant", *McKinsey Quarterly*, Autumn, pp. 58–67 (1988).

(18) Slatter, S. St. P. and King, P. "Stages of Business Development of Small Firms in the Computer Aided Design Industry". London Business School Working Paper, June (1986).

(19) See, for example, Keeley, R. H. and Roure, Juan B. "The

Management Team Element in Technological Start-ups", ibid. note 12.

(20) Freeman, C. *The Economics of Industrial Innovation*, Chapter 5. Frances Pinter, London (1982).

(21) Van de Van, A. H. "Designing New Business Start-ups: Entrepreneurial, Organizational and Ecological Considerations", *Journal of Management*, Vol. 10, No. 1 (1984).

(22) Schon, D. A. "Champions for Radical New Inventions", *Harvard Business Review*, March/April, p. 84 (1963).

(23) Maidique, M. "Entrepreneurs, Champions and Technological Innovation", *Sloan Management Review*, Winter (1980).

(24) "Heel Marks at the Edge of the Cliff", *The Stanford Magazine*, Fall, pp. 12–20 (1982).

(25) Romanelli, E. "Environments and Strategies of Organization Start-up: Effects on Early Survival", *Administrative Science Quarterly*, Vol. 34, pp. 369–387 (1989).

(26) Eisenhardt, K. M. and Schoonhoven, C. B. "Organizational Growth: Linking Founding Team, Strategy and Environment and Growth among US Semiconductor Ventures 1978–1988", *Adminisitrative Science Quarterly*, September, pp. 504–528 (1990).

(27) Aaker, D. A. and Day, G. S. "The Perils of High Growth Markets", *Strategic Management Journal*, Vol. 7 No. 5, September–October, pp. 409–421 (1986).

(28) Angrist, S. W. "Entrepreneur in Short Pants", *Forbes*, March 7, pp. 84–85 (1988).

(29) Kotkin, J. "The Innovation Upstarts", *Inc.*, January, pp. 70–76 (1989).

(30) The terms "hard" and "soft" to describe risk were first used by Bullock, M. in "Academic Enterprise, Industrial Innovation and the Development of High Technology Financing in the United States". Unpublished mimeograph.

(31) Weigner, K. K. "You Can't Keep a Good Technology Down", *Forbes*, 18 April (1988).

(32) Weigner, K. K. "You Can't Keep a Good Technology Down", *Forbes*, 18 April (1988).

(33) Slatter, S. St. P. *Cases in Strategic Management for the Smaller Business*, pp. 329–345, Basil Blackwell, Oxford (1988).

(34) Mosakowski, E. "Organizational Boundaries and Economic Performance: An Empirical Study of Entrepreneurial Computer Firms", *Strategic Management Journal*, Vol. 12 No. 2, February, pp. 115–133 (1991).

3
Product-Market Development

We saw in Chapter 2 how the initial choice of product-market focus determines the long-term potential of the initial strategy. In some cases the initial strategy needs to be adjusted within months of start-up, while in other situations the strategy may hold good for a long time, and growth is a question of pursuing product development and market development opportunities. This chapter assumes the broad product-market focus has been decided and looks specifically at *how* the management team can build product development and marketing capabilities to improve its chance of success in its chosen product-market segments. How well the firm undertakes these activities determines its competitive advantage (or lack of it) and its chances of becoming established in the market-place. The successful firm will understandably be challenged by competitors, both new entrants with alternative or improved technologies, and by larger players with extensive access to finance and know-how. The nature of competition small high-tech firms can expect and the challenges these pose for management are discussed at the end of the chapter, as are various co-operative strategies which small firms can adopt to reduce both their product and market risks.

PRODUCT DEVELOPMENT

Very few firms are able to repeat their early success in designing and launching innovative products. Most firms'

Table 3.1 *Type of subsequent products among 24 small high-tech firms in the UK*

Type of Product	Percentage of Companies
New	4
Incremental	83
Me-too	46

subsequent products are only incrementally better than those of their competitors, and many firms introduce me-too products in an attempt to grow. Table 3.1 shows the results of a study of 24 small high-tech firms in the UK. The emphasis on subsequent product development in the small independent company is on improving and enhancing the first product. New product development is regarded as an iterative and evolutionary process, with new products being derivatives of the first product. Many well-established firms still appear to be single product firms even after substantial new product activity.

Expenditure on new product development is nearly always directed towards development rather than research: few small high-tech firms undertake basic research. New product ideas evolve mainly from the perceived needs of the market-place, although there is a wide spectrum of practice: from the 100% technology-driven company that has little or no accurate information about customer needs, to the truly marketing-led company. Six factors determine the success of new product development activities after a successful first product has been launched:

1 orientation to customers' needs;
2 emphasis on strong technical superiority;
3 continuing involvement of the entrepreneur;
4 focusing scarce technical resources;
5 access to multiple sources of technology;
6 managing sympathetically.

Orientation to Customers' Needs

Most small high-tech firms believe that their product development efforts are geared to meeting a customer or market need, or are geared to overcoming weaknesses in competitors' products. The belief is usually genuine: the problem is that the belief is based on management's mistaken perceptions of customers' needs. Identifying customers' needs for high-tech products is notoriously difficult since customers are rarely able to specify their needs, particularly where new technology is involved. As markets grow, it becomes easier to identify customers' needs but, as shown in Chapter 2, the market opportunity funnel narrows, possibly resulting in limited scope for growth.

Some high-tech entrepreneurs appear to have visionary capabilities which enable them to see needs before the customer realizes he or she actually has such a need. Steve Jobs appears to have had this capacity at Apple. In his book, *Odyssey*, John Sculley quotes Jobs as saying:

> "What we want to do is change the way people use computers in the world. ... What we're doing has never been done before ... my dream is that every person in the world will have their own Apple Computer. To do that we've got to be a great marketing company." [1]

Other less well-known entrepreneurs profess to have this vision, only to be proved wrong by the market-place.

In practice, there is little or no substitute for the old cliché of "being close to the market". Most successful small firms are *close* to their market and gear their product development activity accordingly. Some of the most successful firms have deliberately developed custom or semi-custom products alongside standard products in order to be close to their customers. The identified needs of customers are then fed into their product development programmes. A secondary benefit of developing custom products is that the customer pays for the development work, the firm often later moving into semi-custom products on the back of customer financing. Other ways in which firms keep close to the market are through user groups and their own in-house product support functions that gather first-hand information about customers' needs. Intensive interaction with customers is critical, as indeed is interaction internally between the product development and marketing functions.

Emphasis on Strong Technical Superiority

Successful small high-tech firms place heavy emphasis on achieving technical superiority over competitors. This can be achieved only if the company has strong technical capabilities. In the early stages of the technology life cycle, there are likely to be frequent and major product innovations. Strong technical resources are required to keep apace of these developments, otherwise the firm's product performance will fall behind that of its competitors. In Slatter and King's[2] study of new product development in the computer-aided design (CAD) industry, those firms where the product development team had higher academic qualifications, more experience and had won technical awards, were better able to cope with product competition than their less technically able counterparts. Even when firms relied heavily on outside sources by licensing in or acquiring third-party products, sound in-house technical resources were needed to integrate, commercialize and support such products. One finds that successful firms are continuously in the process of enhancing their technical resources by training, retraining and motivating their staff.

Strong technical resources include not only the ability to design innovative products, but also the ability to design-in quality and to design products which can be manufactured at low cost once margins start to erode. Designing-in quality is critical to success since quality problems are often a root cause of failure in small high-tech firms (see Chapter 8). While there are many reasons for quality problems, good product quality starts with basic design strategy. Designing cost out of products is also critical for competitive success once the rate of growth of the market starts to slow down and price competition emerges. Few high-tech firms find this an easy transition since their early success is usually due to following a high margin differentiated strategy. Developing products for low cost manufacturing requires a different approach and, many would argue, a different development team from that which developed the original innovative product.

While technological superiority can provide competitive advantage for the small high-tech firm, the big danger that goes with it is blindness to the requirements of the market-place (already discussed above) and delays in launching new products. Delays are caused by engineers constantly changing the design to incorporate the "latest improvements" or waiting until they have achieved a major breakthrough, allowing them to leap-frog the competition in a significant way. Such an approach allows the faster competitor to launch more new products and to have a more up-to-date product line than the slower moving competitor. Late product launches lead to products that were intended to be incremental product improvements becoming me-too products. At Oregon-based Lattice Semiconductor, part of the turnaround strategy of Cyrus Tsui, the new President and CEO (chief executive officer) hired in September 1988, has been to improve the speed of product development. Within a year, Tsui reduced design cycle times by 35% to 45%, and new products started to appear. Tsui believes this was crucial to his turnaround success: "The only advantage small companies have over big companies is their ability to execute fast and flawlessly." [3]

The success of Sun Microsystems in the work-station market against Apollo Computer (now owned by Hewlett Packard) has been put down to the successful way that they continually improve their product. By 1987/88 Sun's stated strategy was to double the performance of its work stations every 12/18 months, which was in contrast to most major competitors who were working on a two- to three-year product life cycle. [4,5] By 1991 this had been reduced to about nine months. Sun's emphasis on speed of new product development means that innovation is more or less continuous and that, on average, Sun's product line encompasses more up-to-date technology than Apollo's. Although Sun was started a year and a half after Apollo, it is now almost twice the size and twice as profitable.

Speed of new product development is crucially important, but there is a question as to how fast firms should jump into new product development without carefully defining the price-performance features of the product. Compaq, the portable computer manufacturer, is known to have relatively short product development times, creating new machines in about nine months. However, before development starts the company may spend up to two years deciding what to make. A product definition team, made up of managers from engineering, manufacturing, marketing, sales and finance, must agree on features, performance and price before development goes ahead. "It's better to leave the company in limbo than to head off in the wrong direction," says Joseph Canion, Compaq's President. "Developing a new product is like jumping out of an airplane. One way or another you're going to get to the ground, so you'd better be sure your parachute works."[6] More recently Toshiba has started to gain market share from Compaq and part of its strategy has involved a very large number of new product introductions. It is interesting to speculate to what extent Canion's slightly cautious approach may have helped Toshiba.

Product superiority implies that the small high-tech firm must try to make its product difficult to imitate. If it has patents which it has the time and resources to protect, it may be able to maintain a technological lead until there is a technological breakthrough by a competitor. If this is not the case, then the firm must try to make imitation difficult and expensive for potential competitors. Successful exploitation of a technology typically requires the acquisition or development of complementary technologies. It will often be in the interest of the small high-tech firm to obtain such technologies (usually from external sources) so as to develop a multitechnology-based system. The successful interface of technologies often requires considerable learning and expertise on the part of the organization, a competence which small firms often find easier to develop than larger ones. Multitechnology-based systems can act as a source of competitive advantage for the small firm, since they make imitation more difficult and expensive.

Continuing Involvement of the Entrepreneur

The continued presence of the entrepreneur (the founder or one of the founding team) at a senior level in the organization is critical to successful product development. This point has been frequently made in the literature, and is confirmed by the author's own work in the UK.[7,8] Steve Jobs when developing the Macintosh computer at Apple is quoted as saying: "This product means more to me than anything I've ever done in my whole life. I love this product ..."[9] The critical role of the entrepreneur is to match the technology with the market—or, as one writer observed: "to understand the user requirements better than competitive attempts, and to ensure that adequate resources are available for development and launch."[10] This definition highlights two key aspects of entrepreneurial activity: (a) the need for the entrepreneur to communicate with and understand the firm's technology and market, and (b) the need to have the authority and power to allocate resources so as to drive the new product development process from the idea stage through to successful launch.

The continuing importance of the entrepreneur's involvement and commitment is often only apparent once the entrepreneur is unwilling or unable to perform the new product development role. This is usually a consequence of growth. Growth often leads to a changing role for the entrepreneur within the organization (see Chapter 5), and crisis often leads to his or her removal from the company (see Chapter 8). However, even if the entrepreneur remains willing and able to undertake the role, the climate has to be right for innovation to succeed. It is not always well understood that entrepreneurs are motivated by freedom, power to control resources, creativity and the challenge of identifying new opportunities. Once outsiders, such as venture capitalists and professional managers, have a controlling influence on the firm, the technical entrepreneur may feel demotivated because he or she can no longer be truly entrepreneurial. A good example of this phenomenon is provided by an entrepreneur who sold his successful computer-aided design company to a larger competitor and was then asked to manage his firm as a research and development subsidiary of the acquirer. The marketing of his product was removed from his control and integrated with that of the parent company. The entrepreneur left soon afterwards and remarked:

> "Our acquirers thought we were a clever load of boffins and all that we
> wanted was to go into our research labs and develop new products. But
> we could not do that without closely working with sales, because not

one of our products was developed on our own. Every product was created by a process of negotiation, iteration and working closely with the customers. Since the takeover we have had disastrous development projects where we have tried to develop products in isolation from the customers. Any attempt by development people, however good their record is, will not be successful if done in isolation from customers."

Focusing Scarce Technical Resources

The lack of technical resources is often one of the most significant barriers to growth for small high-tech firms. The technical staff in these firms have to divide their time between designing new products, improving existing products, and providing technical sales support and after-sales service. These four activities involve different time-scales. After-sales service has the shortest lead time—the need is usually immediate—followed by technical support to the sales function, and then improvement to existing products. New product development often comes last in the order of priority. Unlike large high-tech firms, where different staff can be allocated to these four activities, the staff of small high-tech firms have to balance their time between them.

Almost no small high-tech firms identify development expenditure separately in their control systems. Although the total salaries of technical staff is known, the cost is almost never allocated according to the time spent on the four activities identified above. In those few instances where such an exercise is carried out, management is usually shocked to learn how little time (and hence, money) is being invested in product development.

Besides allocating technical resources adequately across the total span of activities, the other major requirement for focusing scarce technical resources is within the product development function itself. Most product development departments aim to work on too many projects simultaneously, with the result that they spread their scarce resources too thinly to achieve results in the required time frame. One often finds that many of the projects are "pet" projects of some engineer for which the technological risk is unacceptable or the market potential is severely limited. Strong management is required to focus the activities of the development department, something which can be difficult to do without lowering the morale of key individuals, many of whom are like artists and see their pet projects akin to creative masterpieces, although they may be technological white elephants. The issue of managing technical staff is discussed in Chapter 4.

What is somewhat surprising is the difficulty management often has in small high-tech firms in getting their product development teams to allocate time to totally new product development as opposed to improving existing products. This is a real problem in those firms designing standard or semi-customized products where the technical staff are often emotionally attached to the products they developed in the past. As a result, they devote more time to improving existing products for which there is a proven market demand than developing new products, the success of which has yet to be proven.

Access to Multiple Sources of Technology

Most firms develop their first product in-house but increasingly use external sources to help subsequent product development. Many small firms find it exceptionally difficult to keep up-to-date in their core technological area, and impossible to have all the necessary technical skills in-house where the chosen product-market requires the use of multiple technologies to meet the customers' needs. We shall discuss later in this chapter how speed is a major competitive weapon in high-tech industries, and that most small firms use speed of response to compete against each other and against larger competitors. The need for speed coupled with the small firm's lack of resources to invest in research and development means that the small firm relies on external sources of technology as a means of accelerating its response time. The major external sources of technology are:

- Obtaining free advice by scouring all available resources. One biomedical company in the UK does this, for example, by talking to doctors at the local teaching hospital.

- Liaison with (usually local) universities. This may be formal or informal, and very often it is difficult to see where the commercial linkage ends and the university's research begins.
- Employing highly recognized experts as consultants or non-executive directors. Many small biotechnology companies, for example, have academic founders who continue with their university posts as well as acting as scientific advisers.
- Spin-offs from another company whereby the "entre-preneurial" group brings technology with it.
- Licensing-in technology from other companies.
- Developing collaborative deals with other companies, often in the same industry, to maximize the synergistic opportunities available. This can involve sharing of proprietary information.
- Exclusive rights to the research and development findings of a research body, e.g Celltech, the leading UK biotechnology company has rights to the R & D output from the British Medical Research Council.

While external sources of technology may lower total costs, avoid "reinventing the wheel" internally, and provide access to specialized or new sources of technology, there are three significant disadvantages if there is an overreliance on external sources of technology:

1 The "imported" technology is not proprietary, even if there is an exclusive agreement for its use. The company's technology strategy, which is basic to its success and its competitive advantage, are outside its own control. Any hiccup in the relationship between the company and its third-party technology supplier can spell disaster for the company. Legal contracts rarely provide much real protection once the agreement starts to go wrong.
2 Internal technical capabilities are not developed, which acts as a severe brake on the future strategic development of the business.
3 Delays in product development are likely due to the difficulty of transferring technology from third parties. Most firms underestimate the time and costs involved in this process. Products that have been designed in research

laboratories and universities frequently have to be redesigned to suit the particular requirements of the market-place.

There is a complete spectrum of companies, from those which rely 100% on internal sources, to those that have none of their own technology and rely exclusively on outside sources. Total reliance on internal sources makes companies very vulnerable to shifts in technology, and it is unlikely that any small company can survive the long term if it believes its own technical people have a monopoly over knowledge. Equally, at the other end of the spectrum, total reliance on external sources will probably lead to a poor product range unless the firm develops its capabilities as efficient marketeers.

Successful firms use multiple sources of technology, and strike a balance between internal and external sources. AGC, for example, a UK leader in the field of plant biotechnology, combines the exclusive rights to the R & D work of the Agriculture and Food Research Council with considerable in-house expertise and continuing strong links with Cambridge and other universities' botany research departments. Proprietary technology, from whatever sources, does not, however, guarantee sustained competitive advantage, due to short product life cycles. Companies need to develop their own in-house technical capabilities to stay ahead of the competition even if they are extensively utilizing external resources. One software company that was licensing-in product designs showed that the development expenditure needed to integrate, commercialize and support products varied from one and a half times to three times the royalty expenditure during the first three years of sales (see Table 3.2).

Table 3.2 *Development costs of licensed-in products*

	Year 1	Year 2	Year 3
Sales ($million)	1.6	13.2	40.0
Royalty: R & D expenditure ratio	1:2.9	1:2	1:1.6

Managing Sympathetically

Much has been written about the management of research and development staff, and Chapter 4 of this book looks very specifically at the characteristics of managing small high-tech firms and some of the difficulties of managing technical staff. However, a section on product development is not complete without mentioning how important the management of the product development function is. Strong technical leadership with clear objectives and deadlines is necessary—yet the leadership style must be sympathetic to the culture of a research and development department. It must allow flexibility and some experimentation if innovation is to flourish. Part of the leadership function must also be to ensure that there is a coherent product development strategy which avoids developing too many me-too products or spreading scarce resources too thinly. Without good leadership, good technical staff will be wasted. Leadership of the product development function requires an unusual blend of technological competence, interpersonal skills and management understanding.

For a firm's product development activities to be robust, all six characteristics must be present. If one or more characteristic is missing, fragility increases. Rarely will everything go smoothly because the resource base of the small high-tech firm is too thin, and unforeseen technical difficulties are inherent in the very nature of high-tech industries. Delays in launching new products and technical problems ("bugs") with recently launched products are the most common symptoms of deeper problems within the product development function.

MARKET DEVELOPMENT

Most small high-tech firms *underestimate* the costs required to establish both their firm and their products in their chosen market segments. Marketing and associated product support costs can be significantly greater than product development costs—often in the order of two times greater, and sometimes more. Part of the reason for this is the time it takes to establish credibility, a problem which almost never goes away as long as the company is small. Even the larger companies find that credibility among customers for high-tech products is a fragile notion that needs constant attention. A few quality problems, for example, and there may be a rapid deterioration in credibility.

Besides establishing and maintaining credibility, the other principal reason for high market development costs is the time it takes for customers to make purchase decisions. Firms always *underestimate* the time between initial customer interest and receipt of order. While this is a problem for all firms selling industrial goods, it is particularly acute for the small high-tech firm, which is likely to have limited financial resources and very quickly finds itself with cash flow problems due to delays in orders being placed. In some high-tech sectors where products have to go through a long customer approval process, as in the aircraft industry, for example, the delays may be considerable. In the UK, the liberalization of the telecommunications industry led to new firms entering the market for equipment and services, but there was considerable time and cost associated with seeking the necessary permissions. [11]

This section excludes discussion of market strategies that take the firm into new market segments: that is the topic of Chapter 6. This section focuses on six market development issues common to the small high-tech firm trying to grow in its chosen target segments. The six issues are:

1   building and maintaining credibility;
2   building market differentiation;
3   linking with large customers;
4   developing appropriate distribution and selling;
5   managing the marketing effort;
6   speed to market.

Building and Maintaining Credibility

During the start-up phase, establishing credibility for the company is of paramount importance since customers are reluctant to place orders, however good the product, since they are concerned that the company may not survive. At BVT, the Finance

Director was involved in many sales presentations in an attempt to convince potential customers that the financial position of the company was sound. This start-up problem lasts at least three years before customers start to have confidence that the firm will survive. However, the problem never completely goes away as long as the firm remains relatively small and independent, since customers know how vulnerable the small high-tech firm can be. Even once the firm's credibility is established, each new product—particularly those that are radical innovations based on new, unproven technology—must establish credibility. The biotechnology industry provides plenty of current examples. One striking example is a company that markets grease-eating bacteria for cleaning drains. Since the end users of the product are industrial and commercial kitchen staff who have little appreciation of the technology, the concept of breeding bugs in the kitchen to keep the drains clean is not easy to sell. Another company which manufactures "natural" food additives using a biotechnological process, takes a great deal of effort to play down the biotechnology origins of its products. Many biotechnology companies now employ public relations agencies to try to project a natural, non-scientific image to customers and the general public.

Building and maintaining credibility with customers is about keeping promises regarding delivery and service, and meeting agreed product specifications. The process takes time. There is no magic panacea other than to stress the importance of constant two-way communication with the customer, which involves both listening to and educating the customer—and the more advanced the technology, the more education that is required. As the customer learns the technology, so the communication process should become more biased towards learning from the customer.

There are, however, two concrete steps that the small high-tech firm can take to develop credibility: obtain a set of key reference customers and build a demonstration product or "demo lab" to prove that their product(s) works. Key reference customers are typically well-known customers who are recognized in their industry as leaders and are satisfied with the firm's product and service. If the firm has a good relationship with these customers, it can use their names to give it credibility, and maybe even arrange for potential customers to visit the reference companies' sites. Where this is impossible, investing in one or more demonstration machines, or even a demonstration laboratory, can be important. Firms selling capital goods find that bringing potential customers to a demo lab or to a reference customer's site is the most effective way of communicating the product's performance features.

Building Market Differentiation

Nearly all small high-tech firms attempt to follow Michael Porter's strategy of focus via differentiation.[12] The principal sources of differentiation are technology and service, although most successful firms strive to develop a reputation as specialists in the eyes of their customers, so that reputation, and in some instances brand names, become sources of differentiation. Designing and manufacturing low-cost products is rarely the basis of a small firm's strategy. Successful small high-tech firms make a continuous and concerted effort to differentiate: they are committed and dedicated to their area of activity, be it a product group, a market or a technology.

Differentiation on the basis of technology is brought about through developing superior product features and superior product performance compared with those of competitors' products. Small firms usually use flexibility as a source of competitive advantage, and give customers a wider choice by offering to customize standard products or by offering very specialized, custom-made products.[13]

Where the small firm is competing against larger firms in the market-place, the most common form of differentiation is customer service. This arises because good customer service is more likely to be sustainable as a source of competitive advantage than the firm's technology, which is forever being "leap-frogged" by competitors. Not only can high levels of service act as a competitive weapon, but close customer relationships also pay off in terms of new product development (discussed above).

Customer service is becoming increasingly important as a competitive weapon in many electronic-related sectors as software, which has been the major source of differentiation in the 1980s, becomes more of a commodity product.

Linking with Large Customers

Large contracts with established customers is one way that small high-tech firms have overcome the credibility problem, built positive cash flows and grown their business quickly. One of the more dramatic examples in recent years is a 1986 start-up, Conner Peripherals, which has become the fastest growing company in US history by forming an alliance with Compaq Computers. Compaq provided $12m of seed funding in return for 40% of the company after the founders, Finis Conner and John Squires, were turned down by several venture capital companies. In its first year (fiscal 1987), sales reached $113m, and grew to $705m in fiscal year 1989. The company started as a captive supplier of $3\frac{1}{2}''$ disk drives to Compaq; Compaq took 90% of Conner's first year production, although this percentage was reduced to 29% by 1989 as Conner made similar deals with other OEMs. Conner Peripheral's current strength comes from its ability to control risk by demanding some form of up-front commitment from customers—either in the form of direct investment (as with Compaq), or in the form of a commitment to purchase a certain number of disk drives once they are ready to be shipped. Conner's Executive Vice President of Sales and Marketing, C. Scott Holt, says: "We are able to reverse the traditional way products are developed: design, build and sell. We sell, design and build, and that has helped us avoid innumerable problems." [14]

A similar strategy was used by the fastest growing high-tech start-up of the 1980s in the UK—Acorn Computers. Acorn grew from start-up in 1979 to sales of £93m in the 1983/84 fiscal year, by doing an exclusive deal with the BBC (British Broadcasting Corporation) to market its products to schools. Other companies like Microvitec, a manufacturer of colour monitors, grew on the back of the agreement.

Software companies, particularly those manufacturing operating systems, have employed similar strategies. Microsoft, for example, which developed the MS-DOS standard for IBM, has enjoyed huge success riding on the back of its OEM contract. Its founder, Bill Gates, became the computer industry's first billionaire, and as of January 1992 is considered to be the richest man in the United States.

Linkages are not always formal contractual relationships. Many small service companies such as custom software companies, hardware distributors and value-added resellers (VARs), have built successful businesses by riding on the back of IBM, for example. Sphinx, a UK company set up in 1984 to develop and distribute UNIX-based application software, is a similar example, riding on the back of AT & T. The benefit of the relationship, however, is not all one way. The larger partner may also gain. Thus, although VisiCorp sold its VisiCalc spreadsheet program on the back of the Apple II computer, the early success of the Apple II in the business market was largely due to the existence of the VisiCalc program. [15]

In many instances the linkages are financial as the large customer has a financial stake in the small company that is acting as its supplier or its distribution channel. Besides Compaq's stake in Conner Peripherals, Olivetti has an equity investment in Sphinx, who are the co-owners with AT & T of a European company selling UNIX operating systems. Besides providing sound financial backing, such a "tie-up" helps the small company keep informed of its customer's or its supplier's technical developments.

There are obvious risks in being so closely associated with one customer or, in the case of a service company, with one supplier. If the relationship goes wrong for whatever reason, or the OEM's business starts to fail, the small firm is extremely vulnerable. Chapter 8 identifies major contracts "going bad" as one of the causes of failure of small high-tech firms. The key to success, therefore, is diversifying the risk so as not to be too dependent on just one customer. Conner Peripherals appears to have been successful in doing this, but not all firms have the opportunity. Some of the small high-tech firms set up in response to the liberalization of the telecommunications industry in the UK which thrived on the back of equipment supply contracts for British Telecommunications (BT) found few other opportunities to diversify their customer base, as BT still had a near monopoly position in the UK market.

Developing Appropriate Distribution and Selling

Direct selling by the company's own salespeople is undoubtedly the most effective way of marketing high-tech industrial products. Where there are few potential customers because there are only a few OEMs, or the company is focusing on a very narrow market segment, this poses few problems—other than finding good technical sales people. This is easier said than done since good technical selling skills are all too rare. Not surprisingly, the computer industry is prepared to allow its best salespeople to earn more than the chief executive, if they are any good. In making salesforce decisions, management all too often forgets to go back to basics to analyze the purchasing behaviour of the customers and the nature of the sales task. Only if the nature of the sales task is clearly defined and competitors' sales tactics have been analyzed can the right type of salesperson be recruited. Some products or services require the salesperson to act more like a technical consultant than a salesperson, while in other situations the task is primarily educational or involves more aggressive selling. In one biotechnology company selling semen, the traditional artificial insemination product, to the cattle breeding industry, the switch to embryo transfer has caused immense selling problems. The company has found out through experience that a more technically sophisticated salesperson is required to sell embryos than semen.

For the small firm the issue is often: what can we afford? In an attempt to keep overheads low, many opt to use commission-only agents (or manufacturers' representatives) as a cheaper alternative. [16]

Where the market is fragmented and difficult for a small company to reach effectively and economically, as when the typical sales value of a single transaction is small, firms must rely on distributors. Building up a good distributor network is one of the most difficult tasks facing a small high-tech company, since technically sophisticated products and services do not easily lend themselves to indirect selling, and small companies find it difficult to obtain "share of mind" from established distributors unless they have a knockout product. Distributors' salesforces tend to be order-takers for established high volume lines. They rarely have the technical qualifications or obtain sufficient knowledge to sell a high-tech product, and rely largely on product data sheets for their information.

Managing the Marketing Effort

In all but a few of the more successful computer hardware and software companies, marketing in the true sense of the word is sadly lacking. Few if any firms have sufficient information about their customers or competitors, and few undertake any marketing analysis. The marketing cultures of the larger high-tech firms such as IBM, DEC and Hewlett Packard just do not exist. Instead, firms rely on the intuition of the entrepreneur or founding team to develop the right product for the right market at the right price. In other words, success is often a question of luck! While the entrepreneur may initially start a company around a significant product innovation for which there happens to be a market, subsequent success always requires a clear view of the market. For the small firm a practical marketing approach should involve:

- an analysis of customer buying behaviour;
- segmentation of the market by type of customer;
- an assessment of the size and growth rates of the major segments (customer segments as well as product segments);
- identification of competitors in each segment, their strategies, and an analysis of their strengths and weaknesses;
- identification and assessment of the major trends in the market and what is driving those trends;
- a review (or audit) of the firm's position in the market-place.

Such an approach is no different from that which should be followed by any small company. The problems are also the same: lack of data, lack of resources to collect the data, and lack of capability in marketing. The special problems of high-tech firms relate to difficulties in identifying market segments in emerging and growth markets, and difficulties in obtaining reliable forecasts of market size in markets which are often global in nature. Forecasts of market growth rates for high-tech products are notoriously over-optimistic. [17]

Speed to Market

The short window of opportunity characteristic of many high-tech sectors makes speed of market development of a new product a critical factor because, in all but a few situations, it is only a matter of time before competitors imitate or improve on the product. Licensing is one way of achieving this (see pages 98–102). The speedy commercialization of a new product immediately after launch is exceptionally difficult for small firms—particularly those lacking marketing skills. If the product is a radical innovation for which the market is ready, the judicious use of public relations in the trade press may create large demand quickly, although the downside of such quick market acceptance may be the firm's inability to gear up manufacturing and meet delivery promises.

COMPETITION

What is the nature of competition for small high-tech firms as they attempt to grow in their chosen product-market segments? Can small high-tech firms develop sustainable sources of competitive advantage to allow them to earn above-average profits (economic rents) against larger competitors when the market matures? These are key questions for the longer term survival of small high-tech firms.

The major competitive weapons used against the typical small high-tech firm are:

- product competition;
- price competition;
- marketing power;
- time-based competition;
- product standards.

As shown below, the small high-tech firm is usually more capable of competing against product and time-based competition than against price competition, marketing power and product standards.

Product Competition

High-tech industries are characterized by short product life cycles and rapid innovation. Leap-frogging competitors with a superior product or imitating them with a me-too product, are common forms of competition. Such competition may come from one small firm or from large players. A superior product based on superior design or technology is clearly a source of competitive advantage, but unless the firm can obtain good patent or copyright protection for its product, the competitive advantage is rarely sustainable. Few small firms can rely on continuous innovation to stay ahead of the competition. The evidence from field interviews suggests that repeating early product success is exceptionally difficult. In theory, patent or copyright protection should give the small firm total protection against imitators. In practice, patents and copyrights only provide limited protection, [18] and for most small high-tech firms none at all, since they do not have the financial or management resources to institute legal proceedings. Furthermore with some technologies, such as vacuum technology, the technology is more of a "black art" than a patentable product, making patent protection difficult or impossible; while for others, applying for patents is likely to alert competitors to future product moves or give them enough information to find ways around the patent. [19,20] The issue of intellectual property rights is a big issue for high-technology firms, but is beyond the scope of this book. Suffice it to say that such rights give little protection to the small high-tech firm.

Whether or not large players are attracted to compete in the market will depend on the potential size of the market and the stage of its development. Unless large companies decide to develop a market themselves based on proprietary core technology, they tend not to enter emerging markets, but wait until the market growth takes off. IBM's decision to enter the personal computer market after Apple and other start-up companies had established that a market exists is a case in point. To attract large players the market potential does not always have to be that big, since the pressure for growth on large companies coupled with a realistic analysis of the forces driving competition in volume markets has caused many large firms to become niche players in their search for growth. In the world market for advanced mass spectrometry, for example, sectors with only about US$50m on a global basis are attracting major Japanese competitors. However, this notwithstanding, the most attractive markets for small firms are still those which are too small to be of interest to larger competitors.

The ability of the small firm to compete successfully against product competition from large players depends on the nature of the technology and the depth of product customization required. In some high-tech sectors, particularly those selling large capital goods, technology tends to develop relatively slowly and size, *per se*, does not determine the rate of product development. Furthermore, a high degree of customization is often required which makes the market less attractive to large players. The nature of technology may, however, change over time, often increasing in complexity and sophistication as large new players enter the market and substantially increase investment levels in technological development.

Price Competition

The entry of new players into any market brings about a battle for customers and market share. Increased competition and the inevitable slowdown in the market growth rate will lead to price competition and decreased margins. As new entrants arrive with me-too or only marginally improved products, the early innovative firms will lose their technological differentiation, becoming more commodity-like in their characteristics. At the same time, the customers' bargaining power increases because they have more choice and become increasingly knowledgeable about purchasing the type of product in question. These forces reinforce each other, leading to more price competition and declining margins. At this stage, the small firm has to either develop a radical innovation to differentiate itself once again (which is likely to be very difficult), or try to defend its market share by becoming a low-cost competitor, or exit the market and refocus on new product-market segments.

Industries or market segments where competitive advantage is determined by cost leadership are a difficult environment for the small high-tech firm whose initial success has been based on product innovation. Even in those few situations where the firm has been set up with the aim of becoming a high volume, low cost producer, low costs have not been sustainable as a source of competitive advantage. The case of Microvitec, the UK pioneer in colour monitors, is just such an example. Microvitec's founder, Anthony Martinez, aimed to follow a cost leadership strategy but purchased his major component, cathode ray tubes, from Japanese television manufacturers. For three years the company was exceptionally successful, increasing sales from £0.2m in 1980, to £14.8m in 1984. The company went public in 1984, but almost immediately the Japanese suppliers started to manufacture their own colour monitors at cost levels which were beyond the reach of Microvitec. [21] In "volume" businesses—those selling standard products in large quantities—the small firm is likely to lack the cost advantages that accrue from economies of scale and learning curve effects.

Where there are no significant cost advantages due to size, the small high-tech firm still finds it exceedingly difficult to become a low-cost competitor. The difficulty arises because the efficiency necessary to be a low-cost producer is in conflict with the capabilities and conditions necessary for sustained product innovations. [22] The culture of the business, the characteristics of the people employed, the leadership style and the organizational structure all need changing. Although senior management may understand the need for such changes, the implementation process is exceptionally difficult. Very few small firms make the transition successfully since it involves abandoning the strengths on which the company grew, and moving into unknown waters. Significant management and staff changes are necessary to accomplish the result. Those companies that have built highly successful growth businesses have typically dealt with the problem by trying to separate the company into two divisions—as Apple did when they formed the Macintosh Division to find a replacement for the Apple II. Such solutions, while correctly recognizing the need for separate cultures, run the risk—as happened at Apple—of generating enormous conflict within the organization. This and other issues related to managing growth are discussed in Chapter 5.

Marketing Power

Even if the smaller firm can hold its own against larger competitors in terms of product competition and costs, it may still find itself at a major competitive disadvantage in terms of marketing muscle. Large companies in the high-tech area, like Hewlett Packard, typically have larger sales and service networks. The smaller firm struggles and often fails to develop the critical mass in marketing necessary to compete against the larger competitor. The classic example is IBM's entry into the PC market. The first generation of IBM PCs was recognized by industry experts as technologically inferior products to those of existing players, but the huge IBM sales and distribution network managed to capture the leading share of the US business market within a year of product launch. The same thing happened in Britain, where Clive Sinclair was the first to market pocket calculators and digital watches but was unable to commercialize his innovations fast enough to stop US and Japanese companies from quickly dominating the market.

While large sales and distribution networks are important ingredients of marketing muscle, one should not forget the importance of service networks in the high-tech marketing mix. Service networks include not only the provision of spares and repair facilities, but also installation and training of customers' personnel. The lack of an appropriate service package is often a major competitive disadvantage for the small firm. Now that large competitors have started to realize that service is one of the sources of sustainable competitive advantage which is most difficult to imitate, small firms are going to have to become more innovative in these service delivery systems when competing against large players. Dell Computer Corporation has shown the type of innovation necessary with its telephone service operation, supported by Xerox Corporation's field service engineers. [23]

Time-based Competition

Chapter 1 looked at how many high-tech markets are characterized by short product life cycles, leap-frogging and windows of opportunity that open and shut quickly. Time is, therefore, a critical competitive weapon since the firm with the shortest throughput time and/or response time stands to steal an advantage in the market-place. Throughput time and response time are different concepts. Throughput time refers to the whole value delivery system: it is the time taken to take a new product from the beginning to the end of the new product development cycle, including market introduction. Response time is the time it takes to develop a new product in response to a competitor's new product introduction. In strategic terms, a short throughput time can give first mover advantages, while a quick response time provides the opportunity for second mover advantages. Both can provide competitive advantage and, in theory, both options are open to small high-tech firms, although the exact nature of the sector will determine whether first or second mover advantages are the most advantageous.

First mover advantages typically provide competitive advantage where property rights (patents and copyrights) can be protected, buyer switching costs can be increased, and critical assets can be pre-empted. [24] Second mover advantages can exist only in the absence of the three first mover advantages. An example of a market where second mover advantages appear to exist is the dynamic random access memory (DRAM) segment of the semiconductor industry. Entry barriers are generally low because competitors did not patent their products (or enforce their patents), large customers follow a policy of dual sourcing, and circuits were made from readily available silicon, often by third-party subcontractors. Firms manufacturing DRAMs that employ second mover strategies, involving rapid response to competitors' first moves, are effective in gaining market share within the cycle of a single generation of products. [25]

The vast majority of small high-tech firms compete on the basis of second mover advantages. They imitate quickly or make marginal improvements to existing products on the market, often relying heavily, as discussed earlier in this chapter, on external sources for their research and development. Speed of response is the basis of their competitive advantage, or lack of it their competitive disadvantage. Reliance on second mover advantages always makes firms vulnerable to price competition since the technology is generally available to all competitors. However, firms that have implemented time-based strategies, such as Sun Microsystems, believe they have a defensible market position. One Sun executive is quoted as saying: "Copying something that moves faster than you can copy it isn't a good business to be in." [26] Another comments:

> "We wouldn't hesitate to bring out a new product at a price and performance level that absolutely destroyed an existing line. Why should we wait for the competition to do it? That's a brand new concept in this business and we've proved you can make money doing it." [27]

First mover advantages are available to only a very few small high-tech firms. A firm developing proprietary operating software, such as Microsoft's MS-DOS system for IBM, is an example of a firm built on first mover advantage. Fast growth companies are often built on such advantages, as can be seen by looking at the history of Intel and Conner Peripherals. Their ability to maintain their competitive advantage and continue growing is dependent on their ability to continue to implement prime mover strategies, i.e. to develop a second and third generation of products which are radical innovations that are difficult to imitate. Research shows that small firms find this exceptionally difficult to do, since only rarely do small high-tech firms repeat their early success. [28]

The well-run, small, high-tech firm should be ideally placed to develop defensible time-based strategies since, in theory, these firms lack bureaucracy and are experienced in operating in a fast-moving environment. In practice, success will depend on the ability of the management to implement such strategies as the firm experiences rapid growth. [29]

Product Standards

Small firms producing a product which requires compatability with complementary goods and services may find that any initial success is quickly eroded by more powerful firms that adopt a strategy for having their product accepted as the industry standard. Strategies for winning standards battles involve establishing a large installed base of both core and complementary goods faster than competing standards and establishing the credibility of that standard. [30] Such a strategy requires not only a proven product, but also the financial resources to invest in distribution, manufacturing capability, maintenance support and marketing awareness programmes. A strong brand image and the ability to attract the support of third-party suppliers of complementary products can also help establish a product as the standard, as was the case when IBM established its PC as the industry standard. Few small high-tech firms have the resources to fight such a battle. Apple Computer's maintenance of its own standard in the face of the IBM-PC standard during the 1980s was very much the exception rather than the rule. MIPS Computer Systems, which is discussed in the next section, may prove to be an exception in the 1990s.

PARTNERING STRATEGIES FOR PRODUCT-MARKET DEVELOPMENT

Strategic alliances in various forms are common in technology-based industries and small firms enter agreements with suppliers, customers and competitors in just the same way as large firms have. On the face of it, co-operation ought to be an effective means of compensating for deficiencies in resources, skills, technology and market access which are so common to small high-tech firms. There are many forms of co-operation, ranging from equity shareholdings and joint ventures to cross-licensing and more specific areas of functional co-operation. The typical alliance between a small high-tech firm and a partner is one in which the small high-tech firm enters into an alliance with a larger company. The small firm provides the technology, while the larger partner provides its marketing, manufacturing and financial resources or expertise.

The narrow and specialized skill base of small high-tech firms means that firms often lack the marketing and other management skills necessary for effective product commercialization. [31] Couple this with their lack of financial resources and the fact that there may be a very short-lived window of opportunity before severe competition begins, and one sees that external exploitation of the firm's technology through partnering can sometimes be the best route to market development. Having one's product marketed by other organizations via a licensing or some other agreement requires few resources, minimizes risk and allows for a wider exploitation of the technology than may otherwise be possible. However, outward licensing tends to be used most commonly as a marginal strategy to exploit market segments or product applications peripheral to the small firm's core business area. The danger of extensive licensing is that it forces the firm to become a research and development laboratory without access to the needs of the market, and to become totally dependent for its own success on the success of other organizations.

One company that was successful in growing fast through partnering is MIPS Computer Systems, based in Sunnyvale, California. MIPS successfully leveraged its RISC (reduced instruction set computers) architecture by entering into licensing agreements with powerful OEM partners such as Digital Equipment Corporation, Tandem Computers Inc., NEC Corporation and Siemens A.G. MIPS' decision to form strategic alliances with major semiconductor and computer companies resulted from the introduction in early 1987 of a new chief executive, Bob Miller, who had previous experience with IBM and Data General. The company was in serious financial trouble, having lost $2.9m in the previous quarter, and was desperately short of cash. Part of Miller's financial strategy was to shift away from chip manufacturing to a focus on technology licensing, software development and systems products. The objective was to reduce capital outlay by licensing selected semiconductor partners which manufacture, market and support products using the MIPS architecture. The success of this strategy allowed MIPS to leverage its technology quickly in a rapidly growing segment of the market, and allowed the company to focus more on its systems business which was more compatible with its resource base. This approach makes sense for a small company trying to compete against larger companies such as Sun Microsystems Inc. (with its Sparc Chip architecture) and Motorola Inc. (with its 8800 microprocessor design). Although some of MIPS' partners are in competition with each other, they regarded MIPS' growing partner list as beneficial because it expanded total market awareness of the design. The short-term success of the partnering strategy is evident from MIPS' rapid sales growth—from $40m in 1988 to over $100m in 1989, with over 40% of revenue coming from royalties. [32]

MIPS Computer Systems is not alone in building its market development strategy around partnerships with major customers. This approach has been very popular in the biotechnology sector, where many of the most successful companies have relied heavily on the pharmaceutical industry to market their products.

One type of marketing partnership common in high-tech industries is the myriad of partnership agreements between hardware and software producers. In spite of the growth of UNIX-based software, most software is still proprietary and in order to sell their hardware, computer manufacturers and others must ensure there is a sufficient supply of applications software written for their products if they are to sell any at all. Thus, MIPS Computer Systems took a 45% investment in a small, independent company, Synthesis Software Solutions, to ensure the acquisition and distribution of third-party software for MIPS-based systems.

Typically, hardware manufacturers seek out third-party software houses—often small companies—to write application software. The hardware company will provide advance information on a confidential basis about its new products to selected third-party software houses. Where these relationships are well managed, both parties end up "pulling through" each other's products into the market-place. In most instances, insufficient time is put into managing the relationships.

What are the typical problems that arise for the small firm? Among the most important are: [33]

- loss of control over key aspects of the business which conflicts with the entrepreneur's inclination for control;
- lack of bargaining power against the larger partner and therefore inability to capture value for its own innovations;
- dependency on a more powerful partner for its success;
- lack of management skills and resources to deal effectively with the complexities associated with managing inter-firm alliances;
- distancing of the small firm's development engineers from the market-place;
- premature exposure of proprietary technology.

There are clearly enormous risks for the small high-tech firm entering partnership arrangements. How can the small high-tech firm protect itself from the obvious dangers? Firms that have developed successful partnering strategies have the following characteristics:

- management with commercial experience in negotiating partnership arrangements;
- a concerted effort to diversify *quickly* their risk of dependency on a single partner—it is much easier to diversify when markets are growing very fast and while the company's principal products still have a clear competitive advantage;
- continuing technological leadership to maintain proprietary technological advantages, thereby maximizing imitation costs wherever possible;
- product and service support to the partner which is second to none—this "buys" partner loyalty and increases his switching costs.

The smaller partner has always to look for ways to ensure that the partnership is of mutual benefit to both sides over the long term. In the short term rapid growth may occur, as at Conner Peripherals or MIPS. This is obviously good news for the smaller company, but such a situation can soon swing to the advantage of the larger partner when the technology matures and there are more sources of supply in the market-place. Maintaining technological leadership is absolutely key for the small firm. Three approaches which firms might consider using to strengthen their position in any strategic alliance are: (1) the development of multitechnology-based systems (described earlier); (2) the pursuit of joint research and development with their partners; [34] and (3) allowing partners to have a minority equity stake in their business. Joint R & D again involves some risk, in that it may involve sharing (or trading) some proprietary know-how, but it has the potential advantage of developing a more stable, long-term relationship with the partner. The same argument applies to equity investments by larger partners.

SUMMARY

This chapter has discussed how the small high-tech firm can build product development and marketing capabilities to improve its chance of success after start-up. Six factors which determine the success of new product development activities after first product launch were identified. They were: (1) orientation to customers' needs; (2) emphasis on strong technical superiority; (3) involvement of the entrepreneur; (4) focusing scarce resources; (5) access to multiple sources of technology, and (6) managing sympathetically.

Most small high-tech firms underestimate the costs required to establish their firm and their products in new chosen market segments. Six critical issues were discussed,: (1) building and maintaining credibility; (2) building market differentiation; (3) linking with large customers; (4) developing appropriate distribution and selling; (5) managing the marketing effort and (6) speed to market.

The small firm is always vulnerable to competition from larger companies with greater resources, particularly competition based on price and marketing power. However, the small firm, if managed well, is potentially capable of competing against product and time-based competition. The inherent resource constraints of the small high-tech firm mean that collaborative or partnering strategies with both competitors, customers and suppliers are quite commonly used by small high-tech firms.

NOTES

(1) Sculley, J. and Byrne, J. *Odyssey ... a Journey of Adventure. Ideas and the Future*, pp. 64 and 74. Harper & Row, New York (1987).
(2) Slatter, S. St. P. and King, P. Stages of Business Development of Small Firms in the Computer-Aided Design Industry. London Business School Working Paper, June (1986).
(3) "Once Bankrupt the Good Times Come Back to Lattice", *Electronic Business*, November 27, pp. 38–41 (1989).
(4) Sun Microsystems Annual Report (1988).
(5) "Sun's Sizzling Race to the Top", *Fortune*, August 17, p. 89 (1987).
(6) "Speeding New Ideas to Market", *Fortune*, March 2, pp. 54–57.
(7) Maidique, M. "Entrepreneurs, Champions and Technological Innovation", *Sloan Management Review*, Winter (1980).
(8) Wiersema, M. F. and Page, R. A. "Managing the Innovative Firm: Strategies for Sustaining Radical Innovation", in M. W. Lawless and L. R. Gomez-Mejia (eds) *Proceedings, Second International Conference on Managing the High Technology Firm*, January 1990.
(9) Sculley, J. and Byrne, J. *Odyssey ... a Journey of Adventure. Ideas and the Future*, p. 83. Harper & Row, New York (1987).
(10) Freeman, C. *The Economics of Industrial Innovation*, Chapter 6. Frances Pinter, London (1982).
(11) Gist, P. "Small Firms in the UK Telecommunications Industry". London Business School Working Paper (1985).
(12) Porter, M. E. *Competitive Strategy*, Chapter 2. The Free Press, New York (1980).
(13) Fiegenbaum, A. and Karnani, A. "Output Flexibility—A Competitive Advantage for Small Firms", *Strategic Management Journal*, Vol. 12, No. 2, February (1991).
(14) "Conner Birdies 3rd", *Computerworld*, February 12, pp. 95–96 (1990).
(15) Sculley, J. and Byrne, J. *Odyssey ... a Journey of Adventure. Ideas and the Future*, p. 147. Harper & Row, New York (1987).
(16) For a more detailed discussion of the role of the salesforce and manufacturers' representatives in marketing high-technology products see, for example: Riggs, H. E. *Managing High Technology*

Companies, Van Nostrand Reinhold, New York, pp. 52–66 (1983); Davis, R. T. and Gordon Smith, F. *Marketing in Emerging Companies.* Addison Wesley, Reading, Mass. (1984).

(17) Wheeler, D. R. and Shelley, C. J., "Toward More Realistic Forecasts for High Technology Products", *Journal of Business and Industrial Marketing,* Vol. 2, No. 3, pp. 55–63 (1987).

(18) Mansfield, E., Schwartz, M. and Wagner, C. J. "Imitation Costs and Patents", *The Economic Journal,* 91, December, pp. 907–918 (1981).

(19) Levin, R. C. "A New Look at the Patent System", *American Economic Review,* 76, 2, pp. 199–202 (1986).

(20) Major, J. D. "Some Practical Intellectual Property Aspects of Technology Transfer", *International Journal of Technology Management,* Vol. 3, pp. 43–49 (1988).

(21) Microvitec plc. Case Study, in Slatter, S. St. P., *Cases in Strategic Management for the Smaller Firm.* Basil Blackwell, Oxford (1988).

(22) Strebel, P. "Organizing for Innovation over an Industry Cycle", *Strategic Management Journal,* Vol. 8, pp. 113–124 (1987).

(23) Angrist, S. W. "Entrepreneur in Short Pants", *Forbes,* March 7, pp. 84–95, (1988).

(24) Lieberman, M. B. and Montgomery, D. B. "First Mover Advantage", *Strategic Management Journal,* 9, pp. 41–58 (1988).

(25) Birnbaum-More, P. H. "Competing with Cycle Time in the Worldwide DRAM Market", in M. W. Lawless and L. R. Gomez-Mejia (eds) *Proceedings of Second International Conference on Managing The High Technology Firm,* University of Colorado, January (1990).

(26) Card, D. "The Maturing of the Workstation Wunderkind", *Electronic Business,* March 15, p. 58 (1987).

(27) Gannes, S. "Sun's Sizzling Race to the Top", *Fortune,* August 17, p. 90 (1987).

(28) Slatter, S. St. P. and King, P. "Management Issues in Small High Tech Firms", London Business School Working Paper, December (1984).

(29) For a fuller explanation of the principles underlying time-based competition, see the excellent book by Stalk, G. and Hout, T. E. *Competing Against Time.* The Free Press, New York (1990).

(30) Grindley, P. "Winning Standards Contests: Using Product Standards in Business Strategy", *Business Strategy Review,* Spring, pp. 71–84 (1990).

(31) See Shan, W. "An Empirical Analysis of Organizational Strategies by Entrepreneural High Technology Firms", *Strategic Management Journal,* Vol. 11, pp. 129–139 (1990) for a study of the

factors influencing biotechnology start-ups to form co-operative relationships.

(32) "Big Lessons for Small Companies", *Electronic Business*, April 3, pp. 32–39 (1989).

(33) Doz, Y. L "Technology Partnerships Between Larger and Smaller Firms: Some Critical Issues", in F. Contractor and P. Lorange (eds), *Co-operative Strategies in International Business*. Lexington Books, Lexington, Mass., pp. 317–338 (1988).

(34) Hebert, L. and Geringer, J. M. "Technology Strategies for Small High Tech Firms", in M. W. Lawless and L. R. Gomez-Mejia (eds) *Proceedings of Second International Conference on Managing The High Technology Firm*, University of Colorado, January (1990).

4
Managing the People

The characteristics of small high-tech companies that were discussed in Chapter 1 create a unique set of organizational values and management requirements. A large portion of the staff typically have some engineering or scientific background, and the average age in many companies is under 30. At Dell Computers, for example, the average age in 1989 was 24—the same age as the founder, Michael Dell![1] The organization is usually informal, egalitarian and in a state of constant change. Small high-tech firms build up distinctive cultures and norms with unique employee profiles and management styles.[2] Successful management of these firms requires a different approach from that which is commonly found either in more traditional business environments, or even among other knowledge-based workers.

This chapter reviews some of the key organizational characteristics of small high-tech firms and draws some conclusions about the characteristics of better performing senior management teams. It is not intended as a comprehensive summary of organizational behaviour in small high-tech firms—that is a subject for a separate book. Instead, its purpose is to highlight some critical areas of human resource management that require special attention by senior management. The more successful high-tech firms have to deal with the problem of managing explosive growth, and specific management issues associated with growth are dealt with separately in Chapter 5. This chapter looks at: the high-tech employee; job excitement, motivation and satisfaction; recruiting and training staff; retaining technical staff; participating in the rewards; corporate culture; managing the functional boundaries; leadership style.

THE HIGH-TECH EMPLOYEE

Most experienced managers of small high-tech firms recognize that their employees are a special breed with unique needs, who create distinct demands on the organization. Yet, to date there has been little hard evidence of exactly how these employees are different. The typical employee is under 35 years of age, and in many companies the average is below 30. There is a very high level of education, with a high percentage holding first degrees and many holding higher degrees, particularly in the more advanced technology companies. It is the preponderance of technical professionals, scientists and engineers that makes the management of small high-tech firms different. Besides being intelligent and well educated, the technically-oriented personality has been described as serious, socially reserved, overly engrossed in their own ideas and projects, possessing poor interpersonal skills, having a high achievement orientation, showing concern for career advancement and being uncomfortable in making quick decisions on the basis of sketchy information. [3]

The motivation profile of employees working in such high-tech firms differs in some significant ways from that of knowledge-based workers generally, and from employees in large high-tech firms. A study of small UK software firms found that employees wanted money, a comfortable life style, recognition and autonomy; but were less motivated by job security, and power and influence over others. [4] It is this combination of motivating influences that gives the high-tech employee considerable job mobility. The high priority given to money was also noted in a Silicon Valley study of software employees. [5] The combination also reflects an expectation on the part of high-tech employees for a high quality of working life in terms of amenities and attractive physical surroundings. [6]

The UK study showed that the profile remained similar across both small (under 50 employees) and medium-sized companies, although in the very smallest companies employees were prepared to trade off some money and comfort for greater autonomy. However, the most important aspect of the motivation profile is that it is quite different from that of any other type of employee. Individuals who are considered very high achievers in large organizations, for example, trade off money and comfort for greater recognition, power and autonomy. [7] The small high-tech employee is different: he or she wants a combination of money with recognition and autonomy.

The implication for managers of small high-tech firms is that employers cannot expect the psychic compensation derived from recognition and autonomy to compensate for low salaries. The typical high-tech employee wants "to have his or her cake and eat it!"

The relatively low emphasis given to power and responsibility by high-tech employees partially reflects the psychological make-up of those attracted to work in small high-tech firms, [8] as well as social trends among younger people for whom self-development in the form of autonomy and creativity is more important than power and influence. [9] This lack of desire for power and influence reflects itself in the difficulty small firms face in finding technical staff who want to be managers. On the other hand, too strong a desire for power and influence would probably not be an appropriate profile for managers of people who require a lot of autonomy and very little security and structure. This may well be a cause of some of the problems firms encounter when they hire managers with big company experience when the firm grows (see Chapter 5).

The different and possibly unique motivation profile of employees in small high-tech firms indicate that management practices and style need to be different from those regarded as "good management practice" in larger organizations.

JOB EXCITEMENT, MOTIVATION AND SATISFACTION

One of the most noticeable characteristics of the small high-tech firm, particularly the successful ones, is the degree of excitement in the air—the "buzz" of the place. As an outsider, one does not see a self-satisfied group of employees going about their tasks in a routine way, but a group of employees who are alert, committed and operating with high energy levels.

In understanding the management problems of growing high-tech firms Garden[10] recognized three different aspects of motivation:

- *Satisfaction*—the state in which employees' basic needs are fulfilled, but a low tension state reflecting contentment.
- *Motivation*—reflects a more positive attitude towards work than satisfaction, if not an eagerness towards work, but without a more highly charged feeling.
- *Excitement*—the peak level of motivation.

The distinction between satisfaction at one end of the spectrum and excitement at the other is an important one, since the task of satisfying employees may be different from the task of keeping them excited. The spirit of excitement in a growing high-tech firm is not obtained by people being satisfied. Observation shows that staff in the most successful growing high-tech firms feel exuberant, excited in their work, energetic, hyped up at work and get a buzz out of work. There is something over and above enjoying work and being "motivated".

The variables over which management has control which are associated with job excitement do not appear to be the same as those associated with overall satisfaction. In a study of small UK software firms Garden[11] identified the critical management variables which were associated with job excitement, motivation and satisfaction. Most of the significant satisfaction variables were found to be things that the company gave to the employee such as opportunities for advancement, sufficient resources and good communications from management. The variables associated with job excitement were very different and reflected the individual contributing to the company, and achieving something useful employing his or her own talents to the full in challenging work. In short, excitement involves "the resources of the individual being fully used, not the resources of the company being given to the individual", as with satisfaction.[12]

Excitement for employees in small high-tech firms is likely to differ from that in larger technology based firms such as IBM or Hewlett Packard. In the larger firms a degree of organizational slack is built in to encourage innovation. In small firms, which are resource constrained and likely to be development or applications oriented (instead of research oriented), Garden's work tends to indicate that creativity, time to explore ideas in depth and freedom in adopting one's own approach, are not generally key to generating excitement.

Chapter 5 returns to the issue of job excitement and satisfaction, since maintaining the spirit of excitement is one of the major challenges for management as the firm grows.

RECRUITING AND TRAINING STAFF

Attracting high quality employees is generally recognized as absolutely critical for the success of a small high-tech firm since the company has few resources other than its people. The quality of the technical staff is particularly important, given the key role product development plays in the success of these firms. Biotechnology firms and electronics firms operating near the leading edge of technology find that good people make it easier to achieve technical success and easier to obtain funding. Biogenetics, a genetic engineering company, provides an example of a company which recognized that the recruitment and development of top scientists was one of the keys to success. A company brochure states: "Biogenetics Inc. began with the selection of scientists and its scientists are its most vital resource." [13]

Attracting good staff is always difficult for small firms, due to the perceived lack of job security, uncertainty about promotion prospects and the fact that it is often extremely difficult for new employees to fit into the existing team. Furthermore, most small firms lack the "pull" that many larger, well-established firms have in attracting new staff. With small high-tech firms, the problems seem even more acute. First, there is a general shortage of suitably qualified technical staff, and secondly, the problem is exacerbated by the fact that many high-tech firms are highly specialized. There are not, for example, many specialists in electro-acoustics, which means that a considerable amount of time and money has to be spent retraining individuals from other technical specialisms.

Attracting high quality sales and marketing people, although perhaps not required in such large numbers as technical people, is even more difficult for small high-tech firms. Good sales and marketing staff are always in short supply but, again, the problem is exacerbated with the small high-tech firm, where both the sales and marketing staff require good technical backgrounds and often need a specialist knowledge of a customer's business. The preponderance of vertical market strategies (see Chapter 3) means that the sales and marketing staff must be fully conversant with their customers' industries. Thus, sales and marketing staff in Stratus Computers (American manufacturers of fault-tolerant computers) have to be knowledgeable about the securities industry, and at Medelec, the Canadian legal software house, staff must understand lawyers' practices.

There is no magic to recruiting. It is hard work and needs to be done at as senior a level in the organization as possible. It is not pure chance that the most successful small firms spend more senior management time on recruiting than their less successful competitors. Recruitment tends to take one of three forms: ex-employees, active "poaching", or usual recruitment methods.

Ex-employees. Given the large number of spin offs in the high-tech industry, it is not surprising that one of the principal sources of talent arises from managers recruiting known individuals from their former employers. As we have seen, this may transmit undesirable cultural characteristics, but the use of "alumni" networks has often proven to be the quickest and most reliable approach to recruitment.

Active "poaching". Recruiting employees from established competitors, often the industry leaders, is common. Small high-tech firms regard the large players in the industry as good training grounds, given they rarely have the resources to undertake extensive training of their own. Raiding other firms may not always be as easy as it seems, particularly when recruiting senior technical staff. Firstly, many firms grant key technical staff an equity position as an incentive to stay.

Secondly, the establishment of non-competition and non-disclosure clauses in contracts of employment makes it difficult to transfer confidential material from one job to the next. Thirdly, technical staff often work closely on one project or a group of projects related to their (often narrow) area of expertise. If the technology is extremely advanced, they will want to continue to work in the area.

Usual recruitment methods. Small high-tech firms also use the traditional recruitment approaches of advertising, headhunting and word of mouth. Graduate recruitment has been used successfully by some small high-tech firms. One firm that has recruited graduates successfully in the UK is Data Connection Ltd, a company writing technically advanced software for computer manufacturers. Data Connection produces a graduate case book which contains write-ups by recent graduates on why they joined and what their experience has been. Below are some excerpts from the company handbook showing what recent graduate recruits wrote about what they were looking for and why they joined Data Connection.

> During my last year at University I made a decision to look for a job in the software industry. A difficult decision as I've never been one of those bleary-eyed hack programmers so favoured by the media and certain kinds of employers. What I wanted was a job that recognised me as an individual, would challenge me and that returned a more than adequate financial remuneration. Data Connection's introduction of themselves seemed to fit in with my requirements, and when I visited their office I was immediately struck by both their enthusiasm and professionalism.

> I was looking for the following features in a job—a technically demanding environment, a small friendly company, flexibility in how I organised my time, reward in accordance with my contribution and the opportunity to learn a wide range of skills. I had two other job offers along with Data Connection's. Deciding was easy—the energy and enthusiasm I'd seen at Data Connection far exceeded that of the other companies I'd seen, and the salary was higher too.

> Having spent a year and a half working for a large computer company, I knew exactly what I was looking for in my prospective employer.

> ... I couldn't resist this challenge, and in August 1984, took up my place at the bottom of the Data Connection line up.

One or two bad hiring decisions can always have a dramatic impact on the performance of a small company. In a fast moving environment the impact can be even greater. Opportunities can be missed and market position lost very easily, particularly when the company is still trying to establish market credibility and has a very short window of opportunity. Few firms have the resources to undertake extensive induction training. A comment from one recent technical employee in a small US software company is typical of what happens to the new recruit: "The flavour of the first month or two was one of me being thrown in at the deep end, with as much help as I asked for but no formal training. You learn quickly in that environment."

Being thrown in at the deep end puts the onus on the individual to learn. In the software industry, reading manuals, talking to experienced colleagues and "learning by doing" are the major learning processes. The development of new employees and their integration into the firm is seen as a major challenge by many firms. At T Cell Sciences Inc., James Grant put it this way:

> "Another major challenge is to develop our people. We now have 55 employees and are adding roughly one person every two weeks. Our target is to have 80 people a year from now and 110 the year after.

> "Integrating the new people into the organization continues to be a problem for us, especially for research. We have to find a way to get people with a university post-doctoral research experience to learn how to work in groups. Among our six technical managers only two have some commercial experience. The other four are new to this. One step we have taken to deal with this problem has been to have a Harvard Business School professor who has had considerable experience working with research organizations meet with our people. We might develop some kind of training program."[14]

Most firms recognize the need for staff training on a continuing basis, particularly where the technology is rapidly changing or the skill base is too narrow. However, only the most successful firms, as measured by profitability, tend to be able to afford much in the way of formal training.

RETAINING TECHNICAL STAFF

Interviews with senior management in the UK and the USA indicate that one of the major challenges facing firms is how to attract and retain good technical talent. High-tech employees are generally regarded as having high job mobility, partly as a result of labour market conditions (a shortage of suitably quali-fied technical staff), but partly as a result of the nature of the individuals attracted to high-tech careers. Job loyalty is low, with individuals being much more concerned about their indi-vidual or personal development, than with job security, *per se.* Individuals obtain security by building up intellectual capital (knowledge and competence) for which there is a ready market in other organizations.

A high turnover of technical personnel has been cited by some writers as one of the unique characteristics of high-tech firms. [15] A Silicon Valley study of 700 technical specialists and their managers found that the desire for challenging work and higher salaries were the major tangible factors in job-hopping, followed by desirable "working conditions". [16] The key intan-gibles cited by the same study were "the opportunity for advancement, to grow and develop as professionals and, most importantly, to do challenging work".

In the UK, Garden has explored the same issue with small software companies in the London and Cambridge areas. [17] Table 4.1 shows the employees' rankings of the potential reasons for leaving their present companies over the next two years, based on a forced ranking of the five main reasons cited. The dominant reasons for leaving were found to be similar across both small companies (those with under 50 employees) and medium-sized companies (those with 50 to 250 employees). The potential reasons for leaving fell into three main groups with six critical or dominant factors. Increased salary was by far and away the most important potential reason given for leaving; but apart from this all the critical factors related to the nature of the employee's job.

Among the secondary group of reasons for leaving an employer was the desire to keep up to date with technical ideas. This may reflect either a lack of opportunity (in the form of time or training) to keep one's intellectual capital up to date in small firms, or a desire by the more ambitious to be at the "cutting edge" knowing that the half life of much technical knowledge is only 3–7 years, depending on the technology concerned. Either way it has significant implications for man-agement, who need to provide constant opportunities for renewing the knowledge base of their employees.

Table 4.1 *Potential reasons for leaving present company*

	Ranking	Reasons for leaving
Critical factors	1	Increased salary
	2	More experience
	3	More interesting work
	4	Need for a change
	5	More challenging work
	6	Promotion
Influential factors of	7	Better location
secondary importance	8	Keep up with technical ideas
	9	Present company getting too large
	10	Run own company
	11	Reasons other than ones specified[a]
	12	More control over own work
Relatively unimportant	13	More structure and clarity in work
factors	14	More flexible working arrangements
	15	Go to more successful company
	16	Difficulties with immediate boss
	17	Friendlier people
	18	Opportunity for equity stake
	19	Go to less commercial company
	20	Go to more commercial company

Source: Adapted by permission from Garden, A. "Turnover Reasons of Software Employees in a Range of Small High Tech Companies", London Business School Working Paper (1988).
[a] Includes personal/family reasons, and various idiosyncratic reasons.

While potential reasons for leaving provide useful insights into the high-tech employees, further insights can be obtained by looking at the time employees expect to stay in their present company, and a range of personal and organizational characteristics. Garden, as part of the same study referred to above, did just this, and found that the average length of time employees had been with their companies at the time of her study was two and a half years, and they expected to stay a further two years ten months. [19] The factors that were found to be important in determining the length of time employees expected to stay were:

- *Education level.* The higher the level the less time employees expected to stay.
- *The nature of the job.* Employees in jobs with a broader range of tasks or activities expected to stay longer. Some job categories show strong dislikes. For example, systems analysts,

engineers and consultants (but not programmers) showed intense dislike of debugging, programming and implementation (in that order), while engineers strongly disliked customer liaison.

- *Perceived comptence of senior management.* Dissatisfaction with the perceived competence of senior management was found to be a critical factor. The competence of senior management tended to be judged according to employee expectations about the continued or future success of the company.

- *The nature of the work and organizational conditions.* Consistent with the reasons for leaving shown in Table 4.1, the following factors were found to be positively correlated with length of time expected to stay (in descending order of importance):

  - perceived level of challenging work;
  - recognition for doing a good job;
  - opportunity for personal growth;
  - opportunity for advancement;
  - interesting work;
  - fun and enjoyment;
  - doing something useful;
  - awareness of making a real contribution to the success of the company.

- *The company atmosphere.* The influence of company atmosphere on the length of time employees expect to remain with their companies varies with size of company. In small companies with under 50 employees a "warm and friendly atmosphere" is critical to retaining staff, whereas in slightly larger companies, a "flexible and open atmosphere" is more important in retaining staff. Unlike the situation in large organizations, satisfaction with one's project team and immediate manager do not appear to be major causes of concern among employees of small high-tech firms.

A high turnover rate of technical personnel can have a substantial hidden cost for the small firm. Not only are there the obvious direct costs of recruitment and training, but there are often considerable indirect costs in terms of management time, lost momentum in new product development and the costs of going down the learning curve with new employees. In fast-moving market-places, the additional *time* that new employees are likely to require to bring new products to market success-fully can put the firm at a significant competitive disadvantage.

The implications of these findings for management are to:

- constantly monitor competitors' salary levels and aim to pay all key staff in the top quartile to avoid high turnover of employees;
- design jobs to provide interesting and challenging work; [20]
- provide comfortable and attractive working surroundings, but without "going over the top";
- assist and encourage employees to keep up to date with technical developments in their area of expertise;
- communicate clearly and constantly with all employees where the company is going, why, and how it is going to get there;
- provide individual feedback and recognition on a regular basis. [21]

PARTICIPATING IN THE REWARDS

Reward systems play a key role in both retaining and motiv-ating staff at all levels. There does not appear to be a general answer as to what is the best reward system. It is heavily influ-enced by the national business culture of the country, by the corporate culture, and by the strategic needs of the business. As with non-high-tech firms, reward systems vary by level of employee and by function. Almost all firms have high basic salaries for technical staff, and relatively lower basic salary plus commission for sales staff. The commission structure for sales staff in many of the computer hardware companies can provide enormous financial rewards for the top salespeople—commonly far in excess of the total remuneration paid to the chief executive.

The main distinguishing feature of small high-tech firms is the relative importance attached to equity ownership for the key executives. Interviews with a wide cross-section of senior managers in small high-tech firms indicated that they were more motivated by equity than younger employees. They tended to have a longer term view and their need for immediate cash benefits was lower. In fact, the better performing UK firms in Slatter and King's research tended to be characterized by a high equity participation from the founder and other key executives. [22] In the USA equity participation is more widespread and commonly includes key technical people in addition to management. The attractiveness of equity, however, is dependent on the likelihood of a public quotation or the prospect of a sale to a third party. The need to share equity among senior managers was observed to be higher in people-intensive service firms than in production-oriented firms.

The particular reward system adopted by a very young firm may be influenced by its financial situation. Those firms with heavy and prolonged cash outflows, such as many biotechnology companies, cannot afford to pay high monthly wages, and many prefer to offer a company-wide share option scheme to reduce their overheads. One company that did this in the UK was Sphinx—the first company set up specifically to exploit UNIX technology in Europe. The company had to spend heavily to develop the market and build customer awareness, and decided to offer a company-wide share option scheme. Now the company is successful in a growing market, the benefits of wide share ownership are apparent throughout the company.

COMPANY CULTURE

Very little has been written about the distinctive cultural patterns of small firms, and yet the media has built up a "picture" in the minds of the public that the firms in Silicon Valley in California, along Route 128 around Boston, and in Science Parks in Europe are in some way distinctive. It is true that many of the most successful high-tech firms that receive a lot of publicity, such as Intel, Apple Computer, Compaq, Lotus, etc., do have strong, distinctive cultures, but smaller firms vary enormously. Some are hardly distinguishable from non-high-tech firms, particularly those that are not at the leading edge of technology, or are primarily subcontract manufacturers, distributors or service operators for high-tech industries. Others have extremely distinctive cultures. One young software writer who had previously worked for a large technology-based company commented:

> "The transition from a large, sprawling organisation to the far smaller world of PCL was immediately obvious. At PCL nobody is more important than anybody else. It is recognised that we each have our own key function and contribution to make to the success of the company. This team spirit was never apparent in the larger company."

Company culture is, as we know, determined by such factors as the firm's history, ownership, size, technology, environment, type of employee and management's objectives. [23] The personality of the founders, particularly that of the dominant founder, is crucially important in all small firms. What is somewhat different about high-tech firms, besides the technology itself, is the nature of the employees and the environment in which the firm operates. The employees are often quite different in type, mobility and motivation to those found in other organizations. Furthermore, the fact that many high-tech firms are located in proximity to one another (e.g. in Silicon Valley in California, along the M3/M4 corridor in the UK), means that much more extensive networking and interchange of ideas takes place among employees than is normal for small firms, who often operate in virtual isolation from the rest of the business community. The rapid change in technology means that employees are obliged to keep up to date with what is happening, and be creative in both their markets and their technological disciplines.

From personal observation, however, it seems that it is the experience of both managers and employees in the formative years of their careers—usually in their mid-20s—that has a bigger impact on how they themselves will act at a later stage in their lives. New high-tech ventures established as spin-offs from other companies nearly always include dominant values from the parent company culture. For example, one UK systems company set up by a group of seven IBM managers, has actively embraced training from the day it started. Forty Friday afternoons each year, the Chairman personally conducts training sessions on different topics ranging from effective communications to understanding the market-place.

In another UK start-up, a spin-off from an old engineering company in the North of England, the two founders resolutely continued the worst habits from their old culture in spite of attempts by the non-executive Chairman and venture capitalists to set the business up with a "traditional" high-tech culture from day one. The company was established in 1983 to develop custom-designed vacuum metallizing machinery for use in a wide variety of end-use industries. The two founders had previously worked together as the R & D Manager and Sales Manager in the old engineering company. Within six months the firm had received its first orders and the founders had recruited a total of 28 staff—many from their old employer— since, although the new company was focused on high-tech applications, the vacuum technology engineering skills of the old engineering company were still applicable. Although the investor directors insisted on setting up the company with no overt distinctions between managers and other employees—no designated car park spaces, one lunch facility, the same conditions of employment for all employees, "clocking-in" for managers as well as non-management staff—the reality was quite different. The founders, particularly the ex-R & D Manager, who was the dominant founder, continued to operate in the same old-fashioned, hierarchical manner and with the same interdepartmental bias as he had experienced with his previous employer, the old engineering company. They declined to eat in the canteen, failed to "clock in", and let it be known that the two prime car park bays were unofficially "reserved" for them! Within months of start-up strong functional cultures had developed with, not surprisingly, the engineering function being favoured ("it was always right") in comparison to the manufacturing and sales departments.

A lack of commercial experience can, however, be just as bad as bad employment experience. In what was actually a successful start-up in Cambridge, England, of a local area network company, none of the four founders had prior commercial experience. They had all previously either been students or academics, and all were perfectionists who openly criticized each other. While the company was small this was not a problem, but caused great difficulties as the company grew (see Chapter 5).

It is exceptionally difficult and dangerous to generalize about the culture of small high-tech firms—given the great diversity of entrepreneurial personalities and firms that make up the small high-tech sector. However, as shall be seen when discussing growth (in Chapter 5) and turnarounds (in Chapters 8 and 9), the cultures of small high-tech firms—like their product-market positions—are very fragile. Almost by definition, small high-tech firms have not had the time to embed their culture into the organization that some of the longer established high-tech firms such as Hewlett Packard, Texas Instruments and IBM have. The fragility is more a function of time than size, since although Apple reached $1.9 billion in sales by 1985, its culture was still extremely fragile, as John Sculley found out when he became President of the company.

There is plenty of evidence that better performing companies tend to have strong corporate cultures, although strong cultures may also have shortcomings. [24] With high-tech firms, the culture should be geared to innovation and customer responsiveness, both of which are key to strategic and operating success. Founders and senior management of small high-tech firms that grow successfully understand that building a corporate culture takes time and effort—and that the process must begin at start-up or even earlier. The process by which the initial business plan is put together, choices about where to locate, and what employees to hire immediately after start-up, can all have a significant impact on the culture that develops. Most important of all the factors that determine culture in the small high-tech company, though, is the personality and vision of the founder. If there is a founding team, then it is either the vision and personality of the dominant partner, or that of the combined team that influences the corporate culture.

The strong influence of product development in many small high-tech firms means that many develop a product or technology-led culture. In the early days of product-market development this culture can often ensure the development of robust products that give the firm competitive advantage. However, if competitive conditions change, new entrants emerge, and the firm has to lower its cost base, a more marketing-led and cost-conscious culture is required. Experienced managers know that changing a firm's culture is extremely difficult, and the ideal situation is where an appropriate culture is developed at start-up and maintained as the firm develops. The details of corporate culture can never remain constant, as the firm's strategy and people have to adapt constantly to the ever-changing external environment. However, many successful high growth, high-tech firms have established a culture that permits constant change to occur. These are organizations that value change, not for the sake of change, but because they allow the firm to be one step ahead of the competition. They are organizations that started out on day one with the founder(s) insisting on operating in a flexible way.

Lotus Development Corporation is one such company that uses the word flexibility a lot, even including it in its statement of corporate values. Jim Manzi, President of Lotus, talks about how flexibility is built into hiring decisions and then constantly reinforced: "We look for people with flexibility because of the rate of change, and so the stress level is fairly severe. Building flexibility into the system and into the expectations of both old-time people and new people is real important." [25]

Irfan Schein, Vice President of Lotus' International Division, says: "people at Lotus just have to accept a lot of flexibility because reporting lines are very easily and very often crossed." [25] Interestingly, Lotus will not recruit the person with the best technical background if their personality does not look like a good fit with the corporate culture.

Implementing a culture that embraces constant change needs the founder or one of the founding team to promote the values that keep the firm successful. Bill Poduska, founder of Apollo Computer Corporation (now part of Hewlett Packard), is quoted as saying:

> "Like anybody else who has that task [of promoting values], I try to condense them down to things that people can remember. The first is excellence. People want to do the best damn job they know how to do in building a product. The second is action—do it today. Third is justice; we really do reward people for the efforts they give. We also stress a simple, straightforward, functional management style. We hold regular and orderly meetings. We have agendas. We also believe in the

> Sloan School Trilogy: authority, responsibility and accountability. We give people the responsibility to do their work, then stand out of their way while they do it."[27]

Promotion of the company's values requires a communication style which meets the needs of the autonomy seeking employees attracted to small high-tech firms. Good communication from top management is, as shown earlier, one of the key variables influencing the satisfaction of high-tech employees: and since these employees are usually well educated, the content of the communication needs to be "substantial". In a recent interview, Steve Jobs, who founded NeXT Inc. after leaving Apple Computer, talked about the need to build an "open corporation":

> "Think of it this way. If you look at your own body, your cells are specialized, but every single one of them has the master plan for the whole body. We think NeXT will be the best possible company if every single person working here understands the whole basic master plan and can use that as a yardstick to make decisions. There is some risk in giving everybody access to all the corporate information and potentially some loss. But what you gain vastly surpasses what you lose. ... The most visible sign of the open corporation at NeXT is our policy of allowing everybody to know what sales everybody else is making. There's a list in the finance department and anyone can go look at it."[28]

Openness is part of a wider notion of integrity which has been identified as one of the characteristics of successful high-tech firms by Maidique and Hayes.[29] Integrity involves not just openness but also honesty, fairness and trust. Such values are seen to be particularly important for firms operating in a highly volatile environment where risks are difficult to assess. Maidique and Hayes concluded that "without integrity the risks multiply and the probability of failure (in an already difficult enterprise) rise unacceptably".

MANAGING THE FUNCTIONAL BOUNDARIES

The key to good strategy implementation is the way in which the major functional areas work *together* to meet customers' needs. Specifically, the interfaces between marketing, operations and engineering/R & D are important, although other critical interfaces may exist as organizations grow and specialisms develop within functional areas. Firms that rely on strategies of differentiation to compete in the market-place, like small high-tech firms, require strong co-ordination between the functions to ensure the firm provides unique products and high service levels. [30] The need is even more acute in high-tech firms, since very close co-ordination and co-operation is required between the functions if they are going to be quick enough to respond to the rapidly changing technology and market conditions in which these firms operate, and provide the necessary level of customer service.

Technology underlies all three major functional areas of the business, and so successful integration requires general management—whose responsibility the integration is—to have a good understanding of the underlying technology. This does not mean that the general manager needs to be a technologist or even have a technical background, although this obviously helps; but that he or she can ask the "right" questions, and has both the ability and willingness to become technologically literate.

The major boundary issues which require co-ordination and co-operation between functional areas in high-tech firms, both small and large, are summarized in Figure 4.1. It is beyond the scope of this book to go into each of the individual issues; see Riggs (1984) for a more in-depth treatment of the issues. [31] Although field service management is shown in Figure 4.1 as an issue at the marketing/manufacturing interface—which indeed it is, many small high-tech firms, particularly in the computer industry, separate out service as a distinct function equal in status to marketing. This will become particularly important in the 1990s for both computer hardware and software companies, as the software in which computer hardware companies are currently trying to differentiate themselves becomes a commodity with the growth of non-proprietary software, notably UNIX.

One of the characteristics of high-tech firms in trouble is a plethora of operating problems relating to the critical boundary

Figure 4.1 *Critical boundary issues which require co-ordination and co-operation between functional areas*
Source: Adapted by permission from Riggs, H. E. *Managing High Technology Companies*. Van Nostrand Reinhold, New York (1984).

issues shown in Figure 4.1. Managing the functional boundaries requires good horizontal working relationships within the firm, and the breaking down of the individual functional cultures which inevitably develop. A strong corporate culture provides the glue for ensuring that the various functional departments work together in the interests of the whole firm. A strong leadership style along the lines discussed below is usually required to make sure the necessary horizontal relationships work effectively.

LEADERSHIP STYLE

There is no one right way of managing small high-tech firms. There is an enormous range of leadership styles and many different ways of achieving the same results. However, the most successful firms (as judged by both sales and profit growth) appear to have a strong but democratic leadership style. Strong leaders with a clear vision and clear objectives are needed to manage the type of people attracted to working in small high-tech firms, but strong leadership does not work with high-tech employees if it is too autocratic. Well-educated staff find a highly autocratic style difficult to get along with and will leave, particularly in the more people-intensive business. What is required is a democratic, or shared leadership style, where the chief executive allows plenty of opportunity for debate, but at the end of the day is prepared to take a decision even if it is unpopular among certain employees.

A style which relies solely on building consensus before a decision is made is likely to be too democratic. It would lead to slow decision making and be seen as weakness by subordinates. The chief executive must always be seen to be "in charge", otherwise frustration and anxiety will build up among the functional executives and spread quickly throughout the organization. Functional vice presidents and directors rarely want to make decisions outside their own areas of expertise although they want to be consulted and involved. If the chief executive has to err on one side or the other of the autocratic/democratic boundary, it is better he or she be more rather than less autocratic. The process by which decisions are arrived at is an important issue for chief executives and they should give considerable thought to when and how they involve their management team.

The requirement for fast, analytical and bold decision making (discussed in Chapter 1) to deal with the extreme uncertainties in the high-tech environment means that one individual is unlikely to have the full range of capabilities necessary for high quality decision making. Chief executives of small high-tech firms need therefore to be supported by a team of functional executives with well-balanced skills. The usual requirement in a small high-tech firm is to balance the technical capabilities with sound commercial sense.

Managers in the better performing firms work as a team rather than as individuals, although this does not imply the absence of friction among team members. The importance of working together as a team is stressed by many chief executives, including Compaq's Rod Canion, who uses a collective approach to decision making, recognizing that no one person on the management team has all the answers.

> "We have a team process," says Canion, "that leads to getting the best answer. We've encouraged all the things that it takes to have a team spirit. All companies want it, most of them talk about it, but few companies really have it, at least to the degree to which Compaq has been fortunate to develop and maintain it."[33]

The chief executive plays a key role in building team spirit by constantly being "close" to employees at all levels in the organization. At Aldus (a producer of software for desk-top publishing), Paul Brainerd achieves this by walking around: "I believe management should be walking around an hour a day and just go and talk to the shipping clerk, the telephone operator, everybody. Just carrying on a casual dialogue is very important."[34]

Frequent interaction with managers and employees alike gives chief executives the real-time information they need to make fast decisions. Chief executives in the more successful firms prefer face-to-face communication, and telephone calls to memos and reports; and have more regularly scheduled meetings with their subordinates. In times of crisis or when important decisions have to be made, the practice of working together as a team using real-time information will help to smooth the decision-making process.

While the chief executive must be decisive and take the lead in making strategic decisions he or she should be careful not to make *all* the decisions. There is some evidence that the more power that is delegated to functional executives to make functional strategy decisions, the better the performance of the firm. [35] This is not to say that the chief executive will not be involved in the decision, only that he or she may be second in influence to the relevant functional vice president. Low performing firms are often characterized by an emasculated top management team in contrast to high performing firms where the team feels empowered. The successful firm requires both a powerful, decisive chief executive and a powerful top management team.

Where decision-making power is kept from senior executives by the chief executive, behind-the-scene politics may emerge and interfere with effective management. [36] When this occurs, conflict between key executives arising from disagreements relating to organizational goals, key strategic decisions and interpersonal difference is likely to lead to secretiveness, the formation of coalitions and other unhealthy political behaviour. Some conflict within a top management team is healthy, and is probably inevitable in small high-tech firms where the top management are more likely to be well educated. However, conflict need not lead to negative political behaviour if the chief executive uses the right processes to encourage constructive debate and is prepared to outlaw behind-the-scenes politicking.

Politics are time-consuming, restrict information flows and create communication barriers within a team. These negative effects are likely to be particularly harmful in fast-moving, high-tech sectors and are likely to lead to slow growth and low profitability. [37]

Being chief executive of a small high-tech firm is an extremely challenging job. It requires a unique blend of leadership and management skills to overcome the forces driving fragility. Few chief executives have all the attributes necessary to ensure success. It is therefore imperative that the chief executive is conscious of his or her weaknesses. This is particularly important where the chief executive is the founder of the company—although the founder may be a good entrepreneur, he or she often lacks people-management skills or specific business skills (e.g. financial knowledge). Founders of some of the more successful firms seem to recognize their weaknesses and take steps before any crisis develops to remedy the situation. This typically involves hiring (or appointing from within) a new chief executive while the founder remains, becomes chairman or "retires" to head up the product development function.

SUMMARY

This chapter has highlighted some of the specific organizational issues which are of special concern when managing small high-tech firms. The motivation profile of the typical employee is often quite different from that found in conventional firms, with the result that the way employees are rewarded and managed needs to be different too. Since it is the high proportion of technical staff among employees that makes the organizational characteristics distinctive, the recruitment, training and retention of such staff are a high priority for senior management. The human resource practices adopted by management in small high-tech firms must take account of both the nature of the workforce and the size of the company. [38]

Many of the most successful firms develop cultures which are informal and egalitarian but are, nonetheless, strong cultures. These cultures, which need careful nurturing by the chief executive, are important in ensuring successful strategy implementation, particularly of those activities which span functional departments. While there is an enormous range of management styles among small high-tech firms, the more successful appear to have strong, democratic leadership, a leader conscious of his or her weaknesses, and a well-balanced management team with team spirit.

NOTES

(1) Whitting, R. "Will Mail Order Image Stunt Dell Computers' Fast Growth?", *Electronic Business*, November 13, (1989).

(2) Among the many books on this subject are: Kidder, T. *Soul of a New Machine*. Avon, New York, (1974); and Rogers, E. M. and Larsen, J. K. *Silicon Valley Fever*. Basic Books: New York (1984).

(3) Golson, H. L. "The Technically Oriented Personality in Management", *IEEE Transactions on Engineering Management*, Vol. EM-32, pp. 33–36 (1985).

(4) Garden, A. "The Motivation and Job Excitement of Software Professionals". Unpublished London Business School Working Paper (1987).

(5) Parden, R. J. "The Manager's Role and the High Mobility of Technical Specialists in the Santa Clara Valley", *IEEE Transactions on Engineering Management*, Vol. EM-28, 1, (1981).

(6) Malecki, E. J. "Hope or Hyperbole? High Tech and Economic Development", *Technology Review*, October (1987).

(7) Hunt, J. *Managing People at Work*. McGraw Hill, Maidenhead, England (1986).

(8) Garden, A. "Organizational Size as a Variable in Type Analysis". Unpublished London Business School Working Paper (1988).

(9) Handy, C. B. *The Age of Unreason*. Business Books, London (1989).

(10) This schema is taken from Garden, A. "Job Excitement, Motivation and Satisfaction of Software Professionals". Unpublished London Business School Working Paper (1988).

(11) Garden A. ibid note 10.

(12) Garden A. ibid note 10.

(13) Harvard Business School. Biogenetics Inc. Case Study No. 9-582-076 (1981).

(14) Harvard Business School. T Cell Sciences Inc. Case Study No. 9-388-001 (1987).

(15) Balkin, D. B. and Gomez-Mejia, L. R. "Determinants of R & D. Compensation Strategies in the High Tech Industry", *Personnel Psychology*, 3, 7, (1984).

(16) Parden, R. J. "The Manager's Role and the High Mobility of Technical Specialists in the Santa Clara Valley", *IEEE Transactions on Engineering Management*, Vol. EM-28, 1 (1981).

(17) Garden, A. "Turnover Reasons of Software Employees in a Range of Small High Tech Companies", *IEEE Transactions on Engineering Management* (1990).

(18) Parden R. J. ibid note 16.

(19) Garden, A. "Correlates of Turnover Propensity of Software Professionals in Small High Tech Companies", *R & D Management*, Vol. 19, No. 4, October (1989).

(20) There are many articles and books about job design, although none specifically related to small high-tech firms. As a start, see: Kleingartner, A. and Mason, R. H. "Management of Creative Professionals in High Technology Firms", *Industrial Relations Research Association Proceedings, April 1986*. pp. 508–515 (1986).

(21) Sherman, J. D. "The Relationship between Factors in the Work Environment and Turnover Propensities among Engineering and Technical Support Personnel", *IEEE Transactions on Engineering Management*, Vol. EM-33 (2) (1986).

(22) Slatter, S. St. P. and King, P. "Management Issues and Problems of Small High Tech Firms". London Business School Working Paper, (1984).

(23) Handy, C. B. *Understanding Organizations*. Penguin Books, Harmondsworth, Middlesex (1976).

(24) Jelinek, A. and Schoonhoven, C. B. *The Innovation Marathon*. Basil Blackwell, Oxford (1990).

(25) Bickerstaffe, G. "The Blossoming of Lotus", *The Director*, September, pp. 113–115 (1987).

(26) ibid.

(27) "The View from Route 128", *Management Reviews*, November, pp. 43–45 (1985).

(28) "Ideas for the 1990s", *Fortune*, 26 March, pp. 37–38 (1990).

(29) Maidique, M. A. and Hayes, R. H. "The Art of High Technology Management", *Sloan Management Review*, Winter (1984).

(30) Porter, M. *Competitive Strategy*, Chapter 2. Free Press, New York (1980).

(31) Riggs, H. R. *Managing High Technology Companies*. Van Nostrand Reinhold, New York (1984).

(32) Kotkin, J. "The Innovation Upstarts", *Inc.*, January, pp. 70–76 (1989).

(33) Whitting, R. "Compaq Stays the Course", *Electronic Business*, October 30, pp. 24–34 (1989).

(34) McCure, J. C. "A Modern Day Gutenberg Readies for the 21st Century", *Management Review*, November, pp. 8–10 (1989).

(35) Bourgeois, L. J. and Eisenhardt, K. M. "Strategic Decision Processes in High Velocity Environments: Four Cases in the Microcomputer Industry", *Management Science*, July, Vol. 34, No. 7, pp. 816–835 (1988).

(36) Politics is defined as the actions (often covert) by which executives enhance their power to influence a decision.
(37) Eisenhardt, K. M. and Bourgeois, L. J. "Politics of Strategic Decision Making in High Velocity Environments: Towards A Midrange Theory", *Academy of Management Journal*, Vol. 31, No. 4, pp. 737–770, (1988).
(38) For further discussion of human resource practices, see Kleingartner, A. and Anderson, C. A. (eds) *Human Resource Management in High Technology Firms*. Lexington Books, Lexington, MA (1987).

5
Managing Growth

The fast growth potential of many small high-tech firms is one of the most exciting aspects of this type of company. Such phenomenal growth is a supreme challenge to management, and makes the firm extremely fragile unless the way the firm is managed changes as the organization grows.

This chapter explores the typical problems that small high-tech firms experience when they go through periods of rapid growth, and some of the approaches used by those companies which have managed growth successfully. All high-tech firms experience major problems as they move from a small, entrepreneurial organization to a larger, more professionally managed organization. Some cope with the problems better than others, but no firm is exempt, since growth means that firms are constantly outgrowing their own capabilities.

All chief executives who have experienced periods of rapid growth acknowledge the difficulties of the management challenge. Paul Brainerd, founder of Aldus Corporation said:

> "In 1988 we went from $40 million to $80 million in sales. It's really a challenge doubling the size. You're always managing at a rapid pace to quickly grasp what the problems will be before hitting a brick wall. Even if you do an excellent job, you are still going to get hit blindside by a couple of things a year." [1]

While recognizing the problem that a firm faces during a period of growth, Rod Canion of Compaq also believes there

are some potential benefits: "If you're growing slowly, problems can sidle up on you almost unnoticed. With high growth
if you don't get out of the way first they knock you flat."[2]

While some firms cope with the problems of growth better
than others there is no magic formula for success. When Scott
McNealy, chief executive of Sun Microsystems, was asked how
he managed fast growth, his response was: "Look, the most
difficult things to do when you're running a fast growth company are getting enough sleep, thinking clearly, having the
courage to make tough decisions, being lucky and working
harder than anyone else. There's no magic to it."[3]

The chapter discusses: stages of growth; typical growth
problems; loss of excitement; the standard recipe—introducing
professional management; the need for stability and flexibility;
successful growth; when growth stops or slows.

STAGES OF GROWTH

Conventional wisdom about growth and the small firm tends to
concentrate on a "stage" model of growth. The small firm is
seen as passing through a sequence of growth stages (the
number varies from model to model), with a discussion of what
the dominant features within the firm are at each stage, and
also what factors need to change in order for the firm to make
the transition from one stage to another. All the models portray
the small firm as a behavioural entity whose focus of activities
changes in systematic and predictable ways. These models
have added to our understanding of growth and the effect it
has on organizations, but the reader should be aware that in
practice the stages are not discrete but are somewhat fluid, with
problems overlapping in adjacent stages, and that there is no
inevitable linear sequence of stages as the firm moves from one
stage of development to the next.[4,5]

In better performing firms, growth is managed as a process
of steady evolution. The culture at Lotus, for example, evolved
gradually as the company grew. The management team continued to be young, laid-back, hard-working and informal.
Interviewed in 1987, Jim Manzi did not feel that culture change

was a problem:

> "I see the culture changing the way it has changed. It's a continuum; there's no specific breakpoint. We do things differently now than we did one, two or three years ago just because of the velocity of the business, the nature of the competition, the graph of our ambitions, the complexity of the organization. As long as we're flexible and as long as we treat our people right—which we continue to spend a lot of time thinking about—it will be fine." [6]

The best-known growth model is Greiner's five-stage model, shown in Figure 5.1, which sees the growth of organizations as a series of evolutions and revolutions precipitated by various crises. [7] However, it is only the first two stages of Greiner's

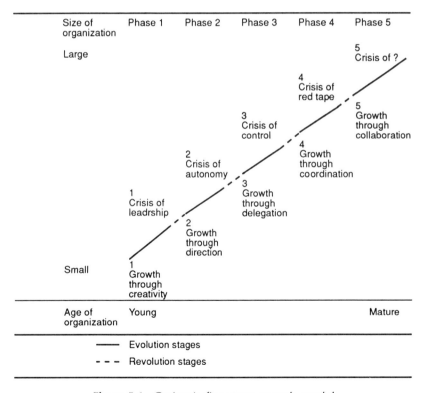

Figure 5.1 *Greiner's five-stage growth model*
Source: Reprinted by permission of *Harvard Business Review* from "Evolution and Revolution as Organizations Grow" by L. E. Greiner, *Harvard Business Review*, July–August 1972. Copyright © 1972 by the President and Fellows of Harvard College; all rights reserved

model that are applicable to the small firms which are the subject of this book. These two stages are interspersed by the classic crisis of leadership where the founder(s) has to accept the need for delegation of authority and be flexible enough to alter his or her position within the company to allow non-founder managers to operate effectively.

More applicable to the small firm are the models developed by Churchill & Lewis, Flamholz, and Kazanjian. The Churchill & Lewis model (shown in Figure 5.2) concentrates on the earlier stages of growth and identifies the company as passing through a series of problems, from getting customers and ensuring the delivery of the product in the start-up stage, through cash crisis as the company grows, to problems of consolidation as the company matures. [8] The model adjusts for

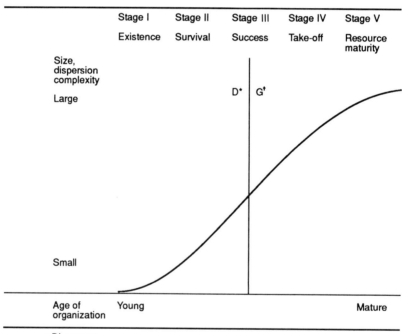

Figure 5.2 *Small business growth model*
Source: Reprinted by permission of *Harvard Business Review* from "The Five Stages of Small Business Growth" by N. C. Churchill and V. L. Lewis, *Harvard Business Review*, May–June 1983. Copyright © 1983 by the President and Fellows of Harvard College; all rights reserved

increasing complexity of operations as the company grows, and also allows for changes in strategies that can cause companies to loop back through the stages. Applying the model to high-growth companies, it assumes that companies will jump rapidly through the stages and, as a result, the "forced evolution" will cause a mismatch between the organization and the needs of the business.

The Flamholz model, which was developed specifically to help firms manage the transition from an entrepreneurial to a professionally managed firm, identifies four stages of growth: (1) new ventures, (2) expansion, (3) professionalization, and (4) consolidation. The key transition is from stage (2) to stage (3) because it is at this time that growing pains emerge. The exact point at which this occurs will vary from firm to firm depending on the industry, the complexity of the firm's product market strategy and the capabilities of its entrepreneurial top management team. There is some evidence, however, that the sales volume threshold at which technology-based firms experience growing pains is considerably higher than for low technology companies. [9] A focused product line with a few distinct market segments reduces complexity and allows the firm to grow relatively large before severe growing pains emerge. Likewise, a highly capable chief executive (or top management team) can extend the point at which crisis occurs. However, there is a danger that postponing the crisis, and continuing to run a relatively large company as though it were a small company, only causes an even bigger crisis eventually.

The Flamholz model is very similar to that used more recently by Scott and Bruce, and Kazanjian when he analyzed the relation of dominant problems to the stages of growth in 105 technology-based new ventures. [10,11] Kazanjian's four stages and the dominant problems at each stage are summarized in Figure 5.3. Not surprisingly, new product or technology applications dominate stage 1 (the development phase), and acquiring resources dominates stage 2 (the commercialization phase). Up to this point the organization is small, informal and dominated by its founder(s), and probably has less than about 40 employees. Some discrete organizational units are probably beginning to emerge. If the firm is successful in the market-place and moves into a period of high growth, the major problem facing management is to organize the firm

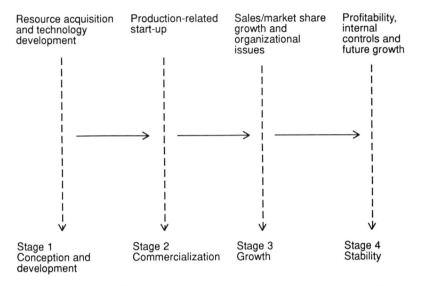

Figure 5.3   *Relation of dominant problems to stages of growth*
Source: Kazanjian, R. K. "Relation of Dominant Problems to Stages of Growth
in Technology-based New Ventures', *Academy of Management Journal*,
Vol. 31, No. 2, pp. 257–279 (1988)

in such a way as to be able to sell, produce and distribute its
product(s) in volume at a profit. Not surprisingly, it is at this
stage that building an efficient and effective organization takes
on increased importance. It is the problems that emerge in
building such an organization quickly that are the focus of this
chapter.

TYPICAL GROWTH PROBLEMS

Growing pains emerge when the small high-tech firm's growth
outstrips its organizational and administrative resources.
Growing pains are unavoidable, and so management must recognize the nature of the problem and act accordingly. The
degree of organizational change that is necessary to solve
growth problems is often considerable and painful for those
involved.

    In analyzing any set of business problems—and growth
problems are no exception—management should always seek

to separate out the symptoms from the causes. Treatment of the symptoms alone will not cure the "patient" unless the underlying causes are also dealt with in an appropriate manner. Many of the most common growth problems are the same for fast-growing high-tech firms as for any entre-preneurial firm experiencing rapid growth. However, the fragi-lity of the small high-tech firm exacerbates the effect of many of the problems, thereby further increasing fragility. Not sur-prisingly therefore, rapid growth is a time of increasing risk for the organization, even though the financial community may be identifying the company as a star performer.

Problems associated with growth usually show up first as symptoms. Familiar symptoms in small high-tech firms include: [12]

- confusion about "what my role in the company is, particu-larly at management level";
- a permanent feeling of crisis: constantly "putting out fires" and "chasing my tail";
- long working hours but "never enough time to get things done";
- interdepartmental bickering and even warfare;
- increased feeling of job insecurity;
- meetings felt to be a waste of time;
- lack of co-ordination between different parts of the organization;
- key people, particularly technical staff, leave the firm;
- cohesiveness and "employee spirit" declines;
- decisions delayed or do not get taken because they fall between two deparments;
- managers begin to design and maintain their own control systems because the corporate systems do not provide adequate information;
- lack of perceived direction;
- friendly and/or exciting atmosphere starts to disappear: firm becomes impersonal.

The effect of these and other similar symptoms is to lead to frustration, stress, poor decision making and declining morale which in turn leads to declining firm performance. It is not always easy to distinguish between causes and symptoms since organizational cause and effect relationships are usually complex and difficult to disentangle. However, failure to analyze the organizational and administrative problems that emerge during rapid growth, identify the causes and take appropriate action, will inevitably lead to a slow-down in growth and possible crisis.

Most of the organizational problems that small technology-based firms incur when they grow rapidly, are common to

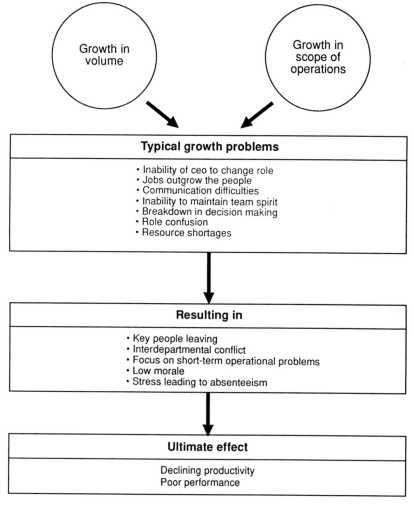

Figure 5.4　*Typical growth problems*

non-high-tech situations as well. [13] There are seven principal problems:

1 the inability of the chief executive to change his or her role;
2 jobs outgrow the people;
3 communication becomes more difficult as the number of intra-company relationships increase;
4 inability to maintain the "team spirit" and cohesiveness of the small firm;
5 breakdown of decision making as demand increases;
6 role confusion among top management;
7 resource shortages leading to stress and burnout.

Figure 5.4 summarizes the typical growth problems, each of which are briefly reviewed below.

Inability of the Chief Executive to Change Role

As the firm grows the nature of the chief executive's role needs to change from one of "doing" to one of "managing". Typically this involves delegating certain tasks which the chief executive did him/herself before rapid growth began; yet for most chief executives of small high-tech firms, particularly if they are the founders or owners, this transition is difficult to make. The need to change from a "doing" to a managing role means more than just delegating tasks and some decision making. It often calls for a substantial change in priorities—spending more time on planning and control, and perhaps more time with investors if the firm has gone public—and less time on operations.

Problems of this nature may arise due to either a lack of capability on the part of the chief executive to play a different role, or from his or her unwillingness to change role. In small high-tech firms, lack of capability to take on a different role is most acute among technical entrepreneurs who have neither the business experience nor management skills to run a medium-sized business. In some instances lack of capabilities may be linked to an unwillingness to change since the chief executive knows his or her limitations. However, a common problem among high-tech firms is an unwillingness of the chief executive and other senior managers to delegate. The reasons given for such behaviour include:

- a fear of breaking up the tight-knit team that has been a cause of the firm's success to date;
- a fear of losing control: inexperienced managers often equate delegation with loss of control, which, of course, it need not be if adequate control systems are in place;
- a belief that middle management is not ready to handle ever increasing responsibilities.

Jobs Outgrow the People

Rapid growth is usually accompanied by employees at all levels, but particularly key managers, being unable to change as rapidly as the demands of their jobs. Not all managers are capable of handling increased responsibility. Skill shortages are likely to exist and attitudes and behaviour may need to change if existing employees are to meet the expanding demands of their jobs.

One problem unique to the growing high-tech firm is that some of the company's most innovative staff may be attracted to managerial work for which they are not ideally suited, by the prestige and rewards accorded to management positions. In this situation, the firm gets the worst of both worlds—poor managers and loss of key technical talent.

Management in growing firms are often hesitant to handle situations where managers are obviously out of their depth. Very often it is members of the "founding team" (one or more of the founders and/or the early employees) that are causing a problem. In such situations, the chief executive or other senior executive responsible feels a strong sense of loyalty and gratitude for past services rendered by the individual(s). The situation in small firms is often complicated by the fact that the founding team may be personal friends of long standing.

Communication Becomes More Difficult

As firms experience rapid growth, the number of intracompany relationships increase, making communications increasingly complex. Informal face-to-face communications which are the norm in small firms become more difficult and are replaced by written reports. Even firms with a relatively narrow product line will experience problems as multiple locations and physical distances between work groups increase even on the same site.

Inability to Maintain Team Spirit and Cohesiveness

Small firms are characterized by informal structures and cultures and a "hands on" top management style. As the firm grows it becomes increasingly difficult to maintain the team spirit, because the number of personal relationships to be managed increases even more than the number of employees. The more relationships there are to manage, the more scope there is for distrust, suspicion, bad feelings and misunderstandings, which not only leads to poor implementation but also to slow decision making and declining morale. These problems are further exacerbated when new levels of management are added (distancing the employees from top management).

It is not just the size and scope of the company's operations that may cause team spirit to decline. Growth often generates considerable internal tension among the founders or within the top management team due to differences in the capability and/or willingness of the individuals to adapt to the changing conditions.

Breakdown in Decision Making

Growth often causes a breakdown in the decision-making processes that worked when the company was smaller. When problems and issues arise in small firms, decisions can be made on the result of face-to-face discussion using informal methods of communication. Beyond a certain size, top management cannot cope with the volume of decisions required, with the result that many decisions are neglected and avoided or made in a haphazard way, or at best severely delayed. Chapter 1 explained why speed of decision making is critically important for the small high-tech firm. Growth makes speed of decision making an even more important issue since the faster the growth, the greater the number of decisions that have to be taken rapidly. The need for so many decisions to be made quickly is often beyond the intellectual and/or emotional capabilities of many managers, particularly those with a technical background who may have an analytical (and sometimes academic) bias towards extensive analysis and discussion.

Role Confusion

As new employees are added, particularly at managerial levels, to cope with the growth in demand, confusion about roles, authority levels and responsibilities sets in. Confusion leads to demotivation and very often to a breakdown in decision making. When few senior people are sure of the answer to the question "Who has responsibility for ...", then confusion exists. What is worse is the impact that such confusion has further down the organization. Confusion at senior management levels is always transparent to those further down the organization.

Resource Shortages

Shortages of experienced senior staff, both managerial and technical, are nearly always a feature of high-growth situations. Large numbers of new people need to be recruited and trained quickly, but only rarely do firms find they can recruit and train people as quickly as required. The problem is often worse for high-tech firms, particularly the more innovative ones, because they often require specialist technical talents which have hitherto not existed. Firms want their new employees to be productive quickly, but very often the pressure to recruit is so overwhelming that insufficient efforts are made to train and assimilate new staff. The result is very often poorly trained and motivated staff which leads to eventual product quality problems and high costs due to inefficiency. The constant shortage of resources puts enormous pressures on the existing, more experienced employees. The likely effects of such pressures are burnout and/or focus on those activities which are obviously urgent. Tasks such as training, the development of new operational systems and planning are ignored in favour of keeping pace with current demand.

Resource shortages show up not just in the form of people problems but also in areas such as physical facilities and systems. Fast growth firms typically outgrow their phone systems, their management information systems, their recruitment and training systems, their customer support systems; in short everything that comprises the infrastructure of the firm.

LOSS OF EXCITEMENT

In Chapter 4, a distinction was made between job excitement and job satisfaction and it was suggested that the spirit of excitement in a firm may not be obtained through people being satisfied. Garden's study of job excitement and motivation in the software industry (already discussed in Chapter 4) indicated that, with only a few exceptions, the spirit of excitement felt by employees is significantly lower in larger firms than in smaller firms.[14] The few exceptions are those firms that have found ways of not losing the spirit of excitement as the firm grows into a larger, more established organization. Garden found that not all the organizational variables associated with job excitement and satisfaction varied with the size of the firm. However, three variables which showed a significant or highly significant relationship with job excitement showed a noticeable decline as the size of the firm increased, and some of the key factors associated with satisfaction increased significantly with size. Table 5.1 summarizes the key variables which appear to change with size. Noticeable change in the variables occurs when the firms are still at a fairly early stage of their growth. Garden's study found significant differences in employee attitude between three cluster sizes of small firms: those averaging 45 employees, 89 employees and 205 employees. While these categories were chosen arbitrarily the findings are consistent with case study evidence in many small high-tech firms.

The growth of LAN Systems, (name changed to preserve confidentiality), a local area network company, provides one

Table 5.1   *Organization variables showing significant change as size of firm increases*

Excitement variables decreasing with size	Satisfaction variables increasing with size
Awareness of making contribution to success of the firm	Education, training opportunities
Ability to achieve something useful	Sufficient resources
Able to make full use of own skills	Adequate security

Source: Garden, A. "Job Excitement, Motivation and Satisfaction of Software Professionals". London Business School Working Paper (1988).

such example. The firm was founded in 1984 by John Andersen, a 26-year-old MBA graduate of the Wharton School, who had a vision of what the office of the future might look like. He brought in two co-directors of a similar age both with Ph.D.s in computer science who were then undertaking research at a prestigious university. The business started in John's house, with the directors working together in the same room developing the first product and undertaking some consultancy work to cover overheads. As the first product emerged, they moved into a small office and recruited about six staff. The atmosphere was extremely congenial and friendly, everybody understood the targets and the newly hired staff soon shared the values, enthusiasm and commitment of the founders. Subsequently the founders referred to this group as the core group.

With the successful launch of the first product into a still emerging market segment, the company grew quite quickly to about 40 to 50 employees without losing the small and friendly atmosphere that had started in John's sitting-room. The core group easily passed on their values and objectives to the new recruits. Everyone worked long hours and was dedicated to the success of the firm. At about this time John and his co-directors developed a typical functional organization structure and began to appoint a supervisory layer of management underneath themselves.

As the business continued to grow to about 75 employees additional recruits were hired, but John noticed that these latest recruits were "nine to fivers". They went home on time and were much less interested in the success of the business. At the same time new senior managers were brought into the finance and sales functions and friction started to develop between John and the other founders. All three founders were perfectionists with no industrial experience prior to starting LAN Systems. They were highly critical of each other, and John's co-directors were dissatisfied with his autocratic style and lack of people-management skills. John, on the other hand, who spent most of his time on strategy was increasingly frustrated by what he saw as a lack of business awareness by his fellow directors and a lack of commitment by the employees, both those recently recruited and some of the earlier recruits. It was quite clear that the early spirit of excitement had disappeared.

What is interesting in the LAN Systems example is the way in which the recruitment of successive waves of employees impacted the organization. The founders and "core" employees were clearly highly motivated and managed to engender a reasonable degree of enthusiasm as the firm expanded to about 40 employees. Beyond that size, the firm found it increasingly difficult to maintain an exciting work environment, and by the time it had 60 to 75 employees it was experiencing severe growth pains. This situation is not atypical. Many small high-tech firms appear to exhibit severe management problems as they hit the 50–75 employee barrier. This is the transition period when the firm is typically trying to move from becoming a small entrepreneurial venture to a more "professionally" managed organization. The key at this stage is to introduce a more professional approach to management without losing the excitement which is important to innovation and building a winning culture (see pages 159–168).

Less obvious, but observable in some small high-tech firms, is another transition point when the firm reaches about 150 employees. At around this size it becomes difficult for the founder(s) to hire and know all the employees individually, and to maintain an environment which motivates innovative technical employees. Beyond this stage management finds it difficult to be "hands-on" and often develops a more indirect method of managing through structure, systems and cultural values, more typical of a large established firm. Such a textbook approach is, as shown later, inappropriate for the rapidly growing high-tech firm that must respond quickly to its environment.

The loss of excitement as the firm grows is due partly to the size factor and the changing patterns of social interaction within the firm; and partly to the characteristics of employees who are attracted to firms of different size (see Figure 5.5). As with many situations, the cause and effects flow in each direction, and management can set up a virtuous or a vicious cycle. If the firm manages to retain an "exciting" culture as it grows, its chance of attracting high quality recruits will be good. This will lead to the development of a high-performance culture which provides the right environment for sustained growth. If, on the other hand, management allows the type of situation described at LAN Systems to develop, a vicious circle ensues

Figure 5.5 *Impact of growth on employee commitment*

and key employees leave. This has the effect of increasing fragility at what is likely to be a difficult period of transition even if managed well.

Before discussing the various options used by high-performing growth firms to avoid loss of excitement, we need to understand how the standard recipe for dealing with growth—the introduction of professional management—is likely to accelerate the loss of excitement.

THE STANDARD RECIPE

The traditional approach, or "standard recipe", for dealing with the many management problems that arise from rapid growth is to introduce professional management. Both academics and practitioners alike talk about how growing firms need to make the transition from entrepreneurial to professional management. (This broadly equates to the first crisis in Greiner's model shown in Figure 5.1.) What this means is not always clear, although there are two features which tend to differentiate entrepreneurial from professional management: (1) the degree to which decision making is delegated, and (2) the degree of formality built into procedures, policies and control systems. The introduction of professional management practices involves the delegation of some decision-making responsibility from the chief executive/owner manager to a group of middle managers on the basis that one-man rule becomes increasingly difficult and ineffective when the firm reaches a certain size. Secondly, it involves the use of more formal systems for planning and controlling the activities of the business. The need for more formal systems and procedures is in part due to the delegation process. Systems are needed to guide and evaluate the performance of middle management, but the need also arises due to the increasing volume of transactions that accompany growth.

The systems and procedures that firms install as they "professionalize" can be thought of as operational systems and management systems. Operational systems are the basic systems which every firm needs to function. Systems are required to facilitate sales, order processing, inventory, purchasing, production, delivery, billing and collection as well as for basic accounting. Without such systems the firm is unable to meet its customers' needs. With growth, firms soon outgrow their existing systems. A continual process of upgrading systems is needed which usually involves the firm acquiring new managerial capabilities from outside. Management systems, on the other hand, are those geared to the general management tasks of planning, organizing and controlling the future development of the firm. Typical management systems include strategic and operational planning systems, organizational systems (appraisal systems, management development systems, etc.) and control systems (budgeting, objective setting, etc.). Formal management systems tend to be introduced when the firm reaches such a size that the original entrepreneur or chief executive can no longer be involved in all aspects of the business. The point at which this is reached depends on the capabilities and work capacity of the chief executive, and the complexity of the firm's business activities.

In theory, professional management as defined above—whether introduced by hiring a new chief executive or by the chief executive changing his or her management approach—should help the growing firm. After all, delegation should allow the firm to remain innovative and adaptive to its environment by pushing decision making down closer to the customers and suppliers, and more formal controls should promote greater efficiency. In practice, however, the introduction of professional management causes its own set of problems, often more serious than the problems they were intended to solve. The typical problems that fall into this category are:

- hiring new "professional" managers;
- the introduction of new levels of management;
- the introduction and growth of functional specialisms;
- the development of structural rigidities leading to poor implementation;
- the negative aspects of formal management systems.

These problems are sufficiently common among growing technology-based firms that each is discussed below separately.

Hiring New Professional Managers

Bringing so-called "professional" managers into growing technology-based firms is fraught with risk. While no statistics are available, the failure rate is very high. The problem starts with the recruitment process. Insufficient attention is given to defining the job, and the type of person required. Many firms experiencing growth problems believe that they should professionalize by recruiting an individual with management experience in a large firm. This is a potential recipe for disaster, since it equates—quite wrongly—large firms with professionalism. The opposite is often true, even in technology-based industries.

Once new managers have been recruited—often into financial and marketing positions—the problem becomes one of fit. The organizational culture and operating style of small but fast growing companies are usually very different from the environments where these individuals have been previously employed. They find it difficult to adapt and to work as part of the management team. Furthermore, an individual who is a good manager in a large organization is often no good at managing the type of people attracted to small high-tech firms: the high need for power of managers from large organizations is often in conflict with the desire of the employee for autonomy and a degree of independence. Nobody "speaks their language" or understands their approach to business or seems interested in learning about it. They wonder why they were hired in the first place, become frustrated and leave. The blame for the lack of fit can lie either with the existing management team or with the new recruits. Many entrepreneurs complain that they fail to see (although they want to) how professional managers add value, and are perplexed as to how they spend their time. What concerns them most is the inability of many of these (professional) managers to understand the business and "make things happen".

New Levels of Management

Delegation invariably means adding a new layer of management and the start of a management hierarchy. As the firm goes through the 50–75 employee transition phase and beyond, a cadre of managers reporting to the board develops: the "dreaded" middle managers. If promoted from within, middle managers in growing high-tech firms usually lack adequate managerial skills, while if brought in from the outside, middle managers have all the problems discussed above. Too often middle management act as blockages to good communications within the firm. At Apple Computer, founder Steven Jobs commented as follows:

> "Go back 10 years, Polaroid and Xerox would have been on everyone's list of the 10 best-managed companies. How did they lose their way when they became multi-billion dollar corporations? When you start growing like that, you start adding middle management like crazy."
>
> "... People in the middle have no understanding of the business and, because of that, they screw up communications. To them, it's just a job. The corporation ends up with mediocre people that form a layer of concrete. We're trying to keep Apple as flat as possible." [15]

Top management's natural reaction to this problem is to by-pass the middle management layer, particularly in owner-managed firms. The time pressures brought about by growth rarely allow top management the time to work with the new middle management to bring about a new style of management. Where new managers are recruited from outside the firm an additional problem arises: the alienation of subordinates. Employees who previously had direct access to senior management perceive themselves to be demoted, which in turn may lead to declining morale and the loss of some key employees.

Introduction and Growth of Functional Specialisms

Professionalization of management also brings with it the addition of technical experts and various staff specialists (e.g. human resource professionals, IT specialists, marketing planners, etc.). Typically the newcomers are required to provide the skill base to allow the firm to grow and to maintain technological competitive advantage. Even though new staff are often brought in to bolster existing management, employees feel threatened. The problem usually involves a mutual lack of understanding between the old and new guards, a situation which is aggravated when new employees try to "take over". As senior management adds new staff positions to provide support for line management, it becomes increasingly difficult to see how the staff specialists add value for the customer. In many cases they subtract value by interfering (to justify their existence) and by slowing down decision making.

Development of Structural Rigidities

Organization charts are not generally a feature of small companies but growth soon brings pressure to formalize structure. Chapter 4 provided an example of how quickly departments stake out their territory and build walls around themselves. So-called professionalization tends to encourage such behaviour and inevitably leads to a breakdown in the all-important cross-functional linkages. The end result is slow decision making and poor implementation.

Negative Aspects of Formal Management Systems

Perhaps the greatest danger of professionalization is the effect formal management systems have on innovation and entrepreneurship. Innovative product development and marketing is the life blood of successful fast-growth technology-based firms, yet time and time again professional managers introduce inappropriate management systems in a desire to improve operating effectiveness. Whereas effective operational systems are a prerequisite for managing growth, the introduction of "professional" management systems (described above) may change the culture of the firm on which its early success has been dependent. Formal management systems can very quickly become bureaucratic processes which stifle initiative, slow down decision making and make the firm less responsive to customers' needs. On top of this, the cost of running the systems often outweighs the benefits.

In addition to the problems brought about by the professionalization process itself, some of the problems caused by growth—role confusion, resource shortages, communication problems, etc.—may continue to persist making the effort to professionalize all the more difficult to achieve. A vicious downward spiral can quickly develop whereby stress increases and morale declines. In the very short term this may be offset by the euphoria often associated with rapid growth, but it increases the fragility of the firm making it more vulnerable to single events which trigger decline (see Chapter 8).

FLEXIBILITY AND STABILITY

How do firms cope with the rapid growth and the issues highlighted above? Most firms muddle through and learn by their mistakes. Few have the capacity to think about their organization analytically. Most are searching for a simple solution to what is, in fact, an extremely complex business problem of managing change. Managing the requirement for rapid change while providing continuity has been identified as the central dilemma facing high-tech firms. [16]

As shown above, rapid growth leads to significant instability in the organization, due to the constant need to reorganize to meet the operational requirements of the business. This would tend to indicate that the organization requires some form of stability, but too much stability will lead to a loss of one of the small firm's greatest assets: its flexibility. Nowhere is the dilemma between the need for stability and the need for flexibility greater than in the growth phase of small high-tech firms. However, the requirements of flexibility and stability are mutually exclusive: the attainment of one is always at the expense of the other. Flexibility implies openness to change, adaptability and freedom from rigidity, while stability implies routine desire to preserve past wisdom and resistance to change.

Flexibility is clearly required to enable the firm to modify its existing practices as it grows in an environment where product life cycles are short. Too much flexibility, however, makes it difficult or impossible for the organization to retain a sense of identity and continuity. The conventional view of stability, on the other hand, is that it is required to permit the organization to exploit "regularities" in an economical way. Regularities are processes and actions which lend themselves to systematization when the organization has a memory and a capacity for repetition. However, complete stability which would imply total adherence to past wisdom can be as dysfunctional as total flexibility: the organization's capability to respond and motivate would be almost nil in such circumstances.

As the firm grows, there are, however, a set of forces that push small high-tech firms towards stability. Six major forces (shown graphically in Figure 5.6) can be identified.

1 *The recruitment of different types of employees.* New employees are often recruited from larger firms who have different motivations from the original employees. Larger high-tech firms tend to employ different psychological types than smaller firms. [17] Smaller firms (under 50 employees) tend to attract people who prefer greater flexibility and openness

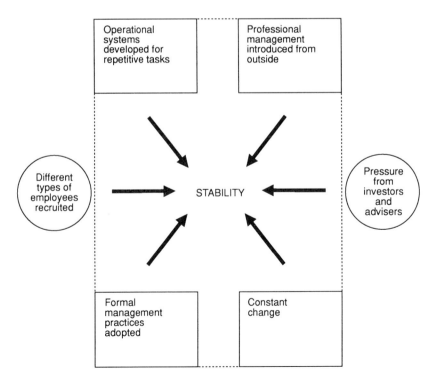

Figure 5.6 *Forces driving the need for stability*

whereas larger firms attract people who like stability and structure. Growth, therefore, changes or severely influences the culture of the firm over time unless the existing corporate culture is strong enough to absorb the new employees.

2   *Influence and pressure from investors and advisers to professionalize the management.* Many professional advisers fail to realize the distinctive nature of small high-tech firms and recommend, or even insist on, the adoption of the "standard recipe"—formal management systems and professional outside management. External pressure for premature sophistication often occurs when companies go public.

3   *The need to develop effective operational systems for repetitive tasks.* Such systems, by their nature, try to put order into a situation where chaos would otherwise ensue. They are needed to cope with both the increased complexity and scope of operations that typically accompany rapid growth.

4   *The introduction of professional management from outside.* Typically, new professional managers bring with them management styles, which are the antithesis of the entrepreneurial culture that characterizes the start-up and early growth phases of the small high-tech firm. Logical decision-making processes which are more analytical and maybe more rational than those found in entrepreneurial firms contribute to organizational stability.

5   *Adoption of formal management practices.* Management systems which "professionalize" the firm reduce flexibility, as already discussed.

6   *Constant change.* Growth is accompanied by constant changes in staff, job demands, organization structures, systems, products and markets; all of which create uncertainty and ambiguity. Some fast growing high-tech firms reorganize four or five times a year. While constant change encourages flexibility, and a few managers actually thrive on it, many people are not comfortable in an unpredictable setting; they prefer and search for a more stable environment. Thus, paradoxically, constant change itself acts as a force driving stability.

Those small high-tech firms that manage growth most

successfully balance the need for flexibility and the need for stability. Three approaches to this difficult management problem are possible: (1) a compromise response whereby the organization tries to achieve balance; (2) alternating emphasis on flexibility and stability (the see-saw approach); (3) simultaneous expression of the two necessities in different parts of the organizational system.

In reality the ideal balance is impossible to achieve. Instead, organizations try to approximate such a state through a compromise response, using constant interaction and experimentation. While constant interaction may at first sight appear laudable because it promotes learning and is a sign of flexibility, it may well have the opposite effect in practice. Change occurs daily in a growing company—often in very minor ways that are too small to be noticed by management. However, the cumulative effect of a succession of minor changes can significantly shift the organizational capabilities of the company before management realizes what has happened. While the most commonly used approach, it is probably the least likely of the three approaches to work in practice. The following comment from a CEO of a company based on Boston's Route 128 sums up this approach: "We must introduce professional management at all levels in the organization but do it in a considerate way so we do not lose our flexibility." To the firm's professional advisers or investors this was probably music to their ears when it was first said, but two years later the company appeared to have lost its way without having introduced professional management successfully, and having lost many of its most creative engineering staff.

The see-saw approach, whereby the firm alternates between periods of stability and periods of flexibility, may sound like an attractive alternative, given that balance can rarely be achieved using a compromise approach. This is the approach advocated by Maidique & Hayes in their study of high-tech firms:

> The successful high tech firm alternates periods of consolidation and continuity with sharp re-orientations that can lead to dramatic changes in the firm's strategies, structure, controls and distribution of power, followed by a period of consolidation ... knowing when and where to change from one stance to the other, and having the power to make the shift is the core of the art of high technology management. [18]

In practice though, it is often extremely difficult to shift direction without a crisis or a change in leadership.

The third approach—the simultaneous expression of the two necessities in different parts of the organizational system—can also be successful. Nevertheless, it can easily deteriorate into conflict and confusion unless managers and employees can learn to live with ambiguity and build constructively on the natural tensions that arise. There are no sure-fire recipes for success, so firms have used a variety of mechanisms to achieve the desired balance. For example:

- The entrepreneurial (flexible) founder moves up to chairman and keeps responsibility for product development and strategic development.
- The organization is split structurally into a "professionally" managed operations and marketing arm and a separate, flexible product development activity. This is the approach Computervision took after they purchased Cambridge Interactive Systems. The danger of this approach is that the product development employees are divorced from their customer base, which is a source of major innovation for all but a few advanced technology firms.
- Strong top-down performance standards are set for each part of the organization which, when taken in totality, achieve the desired balance. These standards are most effective when built into the organizational culture at an early stage and then vigorously maintained throughout the period of rapid growth.
- Complementary appointments. One of the key reasons for the success of many high-tech ventures is the existence of a balanced team—particularly in terms of skills, but sometimes in terms of power also. As small high-tech firms grow, it is common to find efforts being made to ensure the right mix of top management skills and philosophy. Intel, the semiconductor manufacturer, has taken this idea further than most by having two individuals with contrasting backgrounds and experience in most boxes on the senior management organization chart.

The fourth approach involves constant change and is probably more appropriate for the small high-tech firm than the other three approaches, since the small firm's ability to react quickly is part of its competitive advantage. The approach involves a continued process of organizational redesign driven by the chief executive. [19] The aim is to have all employees committed to constant change, since the forces driving stability will provide enough of a natural counterbalancing force that no specific action is necessary to promote stability. There are two principal problems with this approach. Firstly, there is likely to be a firm size beyond which this approach is impractical to implement, and secondly, there is likely to be a limit to the rate of change with which the average employee can cope.

SUCCESSFUL GROWTH

Managing fast growth in entrepreneurial firms is one of the most difficult management challenges that exists. Such firms are inherently fragile for the reasons already discussed in Chapter 1, but fast growth magnifies the weaknesses that already exist and presents a new set of problems. Since the problems cannot be avoided the question to ask is: How can the small high-tech firm overcome the problems associated with growth?

The short answer to the question is to say concentrate on the people issues. The employees are the engine that makes the firm successful. Their commitment and motivation which has allowed the firm to enter a growth phase has to be nurtured through the many changes that are needed to manage fast growth. In reality, management of fast-growth firms are often overwhelmed by the problems and pressures of keeping pace with demand. They approach change on an *ad hoc* basis, improvising as necessary to contain one problem after another. Unfortunately, there is no magic answer, since the most successful fast-growth, high-tech firms often adopt a paradoxical approach to managing growth. The need for both stability and flexibility simultaneously requires a careful balancing act between:

- strong central leadership and decentralized task-oriented management;

- entrepreneurial and professional management; and
- processes providing organizational cohesion and those promoting individual responsibility.

Too much emphasis one way or the other on any of these three dimensions, and the solution becomes part of the problem.

Strong Leadership and a Balanced Management Team

Most high-tech firms that have experienced a period of successful growth are characterized by a strong leader who has a clear vision and objectives. Strong leadership in high-tech firms does not automatically imply an autocratic style as it so often does with small firms generally. The problem with many fast-growth, high-tech firms is that a strong leader exists, who is recognized for his or her entrepreneurial and technical talents, but the individual does not have a broad understanding of what leadership entails. They do not understand how to manage transitions and how to develop and improve the organization on a continuous basis. Good leadership in small high-tech firms involves communicating very clearly the vision, values and objectives of the business throughout the organization. Strong leadership provides a key role in overcoming the confusion that usually accompanies growth, and is necessary to build and maintain the cohesiveness of the organization. All employees need a common understanding of the company that management is trying to build.

Strong leadership, however, must be supported by a well-balanced top management team to avoid any "excesses" on the part of the leader, and to ensure that no functional areas are neglected. Too often strong leaders are interested in only one aspect of the business—often the technology aspects—and become disinterested in the more commercial side of the business. At Lotus Development Corporation, Mitch Kapor, the founder, realized in 1984 that it was time to step aside as president. In a subsequent interview Kapor said: "It became apparent to me that I was getting burned out and unhappy with my experience as the person to whom manufacturing and sales reported."[20] Kapor appointed Jim Manzi, then aged 33 (a year younger than himself), to the presidency of Lotus. Whereas Kapor had a reputation for being mellow and loose, Manzi was the opposite. Manzi saw himself and Kapor as complementing each other.

> "The way we run the company is unique. He [Kapor] works with product strategies, with research and development. I work with organizational entities, with business strategies and take care of day-to-day operations. I'm better with small groups—I'm better with single individuals than with a thousand people."[21]

The importance of team work is stressed by many successful growth companies. Rod Canion the founder of Compaq, says that he soon realized that no one person on the management team had all the answers, which subsequently led to a collective approach to decision-making:

> "We have a team process that leads to getting the best answer. We've encouraged all the thought it takes to have a team spirit. All companies want it, most of them talk about it, but few companies really have it, at least to the degree which Compaq has been fortunate to develop and maintain it."[22]

We saw earlier in this chapter that one of the problems of growth is that the demands of a job outgrow the managerial capability of the individual. For a management team to be well balanced, it is essential that hard decisions are taken about those managers who can no longer adequately perform to the required standard. This is a particular problem in growing high-tech firms where members of the founding team may have great technical skills but no managerial skills. The way successful firms deal with this problem is to distinguish very carefully between directors and managers. The chairman of one software company commented:

> "We have directors who have never been managers, because they're no good as managers. They are software engineers. It's a hard decision to tell one's cofounders they can only be directors and not managers, but intelligent people can be so stupid that you cannot put them in charge of anything."

Throughout the growth process it is important that top management maintains a "hands-on" style for as long as possible to ensure that the focus drive and energy which is characteristic of successful entrepreneurs does not fade. Once top management distances itself from the employees it creates a dangerous gap. "If you can no longer be one of the employees you lose something", says John Gifford of Californian semiconductor manufacturers, Maxim Integrated Products. [23] It is interesting to see just how often the original entrepreneur who has moved himself/herself "upstairs" to the chairman's job has to come back and play an operational role when high growth ends up as poor performance.

Balancing Entrepreneurial and Professional Management

Those firms that have been most successful in managing themselves in a "professional" way during rapid growth have been those that started using professional management approaches at or soon after start-up. Compaq provides a good example of this approach. From the start, Compaq acted like the big company it was quickly to become. Tight financial controls and forecasting systems were put into place even before production began; only big-name banks, attorneys and auditors were employed. "You'll find that our outside advisers have the same profile as our own managers—big, experienced professionals that the company can grow into. There are plenty of opportunities for change when all the underpinnings are solid", said Vice President and Chief Financial Officer, John Gribi. [24]

Good management saw them through explosive growth following their first product shipment in 1983. First year's revenues were $111m, and in 1984 sales jumped to $329m. Company founder and president, Rod Canion, says 1983 was the pivotal period, when the number of employees grew from 100 to 600, and production increased from 200 machines in January to 9000 in December. In 1989, Michael S. Swavely, President of Compaq's North American Division, outlined the company's strategy for dealing with the rapid growth:

> "In terms of managing the company's growth, we followed three major principles. The first was to make sure that we had adequate financial resources. The second was to ensure that we hired the management

talent that could guide the growth of the company in a start-up phase as it developed into a very large corporation, while at the same time maintaining management consistency. The third principle, from a systems perspective, was to install systems from the beginning that could handle growth up through a million dollars or more. The basic concept in the formation of the company was that we would be a large company that happened to be in a start-up phase.' [25]

But despite this strategy, Swavely did not think that managing Compaq had been an easy job.

"It has been difficult in every way. I think that it's almost inconceivable for a manager in a mature industry to understand what it's like to manage growth that's been so explosive, because it's much more than just a company challenge. It's a personal challenge. Your job completely changes at least once a year and probably more often than that as you rocket through these growth stages. Nothing stays the same. If you can't deal with that kind of environment, it would drive you crazy." [26]

A similar approach was used at Xoma Corp, a biotechnology start-up. Pat Scannon, the founder, recognized the need for professional management early in the company's development and hired Steve Mendel as Chairman and Chief Executive a year after its inception. "When you bring managers in late, they come into a situation where spending is unlimited, people have too much freedom, research is all over the place and prospects are not really identified", says Mendel. "Someone has to stop the party. Because we started early we never had that party." [27]

The message from these companies is very clear: start as you intend to continue. Introduce as professional a management approach as early as you possibly can. By introducing certain disciplines and standards from the beginning into the entrepreneurial culture, culture shock can be avoided or substantially reduced when the rapid growth phase actually occurs. [28]

When rapid growth does occur, it is vitally important to maintain those parts of the entrepreneurial culture which are critical to the success of small high-tech firms. Entrepreneurial capabilities necessary for success include the ability to:

● make decisions quickly;
● rapidly re-deploy resources as market and competitive conditions change;

- have fast internal communications;
- obtain rapid feedback from customers;
- be innovative;
- stay flexible.

Entrepreneurial cultures are flexible and informal. The best performing companies make conscious efforts to inculcate flexibility into the organization at an early stage. Successful growth firms achieve this by being *rigid in their demand for flexibility*, and spending a lot of time thinking about the type of people they want to hire. Jim Manzi at Lotus has said: "We look for people with flexibility because of the rate of change. ... Building flexibility into the system and into the expectations of both old-time people and new people is real important." [29] One way of trying to ensure flexibility is to maintain a degree of informality. Manzi stresses this point at Lotus:

> "While hierarchies are required and inevitable, they are not the sole mechanism through which the company is run. ... We use multiple mechanisms, and informality and just walking around and talking to people are part of that—not just for me but for everybody. I really hate being told what to do; so I try to remember that." [30]

Lotus had to deal with explosive growth early in its history. Founded in April 1982 with $1m in venture capital and eight employees, by the end of 1983 they had launched the first version of the 1-2-3 program, had sales of $53m and had grown to 300 employees. By 1986, turnover had reached $283m, with over a thousand people on the payroll.

Maintaining an informal culture requires keeping the number of levels in the organization to an absolute minimum. Although some hierarchy is inevitable, the negative effects of hierarchy can be kept to a minimum by taking steps to ensure the firm is a single status employer. This means that all employees are treated the same where fringe benefits are concerned. All employees attend the annual company outing/party. Although seemingly simple, this becomes increasingly hard to implement as the firm grows.

In nearly all growing firms it is necessary to recruit some senior managers from outside the firm. However, winners tend to devote time and effort to developing senior managers from within the organization. One study of successful mid-size growth companies in the USA found that 75% of senior executives "had risen from the ranks" and that where they had to recruit high-level management skills from outside, considerable efforts were made in "understanding them, reviewing and reinforcing their roles and encouraging supportive interaction with the old guard". [31] Successful fast-growth, high-tech firms adopt the same policy.

The introduction of professional management which involves large company management systems (as opposed to operating systems) being introduced, should be avoided at all cost. Innovation, particularly in the area of new product technology is critical to the continuing success of the growing high-tech firm. [32] Management must ensure that it continues to encourage innovation by tolerating failure, allowing a certain amount of organizational slack, and encouraging a culture in which technically-oriented employees continue to be motivated. Commenting on this issue at Apple Computer, John Sculley said:

> "If I had come in and just tightened everything down and sanitized it, the very things that make Apple an unusual company would have been lost—the creativity and innovativeness to develop new, exciting products that are changing the way people, think learn and work." [33]

At Cypress Semiconductor Corporation, Chief Executive T. J. Rodgers has managed growth through an unusual combination of entrepreneurial activity and highly formalized management systems. In 1986, four years after founding Cypress, Rodgers recognized that the company was starting to slip into the less flexible ways of a big company. To remedy the situation Cypress became a venture capitalist, funding four start-ups over the next three years. At the same time, however, Rodgers kept growth under control through strict management systems which are constantly refined. Since day one, Rodgers has implemented what he calls a "turbo" management-by-objective system which requires all employees to spend an hour a week evaluating their past performance and setting future goals. Every Tuesday at 4 p.m. they must file progress reports which are reviewed by managers, and exceptions are scrutinized by Rodgers. Each of the 1400 employees has both short-term goals and three more ambitious longer-term goals. The product-planning system, head count control, capital spending and expense systems are similarly formalized. All divisions and start-up subsidiaries are required to use the system. Although Rodger's tough control style may not be to everybody's liking, it undoubtedly contributes to Cypress' success. Cypress grew at an annual average annual compound growth rate of 128% from 1983 to 1989, the fastest rate of any company in *Electronic Business'* 1990 listing of the 100 fastest growing US electronic companies. [34]

Organizational Cohesion and Individual Responsibility

Holding the organization together as the firm grows requires both strong leadership and sound management from those at the top of the organization. When the firm is small, top management has direct contact with all employees and is probably involved in most of the hiring decisions, and new employees are easily absorbed into the culture. Beyond a certain size, new employees no longer take on the values of the earlier employees unless specific management actions are taken to reinforce the culture. The culture of the firm is the glue that provides the organizational cohesion.

At Sun Microsystems, sales reached $2 billion within seven years of the company being founded. By 1989 the company had 8900 employees. As numbers grew, some of the classic symptoms of growth started to emerge: labour turnover rates increased as stress began to take its toll. When the company was small, the chief executive, McNealy, was able to deal with such problems by gathering everybody together for pep talks, but as Sun grew a formal, written mission statement was developed; and in 1988 a "quality of life plan" was issued. The goal was to get employees back in touch with Sun's mission and strategy and to regain some of the feel of the start-up period. McNealy started to communicate Sun's vision through quarterly videos on strategic issues, problems and solutions. One such video was on recruitment to help managers understand the importance of hiring the right people. [35]

During periods of rapid growth, successful firms make a

conscious effort to build cohesion. Among the processes used are:

- Intensive training both to develop employees' skills and to reinforce the cultural values of the company. This includes training for senior management on how to manage change.
- Increased emphasis on communications. Communications becomes much more complex as the firm grows, and a greater investment of management time is needed to ensure vision, direction and values are constantly communicated.
- Greater use of integrating mechanisms such as multi-disciplinary project teams, matrix-like organizational structures, job rotation and physical location of people.
- Actions to motivate technical staff who see management reaping the rewards of bigger salaries, titles, etc. Typical actions involve instituting technical forums, dual career ladders, etc.

Simultaneously with providing organizational cohesion, management has to ensure that line management is fully accountable for performance. Accountability requires clear definition of responsibilities and the avoidance of complexity; which can conflict with some of the integrating mechanisms used to promote cohesion. One commonly used approach to encourage accountability and motivation is to break the growing firm down into divisions or smaller business units, to achieve the type of effect obtained at Cypress Semiconductors. Lotus did this in 1985, when management decided to divisionalize its operations "It's very difficult to run a business as a single profit-and-loss centre with more than 1000 people," says Kapor. "It promotes the move to divisionalize." Sandra Gunn started up the Engineering and Scientific Products Division in March of that year. She sees herself as an entrepreneur:

> "I was told that I would have resource commitments and I was told to come up with a plan. There were no parameters, no guidelines. I could do pretty much anything I could justify. ... What we're trying to do here is create an environment inside Lotus as appealing or even more appealing [as starting their own company] for our development people so that they won't feel that the only way for them to achieve their personal goals is to leave." [36]

Small divisions can be made commercially and technically responsible and preserve some of the characteristics of the entrepreneurial small firm. However the danger is that collaboration across the organization declines as the identity of the organizational units increases. The most successful firms try to get the balance right: they recognize that it is legitimate for each business unit to develop its own culture but that the corporate culture must be utterly dominant.

Managing high growth involves managing rapid change. It requires management to embrace constant change. Some of the key points that emerge from this chapter are summarized below as tips for managing growth.

Tips for Managing Growth in Small High-tech Firms

- Ensure strong leadership with clear vision and objectives.
- Have a well-balanced management team.
- Maintain a "hands-on" top management style with active involvement in the innovation process.
- Do not confuse direction and management: take tough decisions on individuals quickly.
- Do not confuse the need for operating systems with a need for professional management systems.
- Stay informal and ensure single status.
- Develop processes to maintain organizational cohesion.
- Develop processes to promote innovation.
- Give clear responsibilities to line management.
- Keep the business simple: avoid complexity.
- Set performance standards: use external benchmarks.
- Make key decisions quickly.
- Rapidly redeploy resources where necessary.
- Divisionalize when appropriate.

WHEN GROWTH STOPS OR SLOWS

High growth rates cannot be maintained for ever: most high-tech firms sell industrial goods which are subject to cyclical demand patterns. Although they may successfully grow through a recession when they are small, this is much more difficult to do when the firm is larger. It is then that the firm has to go through a period of consolidation (perhaps as a prelude to a further period of growth later). The approach to consolidation depends heavily on whether growth stops abruptly and the firm hits a financial crisis, or if growth continues but at a substantially slower rate. In either case, consolidation is a different management challenge to managing growth. The only similarity is that once again it involves change—in the people, the structure, the systems and the culture.

Where the company goes abruptly ex-growth (i.e. it stops growing), it may well hit a financial crisis which puts it straight into the category of a turnaround situation. Managing such situations is the subject matter of Chapter 9. If, on the other hand, growth slows down but there is no financial crisis, consolidation still involves considerable strategic and organizational change. Strategically, the firm will need to rethink its strategy as the key factors for success in the core business are likely to have changed. Most likely the firm will be trying to be "all things to all people", and there will be a need to refocus the firm's product market strategy to take account of the new entrants that are likely to have been attracted into the market. This is likely to involve withdrawing from some product-market segments and employing strategies designed to improve productivity and cost efficiency in others, since the chances are that the firm will have lost some of its technological differentiation. The major challenge for firms at this stage is how to capitalize on their innovative capability by defining new product market areas (which is the subject of Chapter 6) or introducing a new generation of innovative products to differentiate itself technologically.[37] New strategies may also involve developing new strategic alliances, even with old enemies. Thus, Apple and IBM are now working together, something that would have been unthinkable five years ago. In a survey of 100 high-growth, high-tech firms, management consultants, Booz Allen & Hamilton found that 80% of the firms surveyed needed to alter and/or refine their strategy and form new strategic alliances as they grew.[38]

At the same time as re-assessing their competitive position, restructuring and downsizing may be necessary to regain effectiveness and momentum even if the firm is not in a crisis situation. Organizationally, the excitement and strains of fast growth disappear and a new set of problems appear. The pressure to reduce costs which leads to more formal managerial control systems for business planning, resource allocations, etc. tends to stifle radical innovation. Promotion opportunities disappear and key employees leave. The existing management is often unable to cope with the new environment and has to be replaced. In the Booz Allen study referred to above, over 70% of the firms surveyed had to restructure or resize the business at various points in their history even though they were still growing and had ample market opportunities. Even though the firm may not be in a crisis, the types of strategies discussed in Chapter 9 will probably be necessary if the firm is to have any chance of moving back into a fast growth mode or to stop itself slipping into a classic crisis situation.

Fast growth increases the fragility of the small high-tech firm since growth means that the firm is constantly outgrowing its own capabilities. The three "internal" forces driving fragility identified in Chapter 1—resource shortages, the entrepreneur and the nature of the employees—are all stretched to near breaking point. Growth seems to leverage the weaknesses that are inherent in the small high-tech firm.

SUMMARY

This chapter has identified the typical problems faced by small high-tech firms when they go through a period of rapid growth. The standard approach for dealing with growth— introducing professional management—must be implemented cautiously, since not all aspects of classical professional management are appropriate for the growing high-tech firm. Successful growth requires a careful balancing act between strong central leadership and decentralized, task-oriented management, entrepreneurial and professional management, and processes providing organizational cohesion and those promoting individual responsibility. The most successful firms prepare for fast growth from day one of their existence. Managing fast growth is the supreme challenge for those who love managing constant change.

NOTES

(1) McCure, J. C. "A Modern Day Gutenberg Readies for the 21st Century", *Management Review*, November, pp. 8–10 (1989).

(2) Caulkin, S. "Compaq's Compact Fortunes", *Management Today*, May, pp. 92–96 (1985).

(3) Berkman, B. N. "Raising Sun", *Electronic Business*, 1 May, pp. 25–30 (1989).

(4) Normann, R. *Management for Growth*. Wiley, Chichester p. 46 (1977).

(5) Kimberley, J. R. and Miles, R. H. *The Organizational Life Cycle*. Jossey-Bass, San Francisco, p. 7 (1980).

(6) Bickerstaffe, G. "The Blossoming of Lotus", *The Director*, September, pp. 113–115 (1987).

(7) Greiner, L. E. "Evolution and Revolution as Organizations Grow", *Harvard Business Review*, July–August, pp. 37–46 (1972).

(8) Churchill, N. C. and Lewis, V. L. "The Five Stages of Small Business Growth" *Harvard Business Review*, May/June, pp. 30–51 (1983).

(9) Flamholz, E. G. *How to Make the Transition from an Entrepreneurial to a Professionally Managed Firm*. Jossey-Bass, San Francisco (1986).

(10) Kazanjian, R. "Relation of Dominant Problems to Stages of Growth in Technology-based New Ventures", *Academy of Management Journal*, Vol. 31, No. 2, pp. 257–279 (1988).

(11) Scott M. and Bruce, R. "Five Stages of Growth in Small Businesses", *Long Range Planning*, June, pp. 45–52 (1987).

(12) The list of symptoms is based on a combination of field interviews and literature. See, for example, Flamholz, E. G. *How to Make the Transition from an Entrepreneurial to a Professionally Managed Firm*. Jossey-Bass, San Francisco (1986).

(13) Kotter, J. and Sathe, V. "Problems of Human Resource Management in Rapidly Growing Companies", *Californian Management Review*, Winter, Vol. XXI, No. 2, pp. 29–36 (1978).

(14) Garden, A. "Job Excitement, Motivation and Satisfaction of Software Professionals". London Business School Working Paper (1988).

(15) *Business Week*, 20 November (1984).

(16) Maidique, M. A. and Hayes, R. H. "The Art of High Technology Management", *Sloan Management Review*, Winter, Vol. 25, pp. 17–31 (1984).

(17) Garden, A. "Organizational Size as a Variable in Type Analysis", London Business School Working Paper (1988).

(18) Maidique, M. A. and Hayes, R. H., ibid. Similar conclusions were reached by Romanelli, E. and Tushman M. "Executive Leadership and Organizational Outcomes: An Evolutionary Perspective", *Management of Technological Innovation Conference Proceedings*, Worcester Polytechnic Institute (1983).

(19) Soukup, W. R. and Cornell, D. G. "Organization Design for High Tech Firms: The Case for Controlled Instability", Paper presented at Academy of Management Annual Meeting, New Orleans, August (1987).

(20) Juback, J. "What's Next for Lotus?", *Venture*, January, pp. 36–40 (1986).

(21) Miller, R. "Lotus After 1-2-3: Managing Your Money", *Management Review*, September, pp. 14–16 (1985).

(22) Whitting, R. "Compaq Stays The Course", *Electronic Business*, 30 October, pp. 24–30 (1989).

(23) McCreadie, J. and Rice, V. "Nine New Mavericks", *Electronic Business*, 4 September, pp. 30–35 (1989).

(24) Caulkin, S. "Compaq's Compact Fortunes", *Management Today*, May, pp. 92–96 (1985).

(25) "Rapid Rise to the Top: An Interview with Compaq's Michael S. Swavely", *Journal of Business Strategy*, November/December, pp. 4–7 (1989).

(26) "Rapid Rise to the Top", ibid.

(27) Levine, R. "Biotech Firm Seeks Balance of Business and Science", *Management Review*, July, pp. 32–36 (1989).

(28) Bracker, J. S., Keats, B. W. and Pearson, J. N. "Planning and Financial Performance Among Small Firms in a Growth Industry", *Strategic Management Journal*, Vol. 9, pp. 591–603 (1986).

(29) Bickerstaffe, G. "The Blossoming of Lotus", *Director*, September, pp. 113–115 (1987).

(30) ibid.

(31) Schorsch, L. L. "Lessons from Mid Sized Growth Companies", *McKinsey Quarterly*, Autumn, p. 17 (1983).

(32) Moore W. L. and Tushman, M. L. "Managing Innovation over the Product Life Cycle", in M. L. Tushman and W. L. Moore (eds) *Readings in the Management of Innovation*, pp. 131–150. Pitmann Press, New York (1982).

(33) Sculley, J. and Byrne, J. *Odyssey ... a Journey of Adventure. Ideas and the Future*, p. 287. Harper & Row, New York (1987).

(34) Rayner, B. C. P. "For Cypress Growing Fast Means Thinking Small", *Electronic Business*, 30 April, pp. 35–37 (1990).

(35) Berkman, B. N. "Raising Sun", *Electronic Business*, 1 May, pp. 25–30 (1989).

(36) Juback, J. "What's Next for Lotus", *Venture*, January, pp. 36–40 (1986).

(37) Wiersema, Margaret F. and Page, Robert A. Jr. "Managing the Innovative Firm: Strategies for Sustaining Radical Innovation", in M. W. Lawless and L. R. Gomez-Mejia (eds) *Proceedings, Second International Conference on Managing the High Technology Firm*, January (1990).

(38) Summers, W. P. "Rapid Growth and Fast Retreats", *Outlook*, Vol. 11, pp. 48–52, Booz Allen & Hamilton Inc. (1987).

6
In Search of Further Growth

Unless the small high-tech firm is spectacularly successful in its chosen product-markets, a point is reached at which the firm starts to look for growth opportunities either overseas or by diversifying outside its core activity area. Overseas, the firm usually seeks to grow through entering foreign markets with somewhat similar strategies to those that have been successful in the domestic market. More likely than not the firm will have been successful in establishing a profitable business in its domestic market before it starts to look for overseas opportunities. Where further growth is through diversification the stimulus for such a move is usually a slowing down of growth in the core area and/or a change in the basis of competition caused by shifting customer demands, new technologies and competitors' actions.

Further growth, whether through market development overseas or through diversification in the domestic market (or both), places enormous strains on the organization's resources. In both cases it creates major management challenges just at the time the firm is likely to be suffering from significant problems in its core business. Successful overseas expansion and diversification are difficult at the best of times, but for the fragile, small high-tech firm they can be catastrophic. The successful, rapidly growing firm is likely to be struggling with all the problems involved in managing growth; while the firm whose competitive position in its core business area is weakening has (or should have) its hands full trying to strengthen that position. The attraction of diversification for management is that it appears to reduce risk by "not having all one's eggs in one basket", and the fact that in most high-tech industries, firms are surrounded by what appear to be opportunities. In most sectors the number of opportunities are considerably greater than any one firm can cope with. The natural tendency is for management to get sucked into too many diversification opportunities, which ends up being disastrous due to the firm's limited resource base.

The success with which firms develop their business beyond product market segments where they are initially successful is heavily dependent on the depth and breadth of their resource base. Inherently most small high-tech firms have a limited set of core competencies from which they can leverage themselves into new businesses and new markets.[1] The type of competencies that small high-tech firms develop during the start-up and subsequent growth phases, and the way that those competencies are used in searching for further growth, determine the success of both overseas expansion and diversification strategies. Since there is a wide variety of firms that can be classified as small high-tech firms, generalizations about competencies are difficult to make. However, in practice one can identify a number of broad "types" or categories of small high-tech firms, based on different competitive emphasis. Each of these categories differ in the breadth of their competencies and their scope for developing further growth opportunities.

This chapter starts by identifying and describing the different categories of small technology-based firms and then looks at the type of growth strategies each category typically employs. Since many firms use acquisitions as a means of implementing their growth strategy, the chapter briefly looks at the success and failures of acquisitions by small technology-based firms.

TYPES OF SMALL HIGH-TECH FIRM

Chapter 2 showed that at start-up a firm focuses its initial activities according to its resource base. Such a focus usually leads to specialization along one of three dimensions—product (or

Table 6.1 Strategic differences among the different types of small technology-based firms

Type of firm: Features	Niche players	Market specialists	Product group specialists	Technology specialists		Dominant sector players
				Contract R & D	Core technology specialists	
1 Competitive emphasis	Niche specialization	Special needs of customer group	Product leadership	Technological superiority	Technological superiority	Industry or sector dominance
2 Timing of market entry	Varies	Entry during introductory and growth stages	Entry during introductory and growth stages	Early into technology. Timing of entry into different markets varies		Very early
3 Degree of product innovation	Medium	Main emphasis on market specialization	High	Very high	Very High	Changes over the life of the firm and the product life cycle
4 Market strategy	Follow the leader	Applications engineering	Follow the leader	Custom strategy	First to market	First to market or quickly follow the leader
5 Technical skills of the firm	Very narrow	Narrow	Narrow	Wide	Wide	Wide and increases as the firm grows with the market
6 Product type	Standard or custom	Standard or custom	Standard or custom	Consulting (and custom products)	Standard and custom	Varies over the product life cycle—custom to standard

	(1)	(2)	(3)	(4)	(5)	(6)
7 Major weaknesses	Limited resources Single product businesss	Tunnel vision	Tunnel vision complacency with initial success	Loss of technological leadership if products developed take on industry focus		Inability to manage growth need to innovate at a time of growth
8 Major threat	Inability to build a viable business size	Competition from large firms pursuing dominant player strategy	Competition from large firms pursuing dominant player strategy. New product failure	Losing technological leadership Technology with narrow opportunities Maturity of technology		Aggressive competition from other dominant firms striving for market leadership
9 Initial growth rate	Modest	High	High and short term	Slow	Slow	Corresponds with market
10 Firm's potential for independent growth (i.e. scope of development)	Least	Low	Low	Average	Varies	High

service), market segment (or customer group), or technology—and it is this which forms the basis of the classification of small high-tech firms into the following five categories: [2,3]

1 dominant sector players;
2 product group specialists;
3 market specialists;
4 niche players;
5 technology specialists.

This section describes the principal characteristics of each type of firm, their critical competencies and the specific barriers to growth each faces once it has established a market position. Table 6.1 summarizes the key strategic differences between the firms.

Dominant Sector Players

These are firms aiming for a dominant and central position in their industry sector. Typically, they enter their markets early and grow aggressively to achieve a significant share of the overall market. The interests of the firm span across numerous products and customer groups which comprise the sector or industry (see Figure 6.1). The company evolves from a small entrepreneurial firm to a dominant and structured organization. The evolution of the firm tends to follow the evolution of the industry.

Small technology-based firms which aim for a central position in their industry have the following features:

- a major or radical innovation which can revolutionize an existing market or create a new market, such as the invention of the word processor by Wang;
- ambitious and aggressive management team;
- ability to build resources quickly enough to be able to dominate the industry.

Rarely do small technology-based firms have all three of the above, with the result that dominant sector players are not common among small high-tech firms.

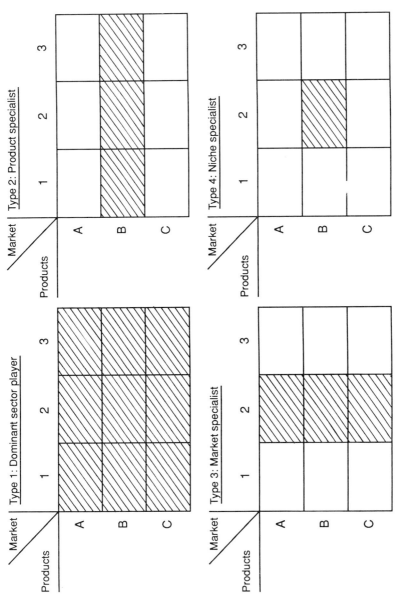

Figure 6.1 *Types of product-market focus*

The industry focus is the result of repeated successes in the company's effort to grow. The history of the company is marked with corporate milestones. One such example in the UK is Domino Printing Sciences which started off designing ink-jet printers for the packaging industry (which comprised a number of customer groups such as food, drinks and pharmaceuticals). Domino later started designing marginally different products to suit other customer groups such as printing, banking, electronic component manufacturers, etc. Today Domino is one of the leading manufacturers in the ink-jet printing industry in the world.

An example of a company which grew from a product focus into a dominant sector player is Apple Inc., in the USA. Apple started life as a pioneer in the microcomputer market with its Apple II, and subsequently brought out more sophisticated versions such as the Macintosh to suit the ever-increasing demands of the business user market. In both cases, the companies entered their markets early, were able to innovate and launch subsequent products to stay in their markets and were led by ambitious and aggressive entrepreneurs.

There are considerable barriers for small technology-based firms attempting to grow into dominant sector players. As the sector evolves the focus of innovation changes from product innovation to product *and* process innovation. Products change from being diverse and customer specific to multi-standard to mostly undifferentiated products. Competitive emphasis changes from product performance to product variation to cost reduction. Few firms have the capabilities to make these shifts without a major crisis. The crisis is often so serious that the company never reaches dominant player status.

The rapid growth that comes with the evolution of the sector brings pressure on the founders to manage the transition from an informal entrepreneurial culture to a more formal and structured culture. The firm has to change from being technology driven to being market driven. Founders may realize this need but may be neither able to manage the transition nor to relinquish control of the management of their company. As the company grows, resources have to be allocated between marketing, manufacturing and R & D more efficiently. Large resources may be needed for establishing distribution channels. Founders may have to part with equity control to bring in new investors, which again is a difficult decision for many ambitious founders. Another challenge is to continue to innovate when the company is experiencing rapid growth in sales and employees. Managing and keeping the motivation high in technical staff when the company is expanding its other functions such as administration and marketing, is quite difficult.

Product Group Specialists

These are firms focusing on a particular product group in the overall market. The same group of products—often standard products—are offered across all customer groups. The emphasis in these firms is on product innovation rather than superior knowledge about customers' needs. As products are standard in nature they can reach all or most segments of the market (see Figure 6.1). Those firms with highly innovative products experience rapid growth. Growth is further enhanced in young and high growth markets.

Firms with "product focus" in rapidly growing markets become the favourites of venture capital firms due to their high potential for growth, especially when they have highly innovative products. However, future growth and viability depends on the firm's ability to continue to develop innovative subsequent products either for the same or other markets. When the firm's focus is on innovating within a large growing industry sector, highly successful product specialists may become dominant sector players.

Not all firms which are successful in their initial product group are able to move successfully into other product groups. When a firm with a highly innovative and successful product enters an established market, it may well succeed and experience rapid growth and high profitability. However, many firms find they are unable to diversify into adjacent product-markets which are dominated by earlier entrants. In such instances, the firm becomes a good candidate for acquisition by the earlier and larger entrants diversifying into the firm's product group. Microvitec is an example of a firm which entered an established market with a highly innovative product. Microvitec entered the UK colour monitor market in 1980 with a low complexity colour display (LCCD) monitor specifically designed for micro-computers. Although the colour monitor market, which was supplied by the TV industry, was reaching maturity, Microvitec created a new market segment. Microvitec's product was superior and was tailored to the top price-performance (i.e. high resolution) segment of colour monitor users, away from the lower segments which are dominated by the large, Japanese TV manufacturers. Microvitec found it difficult to sustain growth with its limited financial and marketing resources. It did not have the financial resources to compete head-on with the Japanese firms in the high volume, low resolution colour monitor market, and its limited technical resources meant that innovative products for new markets were hard to develop. In contrast, firms like Apple Inc. were able to grow rapidly within their initial market by entering the market early, pursuing an innovative product strategy, and aggressively seeking sector leadership.

The relatively narrow technical skills and limited resources of "product focus" firms have made them vulnerable to competitors who have a wider technical base and/or larger resources. These competitors are often able to bring out products which are "me too" or only marginally better than those of the small high-tech firm, but are able to compete on price, marketing strength and by making the product more market-driven. IBM's entry into the personal computer market three years after the launch of the highly innovative and revolutionary Apple II personal computer provides the classic example. IBM's PC was technically a me-too product but it was introduced at a time when the PC market was about to take off and when marketing skills and financial strength (both of which IBM has), were able to make a competitive difference.

Some product specialists become complacent with the success of their first product and neglect to develop new ones. They run into difficulties when competitors design better products or when their markets reach maturity. Others experience rapid growth which often takes them into establishing their own manufacturing and distribution organizations (at home and overseas), around their initial product. They soon discover that sales are tapering off and that they do not have a second product in line to support such investment. Subsequent product development is often not as innovative, causing the firm to start to look for diversification opportunities.

Another common problem faced by product group specialists is that they suffer from tunnel vision. Their relatively small size and limited resources prompts them to adopt a highly focused strategy, but inherent in this is a failure to look constantly for new and related opportunities for growth.

Market Specialists

These firms focus on supplying different products to suit the unique needs of a particular customer group within the overall market (see Figure 6.1). Firms focusing on a particular customer group have superior knowledge of that customer group and products are designed to suit the unique needs of the target customers. Such an approach is called a "vertical market" approach in the software and computer industries.

Some markets are naturally segmented by customer groups. The minicomputer-based CAD software market is segmented vertically. The products are usually technical, complex and expensive, requiring suppliers to design products specific to the application of a customer industry. In other markets, which are not segmented by customer groups, small technology-based firms pursue a vertical market approach to differentiate themselves from those pursuing a horizontal or product specialist approach. The major strength of these firms is the specialist knowledge and experience they have of their customers' requirements rather than any technological superiority. Firms keep close to customer's needs by designing "custom" products. These firms typically aim to achieve significant market share (hence a dominant position) within their target customer groups. These firms are highly market oriented and their emphasis is to supply a fully integrated service to their target customer group.

Customer group focus can be adopted by firms entering either young or mature markets. Such an approach assists firms to establish themselves by building market share rapidly within a particular customer-market. However, growth becomes a critical issue because the major strength of these firms is market specialization rather than technical expertise. In order to maintain growth, they often need to move into other customer groups, but they fear losing the "specialist image" necessary to maintain their position among their current customers.

Niche Players

These firms have the narrowest product market scope of all small technology-based firms. Products often are not only specific to a product group or a price-performance segment but they are also specific to a user group (see Figure 6.1). They are characterized by highly specific and narrow technical and marketing resources, and consist of a single or at best a few products with limited market potential.

The small high-tech firm with niche focus often has a unique product or service which enables the firm to be profitable within a chosen market segment. Market share is defined within the segment. As the size of the segments are usually limited, large firms do not find it worthwhile to participate in them. Products are often customer specific.

In exceptional cases some niche segments may grow into large markets. An example would be the business of Tunstall Telecom in the UK. Tunstall entered the security and emergency communications equipment market in the mid-1960s via the business of supplying paging equipment to elderly people living in local authority sheltered housing schemes. When it started, the EPEC (elderly people's emergency communications equipment) market appeared to be a small market segment, and up until 1980 sales were less than £2.5m. Although the technology and market took a long time to evolve, sales in 1985 were £21m, and Tunstall claimed a 70% share of the EPEC market in the UK. Growth of this type tends to be the exception rather than the rule.

Niche firms usually confront major problems when seeking opportunities for growth beyond their initial segments, due to the narrowness of their competence base. Successful firms may form good candidates for acquisition.

Technology Specialists

Technology specialists are best sub-divided into two categories: those that sell products built around a core technology (core technology specialists), and those that sell contract research and development (R & D) services (contract R & D firms).

Core Technology Specialists

Small technology-based firms have strong technical capabilities and are seen as technology experts in the eyes of their customers. Their businesses are based on an attractive underlying technology which enables them to design products for diverse customer groups and markets. As marketing and financial resources are limited, these firms concentrate on highly specialized and sophisticated technical products and avoid mass appeal products. They differ from contract R & D firms which also have strong technological resources and attractive technology by undertaking speculative R & D and by defining their business around products and not consulting services.

Unlike small high-tech firms with industry and customer focus, which are market driven, core technology specialists aim to be at the leading edge of technological developments. Technological superiority is the key element of their competitive strategy. As the chairman of one such firm in the CAD/CAM industry remarked, "Our main competitive strength is developing products well ahead of the market-place." Another firm in the same industry took pride in saying that its product was an especially advanced system, ahead of "standard" CAD technology that was widely accepted, and consequently their clients tended to be technologically sophisticated. Products are aimed at small segments of the overall market due to the technological sophistication that these firms aim to achieve. Products are often customer specific, low volume, high value and technologically innovative. Product development periods are long, over two years, and may be up to ten years.

Core technology specialist firms are typically started by a team of talented technical entrepreneurs leaving technical universities of excellence. The staff are mostly graduates with higher technical degrees and the staff are motivated more by technical challenge and project variety than by mere growth in sales and profits. R & D can represent a significant part of the firm's expenditure.

The core technology specialists perceive advantages in technological leadership and being first into the market-place with a product innovation. The competitive emphasis is on differentiation in product design: the non-differentiated activities such as manufacturing and marketing are often sub-contracted. Such firms are able to avoid "head-on" competition with the dominant firms in an industry or sector by focusing on high performance segments where cost and marketing muscle are less important. They can often compete in mature markets by adopting a customized product strategy in growing niche segments not attractive to the larger incumbents.

An example of a firm which has successfully grown with such a strategy is Oxford Instruments plc. Oxford Instruments claims to be the world leader in nuclear magnetic resonance imaging (NMRI) technology, which it has developed to suit various markets. It has 90% of the world market for large superconducting magnets used in a variety of applications. Growth can be moderately fast for such firms, once they have overcome the severe credibility problems typically experienced in the first few years after start-up. The nature of many core technologies coupled with wide and superior technical skills enables these firms to look across diverse product markets for opportunities where their technology can compete effectively with existing technologies. However, they can be prime acquisition candidates for large firms wanting particular technical skills. A major challenge facing these firms is managing innovation and flexibility when products and markets are diverse and growing fast.

Technology specialists may introduce products (customized or standard) which may create new markets or revolutionize existing markets. Firms which create new markets can either choose to grow within those markets (and become dominant sector players) or continue with the technology focus by concentrating on the high value product segments of different markets. However, the typical core technology specialist firm faces considerable barriers to growth.

Where firms have been started by technical entrepreneurs,

the entrepreneurs prefer to continue with their innovative work and avoid commitment of their time and resources to marketing effort. Firms which choose to continue with the technology focus, sometimes patent or sell their product design to another firm (often large in size), which has the resources and ambition to take an industry focus. A move from technology-focus to dominant sector player requires a change in organizational culture, commitment and direction of the firm's resources There is evidence in areas like Silicon Valley in the USA and Cambridge in the UK—where academic spin-outs of technology-focus firms are popular—that technology-focus firms which moved into industry focus have moved back to technology focus due to problems in adjusting both their strategy and organization.

Contract R & D Firms

Contract R & D firms define their business around providing bespoke R & D. They are heavily research oriented and have strong technical skills in a particular technology or technologies. Competitive emphasis is on customer service and technological superiority. Products designed for customers may be highly innovative and ahead of industry standards. Marketing is oriented towards identifying "cash rich" technologically competitive customers. Hence, customers tend to be large firms which need assistance in basic R & D, applied R & D in an unrelated technology, or timely launch of a key product.

As R & D is bespoke and commissioned by a client firm, the results are generally "owned" by the customer. Revenue is earned on a consulting fee basis. Contract R & D activity can be profitable with just a few customers even though heavy investments in people and tangible assets may be needed. As the work is very advanced and bespoke, price levels and margins can be high. As the customers finance the R & D, risks are lower than those of product-based firms. Firms experience moderate growth rates due to the nature of their activity, which is based on customer-specific research projects.

Contract R & D firms are typically started by a team of highly talented academic entrepreneurs leaving technical universities of excellence. A high proportion of the staff possess higher degrees (Ph.D.s) in their technical field. The culture is one of maintaining highly innovative and flexible management styles. The structure of the organization is very flat and expands horizontally as the firm diversifies into new technologies.

The contract R & D firm constantly attempts to enhance its technical skills in order to stay ahead of technological developments. This means attracting, motivating and rewarding highly talented technical people. Examples of contract R & D firms are Cambridge Consultants Ltd (UK), PA Technology (UK), AD Little and SRI(US), and Battelle (Switzerland).

As customers finance R & D, contract R & D firms are able to undertake both basic and advanced R & D. As a result of the bespoke R & D, firms may come across product ideas which may be worth commercial exploitation. However, a move into "own product" activity involves major change in resources if the firm is to manufacture and/or market its product itself. Most contract R & D firms deliberately avoid such a move by encouraging employees to spin-off with the product idea and start new firms. The contract R & D firms earn their income through royalties, licence fees or even by taking a minority stake in a new spin-off. If the idea is better exploited by an existing business, then arrangements are made to license-out the product design. In both cases the contract R & D firm will be able to continue with bespoke R & D work while at the same time enjoying royalty or licensing income (or even capital gains from shares) arising from its proprietary product design.

Spin-offs from contract R & D firms are very common and they are often encouraged by the parent firms. The managing director of one contract R & D firm put it this way: "A certain amount of staff turnover is good for our business. If one of our employees is an entrepreneur and wants to start a new company, then we will help him to do it." The spin-offs encouraged by contract R & D firms often benefit their parent firms, when there are formal and ongoing technical and financial arrangements. By contrast, such formal and ongoing arrangements rarely exist in spin-offs from universities.

Some contract R & D firms may decide to participate directly in the commercial exploitation of their products. In such cases, a separate division is typically formed to fulfil the requirements of the product. Although most of the results of the contract

R & D work is commissioned, financed and owned by the client, the contract R & D firm could enter into contracts by which it retains ownership and rights for the product design. In some cases, the firm and the client may have joint ownership. The decision as to who owns the design rights depends on who generated the idea, who financed the R & D and the nature of the contract.

On occasions, contract R & D firms undertake speculative R & D either to build expertise in order to service their technical contracts or to establish industrial property rights which can then be licensed out.

GEOGRAPHIC MARKET EXPANSION

Moving into international markets and branching into new geographical regions of the domestic market are probably the most obvious routes for expanding a small technology-based firm. All five categories of firms identified above can and do adopt this approach, although it may be particularly difficult for firms supplying customized products or complex vertical market products. Both need close customer contact and feedback. It is also a lot easier for the dominant sector player with large resources than for the segment specialist with a limited competence base.

Ideally the small high-tech firm would wait until it reached a certain size and had developed a sufficient resource base before it made the decision to expand geographically. This is not always possible. Unlike their US and Japanese counterparts, many European small high-tech firms have small domestic markets; which means they have to go international very early on in order to build the sales volumes necessary to cover their cost base. Consequently many international expansion strategies of technology based firms are low investment strategies which make extensive use of licensing-out, joint venture and other forms of strategic alliance.

Once the decision to expand geographically has been made, the key strategic question is what market to focus on (with which products) and how to enter the market. Chapter 7 focuses exclusively on the latter point, but as with all product market issues, the decision of where to focus is crucial.

For firms expanding internationally there are three principal geographic markets: North America, Europe and the Far East. Typically, US small high-tech firms have chosen to compete in Europe as their first overseas entry point—Apple, Compaq, Lotus, all started this way. Similarly, the USA has often been the priority market area for European firms. However, there is evidence that some European firms have been more successful at expanding into other European countries than they have into the USA. A study of small UK high-tech firms that had expanded overseas showed that after their own domestic market, countries of continental Europe were a higher strategic priority than the larger US market. [4] Where companies were competing in both geographical areas (the USA and Europe), they were more successful in achieving market penetration in Continental Europe than in the US. While that particular study did not identify the specific reasons for the success, anecdotal evidence would suggest that the European market has been (historically at any rate) less competitive than the US market. When small European high-tech firms enter the US market they have tended to do so with technologies which at best are "me too", whereas within Europe they find they still have a technological advantage.

There is further discussion of successful international entry strategies in Chapter 7.

DIVERSIFICATION

Product-based and market-based diversification within the same general industry based on related technological skills are the most common forms of diversification among small high-tech firms. Diversification into closely related products and markets is, all other things being equal, likely to be more successful than less related areas. However, what on the surface seems "closely related" is usually significantly different in operational terms. Diversification is always a risky strategy for any firm but is particularly so for the fragile small high-tech firm. It is a characteristic of all such firms that they have a very limited resource base where resources encompass the firm's managerial, financial, technical and marketing capabilities.

The firm's core competencies comprise the cumulative technological and marketing knowledge that has been built up and retained by the organization during its lifetime. These competencies tend to be product-market and technology specific, and are not easily transferable in a resource constrained organization. In addition, the small firm often lacks the managerial capabilities to undertake the type of strategic analysis necessary to determine if the diversification opportunity provides the firm with a long-term viable business opportunity. Does the firm have the capability of assessing market attractiveness, the cost of entry and the sustainability of any competitive advantage it may appear to have?

Even if the firm can obtain the necessary analysis, externally if not internally, two key implementation issues are likely to overwhelm the small firm. Firstly, diversification requires a clear "champion" with entrepreneurial ability. The only person(s) likely to have such skills is the founder(s), and then his or her skills may well be market or technology specific. Any other staff that have these skills are more likely to spin off and set up their own new venture than become diversification champions. Intrepreneurs, the name given to entrepreneurs that sometimes operate in large firms, are equally rare in small firms. [15] Secondly—and one of the most common reasons for failed diversification attempts—diversification inevitably involves the top management team diluting its focus on the core business. The inevitable start-up difficulties associated with all forms of diversification mean that the core business receives less attention, which can quickly result in declining performance. This can mean that there is less cash available for investment leading to a half-hearted attempt at diversification (and an increased risk of failure). Even worse, the decline in performance of the core business can rapidly lead to a crisis situation and the eventual failure of the company (see Chapter 8).

The rest of this section looks briefly at four types of diversification: (1) product diversification; (2) market diversification; (3) vertical integration; (4) unrelated product market diversification.

Product Diversification

Product-based diversification for a small high-tech firm involves developing related products for the same group of customers. Thus Microvitec, a UK manufacturer of colour monitors, diversified into manufacturing switch mode power supplies and floppy disk assembly units when its core monitor business came under heavy competitive pressures. Where small high-tech firms go wrong with product diversification is not realizing that although they may have developed customer credibility with their core product(s), the nature of high-tech products is such that they have to start all over again in building credibility if the new product is in a different product class to that of their core product(s). Developing and entering the market with a diversified product puts the firm back almost into the situation of a start-up company. The six critical factors identified in Chapter 2 as important to new venture success are equally important here. Whereas the traditional advice for small firms is to "reject at the screening stage product ideas which demand too great a level of technical expertise and which can be introduced painlessly into the company range",[6] small high-tech firms will not diversify successfully unless they develop products which have a technological edge. In the short term, they might succeed in a fast-growth market, but not for long.

Dominant sector players, technology specialists and customer group specialists are the most likely types of firm to be successful implementers of product diversification, but for different reasons. The dominant sector players are likely to have the technological, marketing and financial resources to allow them a chance of success. The technology specialists can be successful in product development, providing the same core technology is used. And the customer group specialists may be close enough to their customers to design a product which meets their needs.

Product diversification is a very popular growth strategy among small technology based firms.[7] It has been most successfully used where firms have developed a proprietary core technology on which to leverage their future product development efforts.[8]

Market Diversification

When a firm takes its existing product range and begins to sell it to a market segment which it has not previously served, it is called market-based diversification. It requires the firm to learn about the needs of a new customer base and to develop the capability of serving it. It can involve substantial adjustment to the firm's existing sales and distribution system, and may necessitate some product redesign to meet the needs of the new customer group. Some writers refer to geographical expansion as market diversification, but here geographical expansion is restricted to growth in broadly the same product market areas as the firm serves in its local market. Market diversification therefore means growth in market areas that the firm has not previously served.

Most types of small high-tech firm can adopt market-based diversification strategies. Small firms tend to thrive in highly segmented industries which in turn provide the opportunity for early focus on a single segment and later expansion into one or more other segments. In industrial markets, which is where most small high-tech firms compete, close contact with the customers is essential for success. The small high-tech firm's ability to develop such relationships lends itself to market-based diversification.

The software industry is a classic example of an industry segmented by end user (vertical) markets where firms have established a position in one end-user segment and then moved into a related but different customer segment. However, many small technology-based firms have come to grief because market diversification can appear deceptively simple to inexperienced management teams. There are often significant hidden, knowledge-based barriers to entry when moving into a new market segment. In the software industry for example, there are likely to be significant learning and experience curve disadvantages for firms entering new markets. Established competitors will have accumulated a level of market knowledge which may be costly and difficult to imitate.

The niche specialists and the customer group specialists are likely to have the most difficulty implementing market-based diversification. The niche specialists suffer from a narrow

resource base, as discussed above. The customer group specialists, who at first glance would appear to be market-led and
ideally suited to growth in market diversification, often have a
competence base which is not transferable to even closely
related market segments. Table 6.2 summarizes both product-
based and market-based diversification opportunities by type
of firm.

Vertical Integration

Vertical integration—the process of moving backwards or for-
wards in the value added chain to compete with one's suppliers and/or customers—is common among small high-tech
firms. Backward integration is more common than forward
integration as firms start with "soft" strategies and gradually
"harden" (see Chapter 2). It is quite common to see distributors, who are nearly always looking for higher margins,
integrate backwards into designing their own products and
maybe into manufacturing as well.

Forward integration is less common but can be brought
about by the forces of technological change. As silicon chip
technology advances, chip manufacturers are increasingly
finding themselves competing directly against their customers.

Table 6.2 *Product and market diversification opportunities by type of firm*

Type of small high-tech firms	Type of diversification	
	Product diversification	Market diversification
Segment specialists	Lack resources to be successful.	Lack resources to be successful.
Customer group specialists	Closeness to customers may help design of product to meet cus-tomers' needs.	Possible, but must realize that existing skills not directly transferable.
Product group specialists	Danger of producing me-too products that market does not want.	Requires significant shift from technology-driven to market-driven culture.
Technology specialists	Possible, if some core tech-nology is used.	Wide variety of segment options may exist.
Dominant sector players	Potentially capable.	Potentially capable.

The semiconductor industry has historically regarded personal computer manufacturers as their customers, but they are now faced with the fact that they can include all the functions of a computer on a single chip. This poses real problems of business definition since their customers can at the same time be their competitors. Forward integration also occurs when technology starts to lose its ability to act as a key source of market differentiation. Product-based firms start to move down the value chain and focus on building a service business. Such moves are often more associated with survival than growth. They are of course not confined to small firms, since even IBM is currently adopting such a strategy as it builds up its consultancy services.

Vertical integration as a growth strategy is extremely high risk for a small firm. For most firms, vertical integration is akin to diversifying into completely unrelated areas of business. Even the dominant sector players are unlikely to have the resources to implement such strategies successfully. Where vertical integration may pay off for the small firm is where it decides to integrate backwards into component manufacturing to protect proprietary technology. As a growth strategy, however, it is unlikely to be successful.

Unrelated Product Market Diversification

A few small technology-based firms attempt to diversify into unrelated business areas which involve both new products and new markets. Even where such diversification uses related technological skills, this is a risky strategy. A Canadian study showed that unrelated product market diversification was the least successful growth strategy for small technology-based firms. [9] Technology specialist firms are the only category of small high-tech firms to use this strategy successfully. BVT used its specialist skills in depositing thin films in large vacuum chambers to enter product-market areas as diverse as high-speed machinery for the packaging industry and machinery for manufacturing Winchester disks. Such firms grow by applying their specialist technological know-how to selected product areas in diverse end-user markets. They are usually leading-edge firms in terms of technology which have the capability of designing technologically superior and advanced products. They may enjoy protection from patents or other intellectual property rights.

Unrelated product market diversification is too risky for small high-tech firms other than technology specialist firms. There are undoubtedly some examples of firms which have discovered new products by accident which are of sufficient technological superiority to compete in new market areas. However, developing such a product into a viable business is an extremely risky new venture for an established small firm which has a finite set of resources. It would probably have *more* chance of success if it were to be established as a totally new start-up company.

Unrelated diversification involving unrelated core technologies is rare among small technology-based firms, and its chance of success extremely remote.

SELLING OUT AS A GROWTH STRATEGY

A successful initial business does not necessarily mean that the firm is suited for further independent growth. Specialist firms may find that growth opportunities are limited in their existing product market areas and that they lack the resources to diversify successfully. Dominant players may find that they lack the capabilities to succeed in markets where marketing and manufacturing scale is important, and they too lack both opportunities and resources to diversify successfully. Under these conditions the wise small technology-based firm will sell all or part of its equity to a larger firm looking for growth opportunities. Being acquired should be seen as a means of successful business development.

Very few small high-tech firms which are deemed to be successful grow large enough to dominate their industry. Most firms which are successful become leaders in their product class or customer group and are later acquired by larger firms looking for industry dominance. A study of 250 Silicon Valley technology firms that were started up during the 1960s showed that a third of the companies had merged or been acquired by 1980.[10] Not surprisingly, the older the firm the more chance it had of being acquired. The mean age of the firm at the time of acquisition was 6.4 years.

MAKING ACQUISITIONS

Acquisitions should not be regarded by any firm, be it small high-tech or otherwise, as a strategy for growth. An "acquisition strategy" spells disaster: acquisition should be seen only as one method of implementing a growth strategy. Acquisitions are sometimes used to implement the growth strategies discussed in this chapter, or indeed as a means of obtaining further growth in existing product market areas. There are three classic reasons why firms make poor acquisitions:

1 they buy a company which has a weak competitive position or soon develops one after it has been acquired;
2 they pay too much for the company, believing it has more potential for future profitability than it actually has;
3 they fail to manage the post-acquisition period satisfactorily.

The same problems become more acute when small high-tech firms merge or acquire each other, due to the inherent fragility of small high-tech firms.

The speed at which markets, technology and competition change in most high-tech sectors means what appears to be an attractive market sector or the basis of a competitive advantage can disappear very quickly. Even when the firm has the capability of analyzing an acquisition candidate (or acquires it externally by using third-party advisers) the chance of finding an attractive company with a strong competitive position in an attractive market is very low. Such companies are unlikely to be for sale, and are more likely to be the acquirers than the acquirees. The companies that are most likely to be for sale are those that are already in trouble, or are about to be in trouble because the firm lacks the resources to grow organically. Since most small firms do little more than a cursory analysis of acquisition candidates before buying them, it should not be surprising that the experience of small high-tech firms in making acquisitions has been very poor.

The price paid for small high-tech firms is usually too high given the risks involved. The expectation of high growth rates in many high-tech markets raises the asking price. However, the very high level of uncertainty about future profitability engendered by the forces driving fragility is rarely taken into account. Small high-tech firms are risky at the best of times, but those that are "for sale" are likely to be so risky that they ought to be bought at a considerable discount.

Acquisitions are rarely successful when the acquirer takes a "hands-off" approach to the management of its newly acquired subsidiary. For small high-tech firms, a "hands-off" approach is disastrous, since:

- there is a high chance that the acquired firm is in need of a turnaround;
- the purchaser overpaid and hence needs to take action to generate increased profits to justify the price paid;
- the management of the acquired firm is likely to lose motivation if it had an equity stake which was purchased at the time of the acquisition;
- small firms generally have weak financial control systems and need to be brought under immediate control of the new parent to avoid unnecessary losses;
- acquisitions generate uncertainty among employees of the acquired company who need to be provided with strong leadership and a "vision" of the future—if the acquiring firm is not careful it will find the principal asset it has bought (the people) disappearing rapidly out of the door.

Taking immediate control and providing effective post-acquisition management is therefore critically important; but few management teams of small high-tech firms have the capability to manage an acquisition, particularly when the acquisition involves diversification.

ASK Computer System's acquisition of Software Dimensions Inc., a microcomputer software company, in 1983 illustrates the point. ASK had been successful designing and installing computer based management information systems for manufacturing companies, but decided to seek growth in the rapidly developing personal computer software market by acquiring Software Dimensions. After renaming the acquired company ASK Micro they attempted to boost sales by hiring sales people to supplement their distributor network. The result was increased overheads and a group of alienated distributors. ASK Micro went into an immediate loss situation, and the new subsidiary was closed down less than a year after being acquired. [11] Management's failure at ASK to realize that the PC-based software market was quite different from the traditional mainframe market was repeated by endless firms in the mid-1980s.

Not only do acquirers lack necessary detailed knowledge about the products, markets and technologies of their acquired firms, they usually lack both the time and the management skills necessary for post-acquisition management. What typically happens is that the acquired company is left alone after the acquisition until the new owner realizes that its performance is below expectations. Management of the parent company then starts to pay more attention to the acquired firm but in so doing begins to neglect the parent company. The problem of neglect is usually more dramatic with acquisitions than with organic diversification, since once it is acknowledged that the acquired firm is in trouble, the scale of the looming disaster means that top management puts nearly all its time into the acquired firm.

Even where significant "hands-on" efforts are made to integrate acquired or merged businesses, cultural differences are the big killer of post-acquisition management efforts. On the surface one might not expect to find huge differences in the culture of small high-tech firms, particularly if the products and markets are similar or closely related. However, experience proves otherwise. 3-Com Corporation, the local area network company referred to earlier, "merged" with Bridge Communications Inc., a company of about half its size, in 1987. William Carrico, one of the co-founders of Bridge's became President and Chief Operating Officer and Bill Krause became Chairman. The two companies had similar products but the "merger" did not go smoothly. Firstly, at the top of the organization there was a clash of personalities. Carrico is quoted as saying "It is very hard to have two heads, both very opinionated, running one company."[12] But, secondly, clashes also arose further down in the organization due to very different operating styles: whereas Bridge's middle management enjoyed individual offices, 3-Com's management did not believe in them; whereas Bridge relied on paging to improve customers services, 3-Com abstained from such a practice. Despite the efforts by both companies to mix the workforces and gently introduce their own employees to each other's culture, a high staff turnover resulted. Both the Bridge co-founders departed along with a quarter of the Bridge employees.

A similar situation occurred when Legent Corporation was formed in 1985 by the merger of two providers of systems software tools, Morino Associates and Duquesne Systems Inc. A year later, the two companies were still struggling to consolidate. Despite shared goals, ethics, and customers, former Morino founder and later Legent Chairman Mario Morino says there is no such thing as perfect compatibility. Morino Associates had grown through acquisition, and thus tended towards decentralized management, while Duquesne was much more conservative and centralized. "When we confronted each other," said former Duquesne Chairman/CEO and later Legent CEO Glen Chatfield, "we found that we had common views but very different ways of operating to reach them. The differences were bigger than we thought they'd be."[13]

SUMMARY

Few if any firms have unlimited growth opportunities over a long period of time in their core business area. Consequently those firms driven towards continual growth seek product and market diversification opportunities either at home or overseas. For some firms, whose core business is under attack, such strategies are necessary for survival. However, successful development of a high-tech firm beyond the product market segments where it has been initially successful is constrained by the depth and breadth of the resource base.

As small high-tech firms become established, they develop different core competencies which influence the likelihood of successful further growth. This chapter identified five categories of small high-tech firm:

1 Dominant sector players.
2 Product group specialists.
3 Customer group specialists.
4 Niche players.
5 Technology specialists.

The principal characteristics and competencies of each category were described and the specific barriers to further growth highlighted. Product-based and market-based diversifications within the same industry based on related technological skills are the most common forms of diversification, but the fragility of the small high-tech firm always makes diversification a high risk strategy.

NOTES

(1) Hamel, G. "Core Competence of the Corporation", *Harvard Business Review*, Vol. 68, No. 3, May/June, pp. 79–91 (1990).
(2) The classification used here draws on the work by Abell, D. F. *Defining the Business: The Starting Point of Strategic Planning.* Prentice-Hall, Englewood Cliffs, NJ (1980).
(3) The reader may find it useful to compare the five categories identified here with the eight archetypes identified in a study of 247 new ventures in the information processing industry, by McDougall, P. and Robinson, R. B. "New Venture Strategies: An Empirical Investigation of Eight 'Archetypes' of Competitive Strategies for Entry", *Strategic Management Journal*, Vol. 11, No. 6, October (1980).
(4) Slatter S. St. P. "The Internationalization Process in Small Technology Based Firms in the UK". Paper presented at Strategic Management Society Conference, Boston, October (1987).
(5) Pinchot, G. *Intrapreneuring.* Harper & Row, New York (1985).
(6) Mason, R. S. "Product Diversification and the Small Firm", *Journal of Business Policy*, Vol. 3, No. 3, Spring (1973).
(7) Boag, D. A. and Dastmalchian, A. "Growth Strategies and Performance in Electronics Companies", *Industrial Marketing*

Management, Vol. 17, pp. 329–336 (1988). 45% of firms in this study reported that product diversification was their priority growth strategy.

(8) Meyer, M. H. and Roberts, E. B. "New Product Strategy in Small Technology Based Firms: A Pilot Study", *Management Science*, Vol. 32, No. 7, pp. 806–821 (1987).

(9) Boag, D. and Dastmalchian, A. ibid. note 7.

(10) Bruno, F. and Cooper, A. "Pattern of Development and Acquisitions for Silicon Valley Start-ups", *Technovation*, Vol. 1 (1982).

(11) "ASK Computer's Search for a Strategy", *Business Week*, 27 August, p. 88 (1984).

(12) Margolis, N. "Tweaking the 'Ideal' Merger", *Computerworld*, 30 October, pp. 99–102 (1989).

(13) Hoffmeister, S. "Two Men and a Merger", *Venture*, January, pp. 40–43 (1989).

7
Going International

Expanding internationally is one of the most difficult strategic options for the small high-tech firm to implement successfully. There are innumerable examples of firms which have been successful in their domestic market but have failed miserably when they have attempted to enter overseas markets. In many cases the cost of the failure has been large enough to jeopardize the existence of the whole company. This chapter looks at: why small high-tech firms expand internationally; market selection; methods of market entry; factors determining choice of market entry method; overcoming common problems encountered in going international.

WHY SMALL HIGH-TECH FIRMS EXPAND INTERNATIONALLY

Textbooks on international business give many possible reasons for entering overseas markets but not all of these apply to the small high-tech firm.[1] There are five principal reasons why the small high-tech firm seeks overseas expansion, although in many instances it is a combination of the five reasons:

1 to meet ambitious growth targets;
2 to ensure survival;
3 to keep abreast of changing technology and market requirements;

4   to spread the amortization of development costs;
5   to achieve dominance of a global product niche.

Whatever the principal reason for expanding internationally the decision has a lot to do with the mind set of the senior management group. Many US companies that could compete effectively overseas do not because of lack of expertise, perception of risk and parochialism. [2]

To Meet Ambitious Growth Targets

The desire for rapid growth is one of the characteristics of small high-tech firms—particularly in the USA. The pressure for such growth comes from both the entrepreneurs themselves and the expectations of the investment community. Firms that have been extremely successful in the domestic market, achieving a high annual compound growth rate, are expected to continue the same rate of growth, even though the absolute amount of growth necessary to maintain a steady growth rate increases dramatically year on year. The impetus to expand overseas will depend largely on the opportunity for profitable growth in the domestic market, which in turn depends on the degree of market saturation and the strength of the competitive forces driving competition. Most companies will choose to exploit their domestic market before attempting to expand overseas, since that is the market they know. However, as the technology skill base of small high-tech firms is relatively narrow, overseas expansion is usually preferred to extensive product diversification in the home market. In a comparative study of 39 high-growth and 39 low-growth firms in the computer industry there was strong evidence that the high-growth firms derive a significant percentage of their revenues from non-domestic sales. [3]

In the search for growth, overseas markets are often perceived as providing plenty of opportunity. The perception is usually based on little more than a naïve view that the US or European market is "big", yet it is just such a perception that is the driver of international expansion. One cannot help thinking back to the old marketing story about the two shoe salesman in Africa: one returns saying there is a *large* market as none of the Africans wears shoes, and the other says there is *no* market since nobody wears shoes! Two quotes from the principal overseas subsidiaries of a US and British company illustrate the point. The UK managing director of a US-based computer company has said:

> "The Americans just don't understand the European market. They think the US success story can be easily duplicated using US products. They have huge expectations about likely growth rates. In reality the European market for our products is already quite sophisticated and highly competitive."

Similarly, a US vice president of a successful British software company said:

> "UK management views the US as a "land of opportunity". They expect the US subsidiary to do better than it has done ... they do not appreciate the degree of competition that exists in the US market."

To Ensure Survival

For many small high-tech firms, international expansion is a necessity to ensure survival, since the domestic market is too small to provide the sales volume necessary to cover even a minimum level of operating overheads. Firms in highly special-ized niche segments or firms based in countries with small domestic markets are often forced to develop internationally from the first day they are set up. Thus, British Vacuum Tech-nology Ltd, a company set up in late 1983 to exploit the high-tech end of the vacuum metallizing machinery market, obtained its first order from a Californian aerospace company. In fact, the founders were discussing possible orders with several potential international customers, even before the com-pany had been established. The number of potential customers in the UK market for the company's products were so few that there was no viable business without immediately going inter-national. This is by no means an isolated example. Immediate internationalization at a very early stage of a firm's growth is extremely common in Europe, and particularly so in the smaller economies of the Scandinavian and Benelux countries. Going international at such an early stage of a company's development poses some significant problems, due to the limited resource base of the company. Not surprisingly, many fail, but those that are successful provide some interesting lessons in how to reduce fragility.

Internationalizing may also be necessary to ensure long-term survival against potential foreign competitors. This was the rationale for overseas expansion at Aldus Corporation, the desk-top publishing software company. John O'Halloran, Director of International Sales at Aldus explained: "If we didn't go to Europe and Japan we'd run the risk of local companies there not only developing markets, but coming back here to compete in the US." [4]

Historically, the pressure for US firms to expand internationally in order to survive has been less than that facing European firms of a similar size.

To Keep Abreast of Changing Technology and Market Requirements

Plugging into the global information network is essential where technology is changing rapidly. Successful high-tech firms—whose principal skill is matching technology to customer requirements—need to know what the most innovative customers demand, what new technological developments are taking place, what competitors are doing and what new applications are being imagined.

Traditionally, the US market has led the world in technology developments, which has meant that leading European high-tech firms (mainly British) have rightly seen the US market as a place they "cannot afford not to be". However, the USA no longer has a monopoly over technology and it is becoming increasingly important for technology-based firms to have at least "listening posts" in countries such as Japan and Germany. For the smaller company with limited financial resources this is difficult to justify on the cost grounds, but the relatively larger firms ought to be considering such actions.

To Spread the Amortization of Development Costs

The economics of small high-tech firms typically involve heavy up-front product development costs followed by high margins (at least initially) on successful new products. Profits are extremely volume-sensitive since incremental sales have a low marginal cost, and average unit costs are reduced by spreading the amortization of development costs. This is particularly true in something like the software industry, where the direct contribution on a successful product may be in excess of 95% of the selling price. There is no doubt that this economic calculation is firmly in the minds of senior managers when they make the decision to expand internationally. However, what they tend to forget is the higher than expected marketing costs they are likely to incur when they try to enter overseas markets, an issue dealt with later in this chapter.

To Achieve Dominance of a Global Product Niche

Most small technology-based firms, try to establish a unique dominance of a particular skill or application. Since that niche cannot be credibly dominated by selling in only a small percentage of the world market, niche firms may decide to go international. Ideally, such firms would like their name to be synonymous with the provision of their product (or service) to buyers throughout the world. Some firms in the scientific instrument industry fall in this category.

Few small high-tech firms reach dominant niche positions on a global basis, but there is no doubt that an international presence can add to a firm's reputation and credibility, which in turn helps to reinforce the typical differentiation strategy.

MARKET SELECTION

There are three major world markets for high-tech products—the USA, Europe and Japan—although some of the newly industrialized countries of the Pacific Basin (such as South Korea) will become increasingly important markets in the 1990s.

For US small high-tech firms, Europe is usually the first choice market, with priority being put on the larger markets of Germany, France and the UK. Within Europe, the UK is often chosen as the starting point due to the similarity of the language and culture, and the fact that UK buying practices are less nationalistic than those on Continental Europe. Careful market analysis on a global basis, as recommended in text books on international business, is rarely done by small companies since they lack the resources of time and money to undertake such a study. However, the growing high-tech firm, already established in the US market with a winning product is more likely to approach the international market with a planned approach rather than an opportunistic approach. Companies like Apple and Lotus produced business plans before committing resources to international market development.

For European small high-tech firms, the decision to go international is usually one of choosing between entering the large and relatively homogeneous US market or attacking the markets in other European Countries. Many firms have been lured by the size and relative openness of the US market to new ideas, only to be disappointed when they find strong competition from domestic US companies and higher than anticipated standards for product quality and service support. In many product market areas, the US market is more advanced technologically than Europe, so many small European firms who have been successful in their domestic market because they had a superior product find that they only have a me-too product when they enter the US market. However, many small high-tech firms take the view that the US market has to be their number one strategic priority due to the importance of the market. One UK company that took this view was Redwood International, a software company that was founded in 1981 by Peter Osborn. Osborn and his partner Tony Hayward took an early decision to tackle the US market, because, in Hayward's words: "If you are going to be a long-term player in the software market you have to have a global organization, and it is difficult to sustain yourself unless you have a strong presence in the US. The US is half the world market for software while the UK represents only 5 per cent."[5]

Focusing on other countries in Europe has been a lot more common among European small high-tech firms than has been commonly assumed. In a study of the internationalization process in 25 UK small high-tech firms, the US market was found to be the top priority market for those firms who did not consider the UK domestic market their most important market.[6] However, for those firms whose prime focus was the UK, Continental Europe was more likely to be the second choice market than the USA. Table 7.1 summarizes the data.

The Japanese market is a particularly difficult one for both US and European firms due to the many cultural and language barriers that exist. Many small firms are daunted by the task of breaking into the Japanese market. They are particularly deterred by the time and costs of establishing a presence in the market and by the risk of their technology being "appropriated" by Japanese customers and potential competitors. It is common to hear anecdotes of how small western companies with innovative technology have sought to enter the market by designing or building prototype or pre-production equipment, only to have Japanese companies winning subsequent orders. Yet in many high-tech product areas where small firms compete, the Japanese market accounts for over 40% of world demand and cannot be neglected. Entering the Japanese market can help small high-tech firms achieve all the five principal reasons discussed above as to why small firms expand overseas. A lot depends on the ambitions and determination of the management as to whether they see entering Japan to be

Table 7.1 *Strategic priority by geographic region for 25 small high-tech companies in the UK*

	UK	USA	Rest of Europe	Rest of World
Top priority market	15	7	1	2
2nd choice market	4	8	13	–
Overall strategic priority*	1.6	2.3	2.5	3.7

* Mean ranking.

taking advantage of a market opportunity or an action to ensure survival.

Many small firms are content to select foreign markets that are convenient, both geographically (in terms of proximity to the domestic market) and psychologically ("they speak English"). Such a strategy may easily result in missed opportunities, and is probably the case for many UK and Canadian companies who attempt to compete in the US market rather than the continental European and Asian markets. In a study of the Canadian electronics industry, companies that took a global approach as opposed to a "near neighbour" approach to international markets were found to have more than twice the chance of becoming high performers in terms of export growth.[7]

METHODS OF MARKET ENTRY

The 25 companies participating in the research mentioned above had a wide variety of approaches to entering international markets, although two approaches—establishing overseas sales subsidiaries and using overseas distributors— were by far the most common methods of market entry. There was a variety of entry modes which can be classified on a spectrum showing varying degrees of commitment from passive internationalization to acquisition of a local firm. Figure 7.1 shows the range of entry methods, each of which is discussed briefly below. Over time the approach used to penetrate

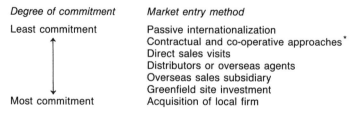

Degree of commitment	Market entry method
Least commitment	Passive internationalization
↑	Contractual and co-operative approaches*
	Direct sales visits
	Distributors or overseas agents
	Overseas sales subsidiary
↓	Greenfield site investment
Most commitment	Acquisition of local firm

*Exact nature of approach determines degree of commitment. Licensing usually shows low degree of commitment while some joint ventures involve significantly higher commitment.

Figure 7.1   *Methods of market entry*

overseas markets changes. Initial methods of entry are often subsequently changed towards approaches requiring greater commitment: either because the initial entry failed or because initial success indicates a clear market opportunity exists.

Passive Internationalization

At one end of the spectrum are those companies, usually at an early stage of their development, who do not actively have to go international, since foreign buyers come to their doorstep. These companies are usually product innovators and near the leading edge end of high technology. They become known to potential customers through technical journals, conferences, university links, and active searching for suitable technology by the customers themselves. Within months of Lotus 1-2-3 software being introduced in January 1983, there was strong demand for the product from overseas countries. In December 1983 Jim Manzi then VP Marketing (and later chief executive of Lotus) said: "We've been getting bombarded with requests. Overseas distributors have been calling to carry our product. ... There's been a flood of telexes from all over Europe. All these signs have been telling us we need to get serious about international markets."[8]

Another example is provided by LaserScan, which developed the world's first automated tracking system for high-energy particles. It found the world's research institutes beating a path to its door, and the first twelve of its machines were sold to overseas buyers without hiring a single salesman!

Contractual and Co-operative Agreements

There are two situations where small high-tech firms use co-operative or collaborative arrangements to help them expand internationally. Firstly, when they want to develop their business very fast before their own technology is superseded; and secondly, and often related to the first, is where they have very limited financial resources to exploit overseas markets. Where this is the situation, the small high-tech firm typically seeks an alliance with a party where they retain the technical expertise and the partner puts in most of the financial resources. There are two common forms of contractual or collaborative arrangement: licensing and joint ventures.

Licensing is by far the most common form of contractual approach used by small high-tech firms, since the set-up costs are low compared to other market entry approaches. Licensing is a particularly useful entry mode in the early stages of internationalization since it provides an indirect means of securing a manufacturing base in a foreign market. It is often seen as a stepping stone in the internationalization process. [9] Chapter 3 explained how MIPS Computer Systems is developing the European and Japanese markets for its RISC technology by entering licensing agreements with Siemens AG and NEC Corporation. Not surprisingly, the results of international licensing are more often than not disappointing as the licensor has no control over what happens in the overseas market-place. Successful international licensing requires:

- clear technological superiority on the part of the licensor;
- competence of and commitment by the licensee;
- products which are *not* high value and technically complex;
- complementary and not conflicting interests between the partners;
- avoidance of very large size imbalance between the partners.

Larger US firms have tended to be more successful licensing European companies than European companies have been in licensing US companies. The experience of British firms licensing CAD/CAM software to US firms in the early 1980s was generally poor. Comments from senior executives in two of these firms illustrate typical problems.

"We appointed a large American computer integrated manufacturing company to sell our product in the US in 1981. Although the US market for our product is about ten times that of the UK, sales in the US were the same as in the UK. It is only now in 1986, that our licensee has come to grips with our product."

"Our product license agreement with ... was initially a failure. Our licensee was ten times our size and they would never take us seriously. It was a very unbalanced relationship. The US market for our product is the same size as the whole of the European market and hence anyone who can distribute through the whole of the US is going to be ten times bigger than you are. Hence it is inevitable that you have a size imbalance. They were very slow in developing the US market, and they were very slow in learning our products. They are a hardware company and we are in software. It took them nearly two years to understand our product." [10]

My own research found few joint ventures and strategic alliances among small high-tech firms and either larger companies or others of similar size. In the previously mentioned study of the internationalization process of 25 small high-tech firms in the UK a group that had, on average 80% of its sales from overseas, only one firm was found that used any form of joint venture or strategic alliance. [11] This may have been the result of too small a sample, since it is known that many large US, Japanese and European companies have been actively seeking co-operative arrangements with smaller technology-based firms as a means of obtaining access to new technologies. Anecdotal evidence would suggest that many more small firms will use some form of alliance as a method of overseas market development in the 1990s.

Direct Sales Visits

Many of the smaller high-tech firms, particularly those in an early stage of their corporate development, locate the focus of international market entry effort in their home country. Such firms employ export sales staff who make overseas sales visits to targeted customers and back this up by frequent telephone, telex and facsimile contact. This approach is rarely ideal as customers like a "local" point of contact and the commitment that goes with a more permanent local representation. However, direct sales visits can be a low-cost way of initially testing out the potential in an overseas market for a firm which lacks financial resources yet needs the face-to-face customer contact which distributors do not provide in the same way. Once the sales visit approach has established that there is sufficient market potential for the firm's product in a particular overseas market, direct sales visits are usually replaced by establishing a wholly-owned sales subsidiary.

While new technology such as videoconferencing, electronic mail, etc., is subtly altering the economic and competitive imperatives of locational choice, and in the case of software, even physical delivery of the product can be done by sending code remotely, successful international expansion is still likely to require a local presence in the foreseeable future.

Use of Distributors or Overseas Agents

The use of overseas distributors or agents by small high-tech firms has met with very mixed results. The best advice for small high-tech firms must be "don't use distributors unless you have to". Unfortunately for firms selling small ticket items (having a value of, say, US$5000 or less), the use of distributors may be an economic necessity. Although the market is deemed to have sufficient sales potential, direct sales visits even by sales staff located in overseas markets may be uneconomical, given the number of calls required to sell a relatively low value product. In small markets or in markets where the firm does not expect to obtain large export sales (due to the suitability of its product or due to intense local competition), distributors or agents may become the only viable option for market entry.

The problem with using distributors for high-tech firms include all those commonly met by firms using distributors: lack of focus on the firm's product range, sale of competing products, acting as order takers but not sellers or marketeers, etc. The problem, however, is complicated for small high-tech firms because they find distributors rarely able to understand their products and who are willing to invest in customer training and product support. Being small, high-tech firms lack the resources (both time and money) to train their distributors adequately. By definition, the small high-tech firm is unlikely to have any bargaining power or obtain a critical level of the distributor's share of mind, a situation exacerbated by distance from the exporting firm.

Where distributors are an economic necessity for small high-tech firms, the most successful firms have been those that have also established a local branch office or subsidiary to work with (but not by-pass) the local distributor. Building relationships with distributors takes time, and quick results should not be expected. Not surprisingly, the high-tech firms that have been most effective in using overseas distributors have been those who have a superior product for which there is a large market demand; but many of these firms have had to learn from their mistakes. When Lotus Development Corporation was founded in 1982 the exclusive worldwide distribution rights were given to Softsel, but within 18 months of start-up these exclusive rights had been cancelled, because Softsel did not offer the end-user or the dealer the support that Lotus felt was necessary. By the end of 1983 a new UK distributor had been found and Lotus' first overseas subsidiary had been established.

Establishment of an Overseas Sales Subsidiary

Establishing overseas sales subsidiaries has been the most commonly used and successful approach used by small high-tech firms expanding internationally. There are many factors (outlined later in the chapter) which influence successful entry into overseas markets. Establishing a sales subsidiary does not guarantee success: it is, however, one of the prerequisites for success. Market penetration is always greater where a sales subsidiary (or branch) exists than where distributors or direct sales visits are employed. The experience of both British companies in the USA, and US companies in Europe, supports this assertion.

Greenfield Site Investments

Warehousing, stockholding and service facilities are the first investments typically made by small high-tech firms after they have established an overseas sales subsidiary. Few, if any, small high-tech firms go further down the investment route, into manufacturing design, research and development, in foreign markets.

Only the very largest high-tech firms have shifted manufacturing successfully into overseas markets. Many source components and whole assemblies in the Far East, but do not manufacture in their principal foreign markets. Companies, like Intel (with 1990 sales of over $3 billion), are only just reaching the stage of establishing manufacturing facilities in Europe: the first time they have undertaken manufacturing themselves outside of the USA or Far East.

Acquisition of a Local Firm

One route to overseas market entry has been the acquisition of one or more small local companies in the chosen market(s). While acquisitions provide quick market entry and a means of overcoming typical start-up problems, small high-tech firms have been particularly unsuccessful in acquiring local firms. They have met all the problems of acquisitions mentioned in Chapter 6, and on top of that have had to contend with their lack of experience in managing a company operating in a different culture.

It is surprising just how many small high-tech firms have used the acquisition route to enter the US market. Five of the previously mentioned sample of 25 UK firms that had "internationalized" had chosen to acquire local firms as a route into the US market for their own product or service. In four of the five cases the company they bought turned out to be a "loser", or entirely inappropriate as a channel for their own products.

FACTORS DETERMINING CHOICE OF INTERNATIONAL MARKET ENTRY

The selection of the appropriate market entry strategy for small high-tech firms depends on a combination of external market factors and company characteristics.

External Market Factors

There are a wide variety of external market factors that influence choice of market entry.[12] Four factors appear particularly important for the small high-tech firm: market size, market structure, government policies and cultural attitudes.

Market size. The larger the size of the target market, the greater the degree of commitment that is appropriate. A small market would require an entry mode with a low break-even point, such as the use of sales agents or licensing. The determination of market size requires unconventional thinking, ignoring national boundaries. For instance, a company might perhaps only target the North East USA, as opposed to the whole country, and yet also include the substantial St Lawrence valley market as well. In Europe, US firms tend to set up subsidiaries in the larger markets of France, Germany and the UK, but rely on distributors in the smaller countries.

Market structure. The degree to which customers are dispersed or concentrated has an important influence on choice of entry strategy. A few focused customers lend themselves to direct sales visits and/or the relatively easy establishment of a sales subsidiary, whereas a dispersed customer base is more likely to need third-party distributors, and/or a sales subsidiary.

Government policies. The way in which government policies affect entry strategies for small high-tech firms are broadly the same as they are for all other firms. The only factor mentioned by interviewees with the managements of high-tech firms was the social legislation in Europe and the US requirements for those selling defence-related products. Social legislation in many European countries (notably Holland and France) makes dismissal of employees difficult and has influenced some small US firms to use distributors in Europe instead of establishing their own subsidiaries. For those firms wanting to sell high-tech equipment to the US Department of Defense, a local US subsidiary is a necessity.

Cultural attitudes. As a general rule, the more alien the culture, the less confident is the management that it can operate in that culture, and the more likely it is to choose a less committed entry strategy, such as licensing or employing local agents. Thus, we find that both UK and US firms have tended to establish sales subsidiaries in each others' countries, but have been more likely to use local distributors and agents in non-English speaking countries.

Company Specific Characteristics

There are four internal factors which tend to be of overriding importance in determining choice of entry strategy: ticket size (the value of an individual sales transaction), the profitability of domestic operations, the state of technology, and management experience.

Ticket size. The nature of the firm's product determines the average ticket size. As the ticket size grows, it is more likely that the product being sold will be a capital expenditure for the customer, or a key component or subassembly for one of the customer's own products. In either case any potential customer will require extensive face-to-face contact with the supplier's technical sales and service staff to convince them to buy the product. The lead time in these situations can be as long as two or three years (and even longer) before an order is placed. The use of distributors or agents is inappropriate in such situations, other than as a means of providing an initial introduction.

For large ticket size products, sales subsidiaries tend to be the most effective method of market entry, but the market entry problems facing the small high-tech firm selling big ticket items will vary depending on the market structure. If the potential customer base is concentrated, a small focused selling effort (using direct sales visits or a small local sales subsidiary) can be effective, but if the customer base is widely dispersed the small firm may find it difficult to develop a cost-effective market entry strategy. There are two ways small high-tech firms commonly deal with this issue. Some decide to sell to original equipment manufacturers (OEMs) in which case they accept a lower margin, since distribution costs have been eliminated. In going to OEMs they swap one type of risk for another: they reduce the risk of failing to gain orders because their marketing effort is too dispersed for the risk of becoming overdependent on the fortunes of one or a few large customers.

Where the ticket size of the firm's product is relatively small, sales visits and sales subsidiaries are still appropriate but only if bulk orders are possible from a relatively concentrated customer base. Where small ticket size products require a large customer base to be economically viable, distributors are always necessary. Figure 7.2 shows how the appropriate

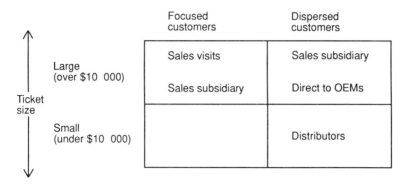

Figure 7.2 *The effect of ticket size and nature of the market on market entry method*

market entry method varies by ticket size and the nature of the market.

Profitability of domestic operations. If the small high-tech firm has already established a strong competitive position in its home market on which it is generating good profit margins, it can afford to invest in the appropriate form of market entry. Thus we find that none of the successful US high-tech firms have approached the European market using direct sales visits from the USA.

State of Technology. Firms at the leading edge end of high technology whose markets are still in the development stage of the product-market life cycle, tend to be short of the cash resources needed to establish overseas sales subsidiaries. Yet these are the firms which need to invest quite heavily in educating their customers, due to the newness of their technology. Consequently, such firms use sales visits direct from their home base and/or go direct to a few original equipment manufacturers.

Management experience. The high-tech entrepreneur's experience before he or she founded or joined the firm, plus that of his or her senior management team, will play an important role in determining how overseas markets are tackled. While international experience can be valuable in helping implement a particular type of overseas entry strategy, high-tech firms differ significantly and cannot automatically afford to adopt the approach that worked well in another high-tech company.

The choice of entry mode has long been recognized as a critical determinant in the success of foreign operations.[13] Different entry modes involve different levels of control, different resource requirements and different risks in the dissemination of firms' specific know-how.[14] No one entry method is invariably correct.

OVERCOMING COMMON PROBLEMS ENCOUNTERED IN GOING INTERNATIONAL

There are eight common problems that face the small high-tech firm contemplating international expansion:

1 the cost of establishing an overseas presence;
2 the management of overseas subsidiaries;
3 managing distributors;
4 product (or service) acceptability;
5 logistics/operations;
6 overseas manufacturing;
7 obtaining market information;
8 lack of top management commitment.

This section discusses each of the problems and some of the ways small high-tech firms have successfully overcome them.

Cost of Establishing Overseas Presence

Most firms underestimate the cost of establishing themselves in overseas markets, whatever entry method they choose. Firms incur incremental costs in doing business overseas, both incremental variable costs in the form of transportation costs, insurance, tariffs, etc., and fixed costs which are linked to establishing an overseas presence. Since firms selling high-tech products tend to obtain high gross margins, often in excess of 60 or 70% of the selling price, most firms do not find it a problem to absorb the incremental variable costs. The problem for small firms is the incremental fixed costs and the time lag before cash is generated from orders (if indeed there are any at all).

First, the absolute level of fixed costs required to establish an overseas subsidiary is underestimated. One small UK computer company estimated that the initial cost for sending one man to the USA for 12 months in 1988 to establish a subsidiary was $250 000. This was regarded as a "shoestring operation" and covered only office rental in Boston, one salary, expenses, legal costs and some secretarial expense. Another small UK company spent $450 000 over 18 months setting up a one-man operation in New York—very expensive since not a single order was received throughout the whole period! These sums of money are significant for firms that have world sales of under $10m per year.

One person, unless he or she is an exceptional sales person, is rarely enough to make much impact on the market-place. A considerable amount of highly focused marketing effort is required to gain a presence. The president of the US subsidiary of a successful UK software company gave one rule of thumb as far as international marketing costs are concerned: "If it takes $x to get to the prototype stage, it will take $3x to get to the deliverable product and then $10x to establish the product in the US market-place."

The fixed costs for US firms establishing themselves in the European market are equally high, if not higher, since in spite of the advent of a single European market on 1 January 1993, most countries still need to be approached on a country by country basis. Strong nationalistic tendencies and local distribution/service needs mean that separate subsidiaries have to be established, or separate agents/distributors appointed for each country.

While the level of fixed costs is an important issue, it is the timing of cash flows that is always crucial to the viability of the small high-tech firm. It is therefore very important for the small high-tech firm to relate projected revenues to costs in planning entry into an overseas market. Critical to relating expected revenues to costs are answers to the following six questions.

1 What is the ticket size of each sale?
2 What is the realistic lead time until the first sale?

3   What is the frequency of subsequent purchases?
4   What is the lead time to the receipt of cash?
5   How legally secure is the sale?
6   What continuing stream of revenue is associated with the sale?

The first two questions—those relating to ticket size and lead time—are particularly important for the small high-tech firm. They are determined by the characteristics of the market and the nature of the firm's products, and will largely determine how risky the entry strategy is, and what criteria should be used for judging its success.

If the ticket size is relatively small, then the firm should see a clear trend in sales, since there should be a large number of separate orders, hopefully building up over time. If the lead time to gain credibility or to persuade customers to use new technology is short, then the firm can get quick feedback as to whether it is succeeding or failing. This is the easiest situation to manage. If the lead time is long, and the marketing effort arduous, then the firm can review success or failure only over the long term. In this situation, the firm needs persistence and an "equity-minded" approach to investment in market development.

For big ticket products, the firm is more likely to encounter a volatile sales pattern. For instance, Miles 33, a UK supplier of front-end computer systems for the printing and publishing industry (later acquired by Quantel), spent about three years wooing certain key customers in the USA and then won an order from one of the biggest US book printing firms, which nearly doubled its US sales at a stroke and repaid all their accumulated costs of entering the US market. Big ticket items often require the demonstration of commitment to the market-place, and hence the establishment of local offices and servicing facilities. Hence the risks involved are far greater than for small ticket product companies. If the lead time is also long, the accumulated costs can be a heavy burden on the small company, and the faith of their financial backers.

Managing Overseas Subsidiaries

Entering overseas markets through the establishment of a

subsidiary has many of the characteristics of new start-up ventures discussed in Chapter 2. Thus those elusive, somewhat undefinable qualities of drive and entrepreneurial flair are required of those entrusted with the task of managing such subsidiaries. However, managing an overseas entity has some unique aspects, due to the cultural difference between doing business in the home country and doing business overseas. The interpersonal skills required by a manager overseas are greater than those required when operating purely in the home country. If the overseas operation employs local staff, the manager has to understand the way they think, and appeal to what motivates them. If the manager or representative is busy selling the firm's services or products to local firms, he must behave according to local customs, and present a face that is sufficiently "native" to give confidence to the buyers. Yet, at the same time, the manager overseas must maintain close links with head office by feeding relevant information back in a timely fashion.

Individual personalities can play a very large part, therefore, in the success or failure of an overseas venture. Failure can be turned to success and vice versa, by changing the manager of the overseas operation. Thus Formscan, a UK supplier of computer interface systems, fired its American manager in 1983, and built up its business from scratch by sending out two young, bright engineers to look around for any work they could. By dint of hard work and some forceful self-promotion, they uncovered a lucrative niche in making computers communicate with each other. One of the founders went out to join them on an opportunistic and temporary basis. In 1987 he was still there, having built up several million dollars worth of business, and a staff of over 20 people.

One of the big questions that continually arises is, should new overseas subsidiaries be managed by newly recruited nationals or by a senior executive sent by the parent company to open up the new subsidiary? At first sight, local nationals might seem the most appropriate route to adopt, particularly if the firm can find a person who understands the market-place and the product. In the previously mentioned study of small UK high-tech firms entering the US market, two-thirds of those that established a new subsidiary used local US nationals to lead the operation. No similar data is available for US firms, but casual contact would suggest a similar ratio of locals to nationals. However, there was no identifiable pattern of success or failure connected with nationality. The only point worth noting though, is that when local managers are deemed to have failed, they are usually replaced by a home country national at least until the subsidiary is "back on course". Success or failure appears to be related to the chief executive or general manager, and in particular to his or her entrepreneurial drive and ability; previous experience of overseas start-ups, multicultural experience, and opportunity for local equity ownership.

One important management characteristic of the more successful overseas subsidiaries of small high-tech firms is the intensity of communication that takes place between the subsidiary and the parent company. The nature of the communication in the more successful subsidiaries involves:

- daily telephone conversations between top management;
- technical support by 24-hour service teams in the parent company;
- extensive personal contact through visits both from and to the subsidiary;
- extensive daily use of facsimile transmissions and, with the larger companies, electronic mail.

Good communications between the parent company and its subsidiary obviously does not guarantee success, but it is worth noting that all the poor performing subsidiaries in the above study were characterized by only poor to average communications. Intensity of communication is not only important for feeding back market information, but is also an additional means of control by the parent company (in addition to the usual financial controls).

While the subsidiary management may resent this, really tight control has to be implemented, since overseas subsidiaries are potentially such a huge drain on corporate cash resources. A poor performing overseas subsidiary can be a major contributor to fragility and subsequent crisis.

US high-tech firms tend to be better at implementing tight control over their overseas subsidiaries than British firms. This is probably a function of size, since the generally larger US firms are more likely to have learned the importance of tighter control than their smaller UK counterparts, but the presence of venture capital backers and more ambitious financial growth targets for US parent companies would also appear to be contributing factors. The new UK managing director of a small but rapidly growing US computer company said:

> "Controls from head office are exceptionally tight but all they are really interested in are the quarterly results. Once we have shipped our quarterly target, the US leaves us completely alone until we're off target again, and then they crawl all over us once more until we're back on target."

"Exporting" the corporate culture is one way firms try to maintain control, although this is not easy given the fragility of the small high-tech firm's culture and the lack of understanding of overseas cultures and working practices. Janet Axelrod, VP of Human Resources at Lotus commented, when discussing the company's cultural values: "These values are important to me and the company, and I have to insist that they'll be transferred overseas. But I am not sure any of us know the various cultures enough to do it." [15]

Selecting and Managing Distributors

Firms that use distributors as a method of market entry, either by choice or necessity, typically encounter major problems selecting suitable distributors. Since high-tech firms are often competing in "sunrise" industries, the distribution section of the industry is also quite immature. Since the barriers to entry for distributors are likely to be fairly low in an immature industry, there are often a wide variety of young distribution businesses, few of whom have established a good reputation for product knowledge and service with potential customers. The small high-tech firm entering an overseas market for the first time not only lacks adequate knowledge about potentially good distributors, but is also in a weak bargaining position unless it is one of the very few firms that has already established a world-class product in its domestic market or other international markets. The marketing director of a UK medical products firm said: "One of the most time-consuming aspects of entering the US market is to find distributors who will put the effort into promoting your products with the same vigour as the large US corporations who are our competitors in that market."

The problem is of course not just selecting suitable distributors but also managing them successfully to sell your firm's products. The medical products firm mentioned above provides an interesting example of how one firm learned the hard way. The UK company signed an exclusive national agreement with a medium sized US firm to distribute a range of portable pumps. The choice seemed ideal, since the US firm manufactured implantable pumps, and was already talking to the doctors who would use portable pumps. Unfortunately, the UK firm underestimated the degree of inherent conflict between the two product lines. Although external and internal pumps typically are used for different treatments, the US distributors' salesmen put all their effort into selling the implantable pump, since it was more technologically advanced and sold for a much higher price. The UK firm was also hurt by staff turnover and low morale within the distributing company after the distributor was acquired twice within two years. They seemed to have learned their lesson, and have altered their strategy for promoting another line of bedside pumps. They have signed up five regional distributors, and have taken the innovative step of also retaining an American agent/consultant, who will closely oversee their interest in the USA. The UK firm retains direct links with the distributors, but obtains detailed market data from the agent, who is remunerated by commission on paid receivables and, therefore, also chases up late payers. However, the company is now convinced that the only way to succeed in the US market is to establish its own subsidiary.

It is not uncommon for firms to use distributors as a low cost, low risk way of market entry, only to realize later that with the margin they are giving to the distributor, they can do a better and more focused job themselves of attacking the market in question. The medical products firm's US distributor was making a 200% mark-up on the cost at which the product was sold to them!

Product Acceptability

It is essential that either the firm's product is perfectly suited to the overseas market, or it must be adapted to suit the market. Too many firms believe that just because they have a well-accepted, high-tech product in one market (either in their domestic market or in another international market) it will be accepted in others. While some technology is directly transferable, different technical standards and different engineering practices exist between the US and Europe and within Europe which make product adaptation a necessity for many firms. Three short examples illustrate the range of product acceptability problems:

1 Macro 4 provides system software for IBM mainframe computers so its products can be sold in identical form in any country where IBM mainframes exist.
2 Cotag manufactures a "smart card" for use in tagging clothes in stores. Although the firm had a unique product and had been successful in the UK, it had to redesign the product to credit card size before it was acceptable to the US market.
3 Continental Microwave, a manufacturer of telecommunications equipment found its product range totally unacceptable to the US market. The price was too high because the product was over-engineered for the needs of the market.

Language differences may also cause problems, as Lotus Development Corporation found out in Europe. Translation of Lotus 1-2-3 software into the relevant languages proved difficult since the original software was not written with language translation in mind.

Although it is important to have the same core technology running through each product line, it is crucial to allow minor adaptation and "repackaging" of the product to suit individual market needs.

Logistics

Assuming the firm has an acceptable product, there are a whole range of logistical problems that have to be faced by the typical small high-tech firm once an order has been placed and the product manufactured. These logistical responsibilities are likely to include all or most of the following:

- delivery;
- installation;
- training customers to use equipment;
- maintaining equipment in working order;
- trouble-shooting if "bugs" are found;
- hand-holding if mistakes are made by users;
- providing spare parts;
- enhancing systems with new functions;
- upgrading systems.

In the domestic market the same logistical needs obviously exist, but the difficulty for the small firm with limited resources is how to provide these "services" in a cost-effective way to satisfy customer needs. The successful firms tend to look for innovative ways of dealing with the problems that arise due to distance, different time zones and the need to duplicate, if one is not very careful, very scarce technical resources. Some of the special steps taken by firms interviewed for this research include:

- Building-in locally manufactured components for ease of service. Thus BVT Ltd, a small British manufacturer of vacuum technology equipment whose major market is North America, designs in as many US-sourced components as possible so that spare parts are readily available and the US manufacturers of those components can do any service that may be needed.
- Having an engineering development team located domestically, dedicated to supporting product modification requests for major overseas subsidiaries.
- Having a dedicated 24-hour per day service team at head office to provide fast response to enquiries from overseas.
- Using a domestically located computerized diagnostic

system to locate faults in equipment installed overseas. Stratus Computers, the US manufacturer of fault tolerant computer systems, used this approach when entering the UK market, although it now has a similar facility in London.

For the small high-tech firm, the provision of adequate service facilities in overseas markets is usually critical to sales success, since the vast majority of such firms are selling intermediate industrial goods. While this can lead to additional fixed costs, most small high-tech firms attempt to operate their overseas service functions as profit centres, which as a bare minimum are expected to break even. The key to providing technical service to international customers is to retain core technological competencies at home to avoid duplicating scarce technical resources.

Overseas Manufacturing

Very few small high-tech firms set up overseas manufacturing facilities, and those that have, have not been very successful. There are some obvious advantages to local manufacture, such as circumvention of tariffs and local content regulations, easier adaptation of products to specific local needs, being seen as a firm committed to that market, etc., but the disadvantages easily outweigh the advantages. The principal disadvantages are:

- additional fixed overheads, further increasing break-even;
- more demands on local management;
- more difficult to control from head office;
- loss of product focus as local manufacture usually leads to product proliferation;
- loss of economies of scale in manufacturing.

The only successful examples of overseas manufacture were found in those companies where:

- The overseas product line was totally different from the domestic product line (usually as a result of an earlier acquisition) and therefore the design and manufacturing facilities were clearly a stand-alone operation that had to be justified on its own performance.

- It was necessary to satisfy customer requirements, as in the case of non-US firms, satisfying US military "made in America" regulations. Thus, Druck Holdings, a UK transducer manufacturer, was required to undertake a considerable amount of redesign and local assembly in the US but it was careful not to duplicate unnecessarily scarce skills and kept its core technological competencies at home.

Obtaining and Communicating Market Information

Another set of problems which become particularly acute overseas are concerned with obtaining market information. The problem is not unique to the high-tech sector. All small and medium-sized firms have this problem when approaching overseas markets. Customized research that monitors the international business environment is generally too complex and expensive for the small firm. Instead small firms have to rely for market information on secondary sources and outsider visits to potential markets. Characteristically, small firms lack the know-how of where to go for these secondary sources, although any good business library is the obvious starting point. Government departments may also have a surprising amount of information available. [16] If used creatively, secondary sources can provide a significant amount of information very cheaply. [17]

Visits by senior executives of the small firms are probably the most widely used source of information. Different languages and cultures impose subtle barriers to understanding, and physical distance and a lack of personal contacts raise practical problems. Not surprisingly, the management of small high-tech firms have little fluency in foreign languages, but they do have a degree of multicultural experience. Many managers in technology-based businesses have worked in the USA, or have worked for American companies in Europe. Several managers I spoke to had made great efforts to visit overseas markets, including visits to China, Japan and Singapore. However, the costs of these trips can be heavy in relation to the amount of information gleaned. For instance, Japan is notorious for the difficulty of getting inside its business world, and for the expense of visiting the country.

High-technology firms which have grown up in a tight local network of business and academic acquaintances (such as in Silicon Valley or around Boston), may feel out of their depth overseas, because they no longer have the support of their network. Somehow they have to get into another network. Fortunately, the truly high-technology firm can become known throughout international academic circles without much effort. The problem is also reduced if the firm operates in a specialized niche, where the number of major world suppliers and buyers is limited. Through specialist magazines, catalogues, conferences and trade fairs, news can travel fast and cheaply. The location of a local partner often provides an entry point into information flows and networks of personal contacts. If a local distributor is systematically "sucked dry" of information, the entering firm can often move on quickly to setting up its own subsidiary.

Other practical ways of dealing with the need for information include hiring managers already plugged into the local network and working with a local agent who is already known as a specialist in relevant technology. Obtaining the necessary market information is of course insufficient by itself: it must be communicated back to the research and development teams, which are usually located in the home market. This requires a commitment to the marketing network—to feeding information from potential users and application ideas back to the development teams. As much of this information as possible should be sent back and acted upon. The best companies have intense daily communications with their subsidiaries and substantial amounts of development time are devoted to the needs of the principal overseas markets. This results in products being more closely matched to market needs and for new application and enhancement ideas being generated.

Lack of Top Management Commitment

A niche firm that approaches foreign markets in a passive or tentative fashion is likely to get poor results, which will usually bring about early withdrawal from exporting activity. A firm with a positive approach will tend to think more strategically and prepare its entry by planning and allocating resources. This is more likely to bring about good results within a number of years, thereby reinforcing the commitment of the people concerned.

Although many of the successful companies have been strict with the allocation and control of financial resources, they have been generous in the crucial area of allocating sufficient management time and other company resources. Top management will typically visit key overseas operations up to ten times a year and it is common to see development teams set up in the home country dedicated to the support of subsidiary requests. Thus Paul Brainerd who founded Aldus Corporation has focused much of his attention to developing international sales since Aldus set up a European operation in 1987. Derek Gray, Managing Director of Aldus Europe Ltd says: "Really, one of the secrets of success with Aldus Europe is that Paul Brainerd has personally always been very interested in international issues."[18]

Looking away from the operational details of modes of entry and towards the mindset of the management and culture of the small high-tech firms, one can distinguish between an opportunistic attitude towards overseas markets, which sees them as a means of attaining extra marginal sales, and the market entry approach, which has a realistic perception of modern global competition.[19] The differences between the two approaches are summarized in Table 7.2. Small companies may be tempted to use the sales approach where they lack international experience and are unsure of their ability to compete overseas, but the research did not find any small high-tech firm that could be described as successful using such an approach. This is supported by a study of 142 Canadian electronics firms which shows that export strategy is closely linked to export performance. The study showed that firms which are content to sell their domestic product abroad essentially unaltered and pay little attention to the nature and selection of segments within its foreign market, are likely to achieve below average export performance.[20] If high export growth is desirable then a careful selection of target market segments with the product as a variable, and not fixed, is essential. Interestingly, the high performing export companies tend not only to use the market

Table 7.2 *Entry strategy approach versus "sales" approach to international markets*

	"Sales" Approach	Entry Strategy Approach
Time horizons	Short-run	Long-run (say, 3 to 5 years)
Target markets	No systematic selection.	Selection based on analysis of market/sales potential
Dominant objective	Immediate sales.	Build permanent market position.
Resource commitment	Only enough to get immediate sales.	What is necessary to gain permanent market position.
Entry mode	No systematic choice.	Systematic choice of most appropriate mode.
New product development	Exclusively for home market.	For both home and foreign markets.
Product adaptation	Only mandatory adaptations (to meet legal/technical requirements) of domestic products.	Adaptation of domestic products to foreign buyers' preferences, incomes, and use conditions.
Channels	No effort to control.	Effort to control in support of market objectives/goals.
Price	Determined by domestic full cost with some *ad hoc* adjustments to specific sales situations	Determined by demand, competition, objectives, and other marketing policies, as well as cost.
Promotion	Mainly confined to personal selling or left to middlemen.	Advertising, sales promotion, and personal selling mix to achieve market objective/goals.

Source: Reprinted with the permission of Lexington Books, an imprint of Macmillan, Inc., from *Entry Strategies for International Markets* by Franklin R. Root. Copyright © 1987 by Lexington Books.

entry approach but also take a global view of their markets. They also tend to be the younger firms and to spend a higher percentage of sales on research and development than the poor performing companies.

The more successful firms commendably conform to the ideal pattern predicted by the theory. They keep very close to their customers, have an ability to pick up their requirements and problems and quickly come up with a solution. Once an overseas market priority has been established they devote considerable resources to developing the international business. Redwood International, a UK software company that in 1990 had 45% of its revenues coming from the US market, is a good example of how long it takes to build an international business. Redwood's Tony Hayward is quoted as saying: "We have been working in the US for six-and-a-half years, but only now are we starting to see a significant return. If you are serious about operating in the US you have to put serious resources there." [21]

SUMMARY

This chapter has looked at some of the strategic and organizational issues that should be considered by small high-tech firms that tend to expand into overseas markets. The five principal reasons why small high-tech firms expand internationally are: (1) to meet ambitious growth targets; (2) to ensure survival; (3) to keep abreast of changing technology and market requirements; (4) to spread the amortization of development costs; and (5) to achieve dominance of a global product niche.

Choice of overseas markets by small firms is often based on convenience factors, but the most successful small high-tech firms adopt a global approach at as early a stage as practicable. In terms of market entry approaches, establishing overseas sales subsidiaries (with service support a necessity) is by far the most successful route for the majority of firms. Both external factors such as market size and market structure, and internal company characteristics influence choice of entry method. One of the most important determining factors for small high-tech firms is ticket size (the value of a typical sales transaction).

Eight common problems encountered by small high-tech firms going international were identified. Various ways in which those companies that had been successful in developing international operations had overcome each of these problems were discussed. Successful firms tend to adopt a carefully planned approach and search for innovative ways to respond to the common constraints.

NOTES

(1) See, for example, Robock, S., Simmons, K. and Zwick, J. *International Business and Multinational Enterprises*, 2nd Edn, Irwin, Homewood, IL (1977).

(2) Malekzadeh Ali, R. and Nahavandi, Afsaneh, "Small Business Exporting: Misconceptions are Abundant", *American Journal of Small Business*, Vol IX, No. 4, Spring (1988).

(3) Feeser, H. R. and Willad, G. E. "Founding Strategy and Performance: A Comparison of High and Low Growth High Tech Firms", *Strategic Management Journal*, Vol. 11, No. 2, February, pp. 87–98 (1990).

(4) McCure, J. C. "A Modern Day Gutenberg Readies for the 21st Century", *Management Review*, November, pp. 8–10 (1989).

(5) Levi, J. "Redwood International", *Business*, October, p. 77 (1990).

(6) Slatter S. St. P. "The Internationalization Process in Small Technology Based Firms in the UK". Paper presented at Strategic Management Society Conference, Boston, October (1987).

(7) Cooper, Robert G. and Kleinschmidt, Elko J. "The Impact of Export Strategy on Export Sales Performance", *Journal of International Business Studies*, Spring, pp. 37–55 (1985).

(8) Harvard Business School. Lotus Development Corporation: Entering International Markets. Case Study 9-387-034 (1986).

(9) Carstairs, R. T. and Welch, L. S. "Licensing and the Internationalization of Smaller Companies: Some Australian Evidence", *Management International Review*, Vol. 2, No. 3, pp. 33–44 (1982).

(10) Slatter, S. St. P. and King, P. "Stages of Business Development of Small Firms in the Computer Aided Design Industry". London Business School Working Paper, June (1986).

(11) Slatter S. St. P. ibid. (note 6).

(12) For a discussion of the importance of macro-economic factors, see, for example, Goodnow, James D. and Hanz, James E. "Environmental Determinants of Overseas Market Entry Strategies", *Journal of International Business Studies*, Spring, Vol. 3, No. 1 (1972).

(13) See, for example, Root, F. R. *Entry Strategies for International Markets*. Lexington Books, Lexington, MA (1987); and Davidson, W. H., *Global Strategic Management*. John Wiley & Sons, New York (1985).

(14) Hill, C. W. L., Hwang, P. and Chan Kim, W. "An Eclectic

Theory of the Choice of International Entry Mode", *Strategic Management Journal*, Vol. 11, pp. 117–128 (1990).

(15) Harvard Business School. Lotus Development Corporation: Entering International Markets. Case Study 9-387-034 (1986).

(16) Seely, Richard L. and Iglarsh, Harry J. "The Informational Needs of the Small Firm Engaged in International Dealings", *American Journal of Small Business*, Vol. VII, No. 3, January–March (1983).

(17) Douglas, Susan P., Craig, Samuel C. and Keegan, Warren J. "Approaches to Assessing International Marketing Opportunities for Small and Medium-Sized Companies", *Columbia Journal of World Business*, Fall, pp. 26–31 (1982).

(18) McCure, J. C. "A Modern Day Gutenberg Readies for the 21st Century", *Management Review*, November, pp. 8–16 (1989).

(19) Root, F. R. *Entry Strategies for International Markets*. Lexington Books, Lexington, MA (1987).

(20) Cooper *et al*. "The Impact of Export Strategy" ibid. note 7.

(21) Levi, J. "Redwood International", *Business*, October, p. 77 (1990).

8
The Inevitable Crisis

Sooner or later everyone involved in the management of a small high-tech firm has to manage a crisis which threatens the very survival of the business. Few firms have managed to grow into large, well-established firms without facing at least one major crisis. The crisis can come at any point in the firm's development and will be characterized by severe cash flow problems, often accompanied by a sharp drop in profits in a very short period of time. Small high-tech firms differ from more conventional firms in the speed with which a crisis develops: they can look comparatively healthy one day and be heading for oblivion the next.

This chapter and Chapter 9 are based on a detailed analysis of the causes of decline and recovery in 30 small high-tech firms in both the USA and the UK. The findings show that, although there are some similarities, significant differences exist between the decline and recovery of small high-tech firms and well-established, "conventional" firms not operating in areas of high technology.[1] This chapter, which focuses only on the causes of decline and the nature of the resulting crisis, shows that a single causal factor may trigger off a chain reaction in small high-tech firms which rapidly leads to a crisis situation. In the more "conventional" turnaround, it is usually a series of factors occurring simultaneously that leads to a severe crisis.[2] The research on which this book is based identified ten principal factors which are the main causes of crisis for companies which have already established themselves as profitable

Table 8.1   *Frequency (in %) of major causes of crisis among thirty small high-tech firms*

Causal Factor	Percentage Frequency
1 Weak general management	53%
2 Poor financial controls	50%
3 Product competition	50%
4 Diversification and acquisition	50%
5 Changing market demand	40%
6 High overhead structure	40%
7 Manufacturing and operating problems	40%
8 Cancellation or delay of major contract	30%
9 Poor marketing	23%
10 Price competition	23%

businesses. Other problems exist but do not occur so frequently. The ten factors and the frequency with which they were found in the research project's group of 30 companies are shown in Table 8.1. This chapter discusses each of the ten causes and then suggests some reasons why there is usually a rapid escalation of crisis, and how the causes differ by size and growth rate of the company, and between manufacturing and service businesses.

CAUSES OF DECLINE

This book distinguishes between causes and symptoms of decline since, although symptoms give clues as to what *might* be wrong with the firm, they do not provide a guideline for management action.[3] To help the small high-tech firm through crisis, the basic causes of the firm's troubles must be identified and analyzed. This is not always an easy task, particularly where there is a sequential chain of causes with multiple symptoms (of the type shown later in Figure 8.1).

Weak General Management

A simplistic view of management can trace almost all the reasons for poor financial performance back to "bad management", arguing that it is either poor decisions or management inaction that are the causes of all the company's problems. Even where the cause of decline and subsequent crisis is due to external events such as changing market demand, it can be argued that management should have forecast such events and planned accordingly. While there is an element of truth in the argument, it is particularly difficult to defend in the case of small high-tech firms where there has been a rapid onset of crisis, primarily due to changes in technology and market demand.

Nevertheless, over half the small high-tech companies that participated in the study of turnarounds had problems at the time of the crisis, which could be attributed to the chief executive officer. As with non-high-tech crises, the problems were generally worse when one person assumed both the chairman and chief executive roles.

Most of the problems of weak general management fall into one or both of the following categories:

- *The technical founder(s) who lack(s) management experience*: The individual is often the "inventor" of the product which launched the company. He or she immerses him/herself in the technical details of the business and neglects both the general management role of planning, organizing and controlling, as well as other key functional areas.
- *The chief executive who cannot manage growth*: Even if the founder has some management experience and is able to cope with initial success, rapid growth changes the nature of the management task—as shown in Chapter 6. At start-up, the focus is on product development and finance, but additional requirements of market development, planning and co-ordinating are soon needed. The chief executive is unable to adapt to the changing requirements of the business—particularly the requirements for effective planning and effective organization building.

Small high-tech firms have all the usual problems of poor general management: inability to make decisions, focus on operations at the expense of strategic thinking, lack of planning, eternal optimism that "things will be all right", etc. A non-executive director of a company making specialized circuit boards for the telecommunications industry commented on the declining performance of the company:

> "We all knew what was needed. What little profits there were in the circuit board division were being swallowed by the massive losses in the component division. It had to be sold off. In addition, the substantial profit potential of the new products was inhibited because the overhead of the company was just too high. Yet board meeting after board meeting the CEO persuaded us that it would be all right.
>
> Finally, a new chief operating officer was hired who had a background of trouble-shooting in large companies and had turned round many loss-making subsidiaries. The root of all the firm's problems was that there were some very hard decisions to be taken, and the chief executive could not face up to them. He was too emotionally involved.
>
> By the time the loss-making component division was sold, problems had developed in the circuit board business, which meant that the business was no longer in profit. Most of the senior managers had been promoted, not for their ability, but because they were either friends or family of the chief executive. Al knew they were ruining the company, but he could not let them go. As an outsider, the new chief operating officer has been able to ask those people to leave. Al has accepted that he cannot manage the day to day affairs of the company. It has not been easy for him."

Besides these general problems, small high-tech firms tend to suffer from two special management problems which inevitably lead to, or at least contribute to, crisis: failure to delegate, and big company attitudes towards expenditure. Both these problems are common characteristics in small firms, but they appear to be more prevalent in the high-tech sector, due to the type of entrepreneur and senior management attracted to these firms.

The high-tech company founder is often a creative genius, like Steve Jobs was at Apple, and is now at NeXT. These technically brilliant individuals are, unlike many entrepreneurs, capable of understanding intellectually the need to delegate, but emotionally they are unable to do it. In one company, the chief executive was explaining his organization to me on a flip chart, and I was interested to see that he had so many boxes with functional vice presidents. This apparent bureaucracy was swept aside when he took the felt-tip pen, ringed *all* the functions and proclaimed ... "and I do all of this"! The inability or unwillingness to delegate among founders is partly a function of unwillingness to give up control of the company to which they have given birth, but may also reflect the preference of many managers with a technical background for immersing themselves in detail.

One-third of the companies in my study of small high-tech firms in crisis had problems resulting from the attitude of senior executives towards expenditure. This was often referred to as "the big company" mentality. Executives, including some founders, who had previously worked in a large company environment, often sought to spend money and live an existence more in keeping with companies not short of financial resources. The prevalence of this attitude reflects the fact that small high-tech firms attract experienced managers from larger companies as they grow, which is not typical of small firms at large; and venture capitalists often favour senior managers with "blue chip" resumés. One chief executive commented: "… They like large expense accounts, to travel first class instead of economy class, to stay in the Hilton rather than Howard Johnsons and they are used to the luxury of several specialist departments around them. …"

Oregon-based Lattice Semiconductor Corporation, which was founded in 1983, is just one example of the "more is better" spending philosophy. By 1986, Lattice boasted 140 000 square feet of office space for 176 employees, an Italian marble entrance way, and 63 staff in sales and marketing. It filed a petition for re-organization under Chapter XI of the US Bankruptcy Code in July 1987, with a loss of $8.5m on revenues of $11.7m. [4]

Poor Financial Controls

Good financial controls and information systems are important for all companies, but vital for those which are growing quickly, or which operate in unstable or rapidly changing markets. In the small high-tech companies in the study, financial controls were considered to be poor for two main reasons: either the company had inadequate cash flow forecasting, costing systems or budget processes, or the information gathering systems focused on matters which were wrongly assumed to be important to the success of the business.

The problem is not just lack of systems but the way in which management uses the data for control purposes. In one software company, staff were able to order computer hardware without needing to obtain authority from their manager. If they wanted something, they just rang up the supplier and ordered it. Costs rose rapidly.

An example of an information system which was analyzing the wrong information is provided by a company which produced its financial reports on a geographical basis. It failed to detect that the sales of a particular product were declining because its figures were included with all the others sold in that region. It took a "gut feel" decision on the part of the marketing director to initiate product improvements because he felt that the product was outdated. It took several months to unravel the figures and prove that sales were indeed declining as a result of a competitor bringing out a superior product. If the information had been available on a product by product basis, then the problem would have been spotted and addressed much earlier. Adequate financial controls are vital to detect changes in the operating performance of a company, but particularly so where product life cycles are short and erratic.

The dynamic nature of high-tech companies and the speed at which they have to change their product-market focus, means that financial control systems may need to be constantly revised. Thus, a manufacturing company which made the decision to move to higher value-added products, failed to allow for the increased inventory-carrying costs associated with more expensive products.

Problems with bad debts and the collection of receivables are strong pointers to weak financial control. One company employed a part-time financial controller prior to the crisis, a legacy of when it was a small firm, and had real problems with bad debts. In another company there were bad debt problems resulting from lack of attention to receivables collection.

Acting against the implementation of adequate financial controls is the high growth rate experienced by many small high-tech companies. This leaves them prone to using systems which were good enough last year but are inadequate today. Another consequence of the high growth rate is that the original financial officers find themselves out of their depth. This is evidenced by the high attrition rate of chief financial officers during the turnaround process. The high growth often acts as a deterrent against hiring in a chief financial officer from a large established firm. They might have experience of budgeting and control systems, but can be unsuited to the culture and environment that exists in a dynamic, growing high-tech firm. The firm is then faced with a dilemma—does it keep going with the existing financial manager and hope that (s)he will grow with the firm, or hire in somebody with experience of managing finance in a large firm, but who may not fit in well with the firm's culture?

Product Competition

Small high-tech firms outside of the service sector compete on the basis of product technology, usually in one or more niche markets. Few small firms are able to develop proprietary technology which can be easily defended through patents. The product life cycle may be shorter than the time it takes to obtain a patent, the time and costs involved may be too high for the small firm and, lastly and most importantly, large competitors will typically find a way around the patent. [5] A panel member from a large biomedical electronics company at an MIT Enterprise Forum, when asked to comment on the business plan of a fledgeling company with a new analytical instrument, said: "The entrepreneur thinks the patent will protect him in the US market. I can tell him that we monitor all new products coming onto the market and if we see a market potential developing we will be the first to invest in the necessary research and development to break the patent."

Severe product competition which supersedes existing products comes from three principal sources:

1 Fast growth start-ups that revolutionize the market by developing a new or superior technology. Thus, a number of small, bespoke software houses failed when Lotus became successful in 1983, and sales of VisiCorp's VisiCalc, the product which it superseded, declined by 75% in 12 months. [6]

2 Large technological competitors such as IBM, AT & T and Xerox, who have huge resources to invest in research and development of the market segment that looks potentially large enough to be of interest to them. They enter with superior products.

3 Changing industry standards. One company that manufactured a reading system for 12" compact discs for use in data storage found itself in deep trouble when CD-ROM technology became the industry standard. The current chief executive described the situation as follows: "... It was really bad luck. You develop a proprietary technology. Your customers love it. The venture boys love you. But suddenly the product is superseded ..."

While external sources provide the product competition, another way of looking at the issue is to see the real cause of product competition as being the company's failure to develop good new products quickly enough. Chapter 3 showed that firms often find it impossible to develop a good, second generation product, with the obvious result that the product line soon becomes obsolete.

Diversification and Acquisitions

Problems associated with new strategic initiatives such as diversification (by start-up or acquisition) and expansion into new markets, particularly overseas markets, are a classic cause of decline and failure among small high-tech companies. It has already been pointed out, in Chapter 6, how the search for further growth through diversification and overseas expansion is extremely difficult for the small high-tech firm, because its financial resources are generally weak and its skill and knowledge base very narrow.

The typical problems revolve around the new business venture being characterized by one or all of the following problems:

- the market is very competitive;
- the new venture has significant competitive disadvantages against competition;

- the parent company does not have the capabilities to implement its desired strategy;
- the parent company does not have sufficient financial resources to see it through any hiccups.

In some cases, chief executives of small high-tech companies argue that the acquisition, diversification or expansion move *per se*, while a cause of their problem, is not the root cause. They argue that it is pressure for growth from the investment community that is the real cause of trouble, an issue discussed in more detail later in this chapter.

Diversification

Always a risky strategy for small firms as it dilutes focus on the core business area; diversification is nevertheless used by high-tech companies to reduce their dependence on a single successful product and/or to achieve ambitious growth targets. Diversification, however, usually implies lack of focus which, as discussed in Chapters 2 and 3, is critical for the success of small high-tech firms. One of the contributory causes to Lattice Semiconductor's failure was the company's "kitchen sink" product strategy which included everything from SRAMs to programmable array logic devices. [7]

The story of a UK distributor and customizer of computer printers is a classic example of how what appears as a simple move can lead to total disaster. Their core business was under pressure in the early 1980s as the demand for customized printers dropped when software and hardware became more sophisticated. At the same time, the directors were witnessing the microcomputer become a commodity product in the consumer market. This made them think about opening a retail outlet to sell personal computers. The directors had visited the USA when dealing with their main printer supplier, and had seen the rapidly expanding retail computer market. They decided that a similar process would take place in the UK and they approached IBM with a view to becoming an authorized distributor for their personal computer. On the back of the blessing that IBM had given to them and the understanding that IBM would have 230 such dealers in the country, the company opened a store in the City of London. The retail outlet proved to be the principal cause of the decline in the company's performance.

The company had a history of providing value-added services to its customers (the printer customization was a good example). It is, therefore, not surprising to find that the staff the company put in the store were computer professionals who could provide expert advice to the clients who came to their shop. The problem was that the customers were "using us as a free consultancy and then walking down the road and getting a better discount".

The shop obviously had start-up costs and they did not expect it to start making money immediately. By the second year of trading, the retail market for computers had become so competitive that massive volumes were required to make any money. IBM were offering bulk discounts, and it is claimed that a competitor was "making their money out of the delivery charges". Another problem was the number of dealerships that IBM had awarded; it was between 400 and 500, not the 230 they had indicated to this company. During the decision-making process which led to the ultimate closure of the shop, one of the directors estimated margins had dropped so much that the shop was physically too small to handle the volume of goods that it would need to sell in order to be profitable.

Acquisitions

One poor acquisition is enough to bring a small high-tech firm to the point of insolvency. Even if the acquired company has been purchased out of cash flow generated from operations or by an issue of new equity (rather than from bank borrowings), any problem with the acquired company has to be met with an injection of both cash and management time from the parent company—just the resources that are scarcest in small companies. While poor acquisitions require the same scarce resources as new ventures, the nature of the risk is somewhat different. Whereas in new ventures the risks of failure are those associated with start-ups (see Chapter 2), the acquisition risk is much more likely to be in the area of poor post-acquisition management, and in high-tech firms often in the area of product quality. The acquisition of a small company making robot kits for assembly by home hobby enthusiasts for $1m provides a good example. The acquirer, who designed and manufactured microprocessor-based equipment for the educational market, saw the potential for selling robots to his existing customer base in the higher education sector. However, there were two problems. Firstly, there was a post-acquisition problem: the original founders (a husband and wife team) lost motivation after they had been acquired since they no longer had a stake in the company; and a year later became divorced. To quote a senior executive, "... the wrong one stayed". Secondly, management underestimated how the product quality requirements of the educational market were considerably greater than the hobby enthusiast market. Consequently, the company had to redesign the product at a cost of $200 000, to say nothing of the management time that went into solving the problem.

In another case, a Professor of Physics at Yale had established a successful company designing, manufacturing and marketing digitizers (machines which translate graphic information into digital form) to the computer-aided design industry. The company then purchased a subsidiary of the Bendix Corporation for $20m which produced CAD systems. Within two years it became apparent that the acquisition had been a mistake. In the words of its current President and CEO: "... the founder had made a terrible strategic blunder". In one fell swoop the company found itself in competition with its own customers, the established CAD systems builders. It became overwhelmed by the unfamiliar problems of selling systems rather than selling components, and it committed enormous amounts of investment to stay in touch with competitors such as IBM and Computervision. Within three years the company had invested a further $20m in the systems company, using both retained earnings from the digitizer business, and new venture capital. A great deal of management time was devoted to the troubled subsidiary. The company's core digitizer business began to suffer and losses grew.

International Expansion

The costs involved in expanding overseas and the length of time it takes to establish a profitable overseas presence means that international expansion is often one of the main causes of failure. In late 1985, Compsoft, a British software company, announced ambitious expansion plans to enter the Continental European market with the establishment of sales offices in Germany, France, Spain, Italy and Switzerland. This was described as "risky but necessary" by an industry commentator at the time. A major problem with the planned expansion was that it really fell between two stools; while the geographic coverage was wide, some of the offices were only staffed by one person, so could not really be expected to be a credible force. It was a compromise restricted by the financial resources of the company, and was too much of a low key approach to bring results. Another problem with the geographic expansion was that the overseas operations were being run with little apparent control from the UK directors. The impression was obtained that the UK management had little idea what was actually happening in the European market, or what the offices were doing.

Where international expansion involves the establishment of international manufacturing facilities before the firm becomes a "large" corporation, disaster is almost certain to follow. It is very hard to find examples of small high-tech companies that have successfully managed overseas manufacturing subsidiaries.

Changing Market Demands

Changes in market demand—some sudden and quite dramatic—are a common cause of failure among small high-tech companies. If such a change occurs where the company has weak management and/or a weak financial position, it may not be able to adapt to the changing market conditions. However, even when management and finance are not a problem when demand drops, the magnitude and speed of the drop may precipitate an immediate crisis. In *Corporate Recovery:*

A Guide to Turnaround Management (Slatter, 1984), it says that where volume drops by more than 25% in a single year, large, non-high-tech firms are likely to have extreme difficulty in surviving as independent businesses. In some high-tech firms the drop can be 75% in a matter of only three months.

Four types of changing market conditions can be recognized in the high-tech sector:

1 sudden shocks due to external events which cause most customers to stop or delay buying;
2 evolutionary (albeit quite fast) market changes;
3 cyclical changes in demand (which are a regular feature of the electronics industry);
4 expectations about market growth are not met.

Sudden Shocks

Small firms are always more vulnerable than large firms to sudden changes in market demand, and high-tech firms are no exception. Two UK examples will illustrate typical problems. A company which rented electronic logging equipment to the oil exploration industry was hit badly when the oil price collapsed, causing new exploration to drop sharply. The rental equipment was returned: no rental, no revenues and, hence, no business! Another UK company hit by changes in the market demand for two of its products simultaneously was involved in software production for the financial services industry. One of the markets it worked in was stockbroking, which slumped in 1984. At the same time, the announcement of deregulation ("big bang") threw the London stock market into a period of indecision. The result was that no companies were prepared to order software until they had evaluated the implications of deregulation. As these two areas accounted for over 40% of their normal sales revenues, the impact was dramatic.

Evolutionary Changes

Market opportunities can disappear as new markets grow and develop, due to technological advances. The PC market is rich with examples of how small high-tech firms that had jumped

into the microcomputer market in the late 1970s found themselves in trouble in the early to mid-1980s. Two US examples
illustrate the problem. A company which wrote software for
major hardware manufacturers had been very successful from
1978 to 1982, but as the PC market started to take off for business use, two events changed the company's fortunes. Firstly,
a whole new series of software applications were demanded
aimed at management use (e.g. databases, spreadsheets, etc.)
and, secondly, IBM decided to enter the market. The response
of this company's hardware customers was to make their
machines compatible with IBM. This move meant that there
was now little need to align software to hardware. As long as
the software could run on an IBM operating system, it would
be readily acceptable to the majority of the market. The company's relationship with the hardware manufacturers became
redundant.

In another example, a Chicago-based third-party maintenance company hit problems in 1987 as improved hardware
reliability reduced demand and some of the big hardware
manufacturers (notably IBM) started to offer attractive maintenance services to corporate customers.

Cyclical Changes

High-tech industries respond to different demand cycles, since
most small high-tech firms are selling intermediate industrial
goods, the demand for which is derived from the customer's
industry. Companies selling capital goods are heavily dependent on the vagaries of the business cycle, while those in the
semiconductor industry tend to be on a completely different
cycle of feast and famine. Cyclical changes in demand, however, do not appear to be a principal cause of failure, although
they may contribute to a company's overall decline when
combined with a number of other causal factors.

Expectations About Market Growth Are Not Met

The difficulty of undertaking market research for new products
and emerging markets has already been discussed in Chapter 3.
Yet, one of the most common causes of failure is management's

unerring belief in its own, or its industry's, market growth forecasts. It seems as though industry followers and those within the industry take great pleasure in hyping forecasts which are based on scant factual information. Arguments that "every office needs one" or "every home should have one" have in the past been the basis of many forecasts. Not surprisingly, the companies that gear up to meet such phenomenal growth are often disappointed—and left with large inventories to prove it. Acorn Computers—one of the UK's fastest ever growth companies—grew from sales of £430 000 in 1980, to sales of £93m in 1984. The company manufactured micro-computers and focused on the educational market, where it had over a 70% market share, and in the autumn of 1983 it launched a new product specifically aimed at the home market. In the company's 1984 annual report, the Chairman stated: "We anticipate another boom in home computer sales this Christmas in the UK", and high inventory levels were built in anticipation of record demand. Sales, however, never materialized: as one analyst put it, "quarter four of 1984 did not happen".

High Overhead Structure

The initial success of many companies encourages them to take on overheads at a rate which the business cannot sustain when market demand or competition increase. Mentioned previously were "big company attitudes" about expense accounts among management, which are, of course, only one of the many contributing factors associated with high overheads. The resource base of most small firms is just too small to permit management to indulge in luxuries. Compsoft, a UK software house, for example, which floated as a public company in 1984, used most of the proceeds from its Stock Exchange listing to purchase a large manor house which was to act as the company's head office and training centre.

The more common problem is overstaffing—staffing ahead of current needs so that expected market demand can be met. Chapter 3 looked at the optimism of most forecasts for new high-tech products and, therefore, it should not be surprising that when demand does not materialize as forecast, the company finds itself overstaffed. One vice president of finance in Silicon Valley said of the former chief executive: "He pictured the company as a $100 million revenue enterprise and staffed accordingly to his over-ambitious plans." Both Lattice Semiconductor and 3-COM experienced this problem. Talking of the 1987 crisis at Lattice, Jan Johannessen, Vice President of Finance (and in marketing at the time of the crisis) said: "We didn't pay attention to the revenue levels compared with expense levels. Sales were always going to take off next quarter. ..."[8]

At 3-COM, founder Bob Metcalfe decided to hire professional management in March 1987, less than two years after start-up. He brought in as President, Bill Krause, who had been running Hewlett Packard's General Systems Division. Krause immediately started hiring people and moved into new premises, but within months it was clear that the company would run out of cash by the end of the year. Krause had expanded too quickly to handle business that was not materializing fast enough.

While high overheads may be a cause of decline, they may be the result of failure in other areas. Unanticipated costs associated with new product development or diversification, particularly international expansion, can mean that overheads escalate quickly. In one company interviewed there was a fully staffed marketing department with no products to sell because of problems in new product development.

Manufacturing and Operating Problems

In conventional turnaround situations, high manufacturing costs are a common cause of decline, but technical problems rarely play a major role. Among small high-tech firms, however, technical manufacturing problems are often major causes of a company's slide into crisis.

The common problem areas are:

• production process engineering;

- component and subsystem suppliers;
- problems with subcontractors;
- quality;
- poor delivery;
- inability to lower costs as volume increases.

Production Process Engineering

Process engineering failures were central to the decline of 40% of the US small high-tech turnarounds in the study. It is difficult to determine how much of the problem was due to poor product design and how much to poor manufacturing. Within the companies each function tends to blame the other—but one thing is for sure—it is always an engineering problem and usually the result of a lack of engineering focus on the "things" which need to be done. The objects in need of focus vary by industry sector. In the semiconductor industry, for example, yield (the number of good or usable products that come off the production line) is a particularly important guide to manufacturing efficiency.

Supplier Problems

Finding reliable suppliers and subcontractors who deliver reliable quality products on time is critical to the success of small high-tech firms. A Californian company which manufactured thin film recording head components used in magnetic disk drives illustrates the problem. The production of these thin film head components required complex processing and advanced technologies. Process engineering involved using very small quantities of a specialist chemical, a light-sensitive polymer. The company had received just two batches in two years. The third batch, however, started to create problems in manufacturing, and product yields went down substantially. The company could not find another satisfactory source and had to redesign the process around a different chemical. This, too, proved to be difficult and as the problems continued the company was driven near bankruptcy.

Problems with Subcontractors

Subcontracting of various functions—but particularly of parts of the manufacturing process—is a common way by which small high-tech firms attempt to cope with their resource constraints (see Chapter 2). The use of subcontractors has all the risks associated with regular suppliers (quality, delivery, etc.) but, in addition, has all the risks associated with small high-tech firms. The position is often extremely fragile since the subcontractors themselves are prone to all the causes of decline discussed in this chapter. Consequently, those small high-tech firms that make considerable use of subcontractors are vulnerable not only due to their own fragility, but also to that of all their high-tech subcontractors.

Poor Product Quality

Poor product quality is undoubtedly a cause of failure since it directly affects sales and customer confidence. However, it is not a root cause of decline, since poor product quality is the result of other causal problems. The three problem areas already discussed in this section are themselves major causes of poor quality, but there are many others such as poor product design, product obsolescence, badly trained and poorly motivated employees, and inadequate investment in plant and machinery. Whatever the exact cause, product quality is a key issue for the small high-tech firm since its strategy is usually built around notions of product differentiation.

The question of product quality must, in part, relate to the use to which the product is going to be put. Is it a critical component in sub-assembly for the customer so that if it fails, it is the customer's own business which is put at risk? The VP Marketing of a company manufacturing in-flight equipment for aircraft commented on his firm's quality problems:

"When we finally managed to get the equipment into production, the returns among the few units that were sold were unacceptably high at 20%. We were trying to persuade pilots, whose lives depended to some extent on our equipment, to relinquish the tried and trusted product technology in favour of our technology. And yet our equipment was proving unreliable."

Poor Delivery

Poor delivery is usually the result of a failure in the manufacturing process, which in turn can be the result of any one of a number of causes ranging from unforeseen technical problems, a failure in management systems, to poor forecasting and over-optimistic promises made to customers by the sales and marketing staff. While strictly a symptom of trouble, poor delivery nevertheless plays a significant role in reducing customer confidence, which is a critical issue in a high-tech crisis situation (see later). In the study, 40% of the small high-tech firms in crisis were characterized by poor delivery. In a minority of situations—but still frequent enough to be evident—poor delivery is the result of the firm having order backlogs which it cannot meet. Aldus, the desk-top publishing software firm, encountered this problem in 1988, when sales doubled from $40m to $80m. The company's manufacturing capability was unable to keep up with demand and it took nine months for them to catch up.

Inability to Lower Costs

The need to lower the firm's cost base as the perceived technological differentiation of the product declines is well known. Small high-tech firms are usually hampered both by their size in not being able to take advantage of manufacturing economies of scale and by their culture, which is geared to innovation rather than efficiency. The need to lower costs in the first place usually results from competition from larger companies who enter the market with a me-too or equivalent product after the small high-tech firm has developed a product and had it adopted in the market-place.

Service businesses exhibit many of the same "manufacturing" problems as discussed above, in the guise of operational difficulties. Firms writing customized software provide a good example of many of these problem areas. They may have technical problems on projects (akin to process engineering problems), as well as quality and late delivery problems. Very often these are project management problems,

but sometimes the fault lies with the original project specification (i.e. the initial product design is wrong).

Cancellation or Delay of Major Contract

In common with many small to medium-sized companies,
small high-tech companies often obtain a large portion of their
sales from a single customer. Conventional business wisdom
has always said that overreliance on a single customer or contract is a dangerous move, since loss or even delay of the
contract can lead to substantial financial difficulties. A fairly
high percentage of the companies in the study of high-tech
turnarounds experienced difficulties due to this factor. Most
managements are aware of the risks and where they exist try
to diversify their activities in some way, but this is often easier
said than done.

The cancellation of a contract is usually the result of an unexpected decline in the customer's own business (for whatever
reasons), although it could reflect customer dissatisfaction with
quality, service or price, or even a failure of the firm to develop
new products when it knows that existing products must
become obsolete sooner or later. Thus, a UK company that built
up its business almost exclusively on a product which it sold to
British Telecom for use in their exchanges, had not developed
a successful replacement product by the time the next generation of exchanges was introduced.

Distribution businesses are always particularly vulnerable to
the whims of their suppliers, especially if the suppliers are
powerful companies. Two UK companies in the computer
industry illustrate the risks involved. MBS plc was set up in
1979 and rapidly became the largest UK distributor of IBM personal computers after they were introduced into the UK in
1983. Between 1984 and 1985, MBS increased capacity (and
hence overheads) at the same time as the rate of growth of the
market started to slow down. In an attempt to gain market
share MBS cut prices, turning the company from an after-tax
profit of £2.1m on sales of £42.9m, to a loss of £2.2m on sales
of £66.8m. Two senior marketing executives from IBM were
hired to turn the company around, but just as they started to

see light at the end of the tunnel, IBM substantially increased the number of distributors for their PC products, depressing margins even further. [9]

The other company, a manufacturer and distributor of computer accessories, enjoyed enormous success by distributing a single product. The product was a real "money spinner" since IBM had chosen the product to use in its PC, which made it a "safe standard". There was no need for much sales effort because everyone recognized that the product was the best. The company grew very quickly, but became almost wholly dependent on the product, with about 80% of its revenues generated by it. Consequently, the other business activities of the company, maintenance and the manufacture of computer accessories, did not receive the attention that they might have done.

The supplier of the product could see that the distributor was making too much money out of the deal that had been agreed and wanted to tear up the contract. At this stage, the company should have been looking for other sources of supply, since the supplier was now in a position to do the distribution themselves and had other distributors who would have been prepared to have given them a better deal. The situation was eventually resolved when the founder of the supplier sold out. A month before this happened, the distributor's sales of the product was over £800 000 per month; the following month sales were only £150 000.

Poor Marketing

The research showed that there are four principal areas where marketing tends to be a problem: (1) poor sales targeting, (2) incorrect pricing, (3) poor technical selling ability, and (4) inappropriate marketing approach.

Poor sales targeting. In almost half the companies in the study, poor targeting of the selling effort could be identified. This was more often than not a problem that resulted from a lack of clear product-market focus for the company, but it also reflected weak sales management.

Incorrect pricing. On balance, companies tend to underprice rather than overprice, particularly in the early stages of the product life cycle. The reverse is more likely to be true in the later stages when competitors have entered the market and forced price levels down.

Poor technical selling ability. In the early stages of the development of a small high-tech firm, the chief executive (often the founder), together with some key design engineers, takes the lead role in selling. At a certain size, however—usually not very large—salespeople are recruited. Good technical selling skills are all too rare and the temptation is to have professional salespeople with no industry experience rather than people who are capable of relating to the customer and can understand the product. This is almost the reverse of the conventional wisdom for small firms at large, who all too often hire product enthusiasts when they need professional selling capabilities.

Inappropriate marketing approach. Examples vary from use of the wrong channels of distribution to use of the wrong promotional approach. In all cases the problem usually boils down to a lack of understanding of the customer's buying behaviour. The most startling example of inappropriate promotional marketing was with the company providing critical in-flight information to pilots. At one stage they decided to promote their product, on which the pilots lives depended, by giving away a cheap watch with each unit sold. As the venture capitalist explained: "The Vice President of Marketing had a strong background and came very well qualified. He simply had no idea of what it took to sell the units. We were trying to persuade cautious pilots of the reliability of our products with watches which failed after a few hours of use."

Price Competition

While nowhere as important a cause of decline as in non-high-tech companies where severe price competition can make a successful turnaround almost impossible to achieve,[10] price competition can be the "killer" for some small high-tech firms. The nature of the product and technology, and the potential size of the market, determine whether imitators enter the market with a me-too product. Sometimes imitators add features or functions to try to differentiate their product, but if the core product characteristics are still broadly similar, the presence of imitators makes the product start to behave like a commodity. Customers have a wide choice of suppliers and do not perceive much product differentiation, with the result that price competition soon develops. In some instances, the power of large customers who want more than one source of supply encourages imitation. The chief executive of a manufacturer of bespoke circuit boards, who had several very large customers such as AT & T commented:

> "They [the customer] would push us very hard to license our products to competitors so that they would have two sources of supply. Worse, they would show our products to competitors and ask them to copy them ... We had very little success in forcing competitors to use our designs. The only way the company could find to combat the problem was to push the design team to innovate constantly so that we always had a better product on the market."

Price competition can be both sudden and severe, as Seeq Technology discovered in 1984/85. Seeq was finding the market for EEPROMS (E-squares) more difficult to develop than had been originally anticipated, so decided to begin manufacturing the older EPROMS to produce revenues. The impact on sales was dramatic—from $9m in 1983 to $43m in 1984, with EPROMS accounting for 75% of Seeq's revenues. The success, however, was short-lived as the Japanese started to flood the market with EPROMS in 1985. Between the last quarter of 1984 and the third quarter of 1985, the price of a standard 128K EPROM fell from $15 to $2. Seeq's manufacturing costs, however, were $5 per unit. [11]

PRESSURE FOR GROWTH

Although not specifically identified as a cause of decline, small high-tech firms are typically expected to grow fast. Such expectations are paramount in the minds of stock market investors, venture capitalists and other investors, but are also engendered by industry hype about potential market size and by the way that role models exist in Silicon Valley, and elsewhere, of entrepreneurs who have amassed enormous fortunes in a short period of time. The media naturally pick up on the good news, building expectations in the community at large, which in turn influences the workforce from which small high-tech employees are recruited. The expectation of high growth is, therefore, built into the culture of the small high-tech company: optimism is pervasive. Early success breeds further optimism and quickly management begins to believe that it is invincible.

The end result of such optimism is, of course, unreliable sales forecasts. Thus at Apple, after the successful launch of the Apple Mac computer, forecasts were set at 80 000 to 100 000 Macs per month. John Sculley's account of how these targets were set is illustrative of what happens, albeit usually on a smaller scale, in many small high-tech companies. Within months Apple was selling less than 20 000 units per month. However, even in the depths of crisis, it is not unusual for considerable optimism still to exist, something which can be a problem for a new turnaround manager, who must bring realism to the organization.

The pressure for growth can lead management to the following actions, all of which are themselves causes of failure:

- building higher overheads than currently necessary in anticipation of a higher level of activity;
- building manufacturing capacity ahead of demand;
- building inventory levels ahead of demand, thereby putting strain on working capital;
- taking short cuts on product development with the result that new products are launched before they are at a quality level acceptable to the market-place;
- aiming for volume growth without paying attention to gross margins;
- diversification through acquisitions.

Once a small high-tech company has gone public (obtained a Stock Exchange listing), the pressure for growth accelerates. High-tech stocks are expected to provide high growth to give investors capital appreciation rather than dividends. A rapidly growing UK company involved in computer equipment distribution and third-party maintenance provides an example. The company grew rapidly in the early 1980s, and to maintain this growth it was realized that further financing would be required. So in February 1984 the company joined the Unlisted Securities Market (USM) at an offer price of 116p. The issue raised £1m, of which half was reinvested in the company and half divided between the directors. Less than a year later, after a period of growth, expectations in the market were still high and the share price reached 295p, placing the company on a price earnings ratio of 33 times earnings.

After the USM listing, the company exceeded its first profit target by 10%, and for the year ending April 1985 profits increased from £663 000 to £1.1m. In the following year, the push for growth continued and there was heavy investment in people—their main resource. The average number of employees increased by 54 to 137. However, as the company geared up for an expected 80% growth and "strove to meet USM targets", *the market for its products turned down*. This created considerable control problems—stock levels increased by £1m as the stock turnover ratio fell, the average length of time taken to collect receivables rose to 3.5 months, while staff wages and salaries almost doubled. This created cash problems and the bank overdraft rose to £2.5m.

As in the above example, it is usually a sudden drop in market demand at the same time as the firm has geared up for growth that causes the crisis. Revenues drop just as the break-even sales level has been increased. An immediate cash crisis emerges. Most small high-tech firms that have gone public see a public listing as a double-edged sword. The benefits are access to funds which reduces risk by keeping financial leverage low or non-existent, and an increase in credibility in the eyes of customers and suppliers. However, the pressure to grow is seen as a distinct disadvantage. There are many examples—particularly in the UK—of companies taking on acquisitions and projects which they might not have done if they had remained in private ownership. When things start to go wrong the public company is more exposed to commercial pressures than the private one: knowledge of the company's problems receive wider publicity, which in turn makes recovery more difficult.

FACTORS INFLUENCING CAUSES OF DECLINE

The causes of decline vary enormously, both across the different high-tech sectors and within the individual sectors. Considerably more research is required than was possible for this book to identify exactly how the causes vary by industry segment and type of company. This section takes just four factors and looks at how causes of decline vary with the size of the company, its growth rate, the rate of technological innovation, and type of business (whether the company is a manufacturing or service business).

Size of Company

How does the size of the company influence the causes of decline? The sample companies were divided into small companies (under US$5m sales revenue per year) and large companies, and four differences worthy of discussion were found.

Firstly, large companies tend to have more causes of decline than small companies. The major reasons for this are:

- Smaller companies are more fragile: they have a weaker resource base than large companies, which means that a full-blown crisis can develop from just one or two causal factors. Larger companies are slightly more robust and require multiple causes of decline, as do conventional firms, before a crisis is reached.
- Larger companies tend to have a wider product-market scope, which tends to give some of the traditional benefits associated with diversification. Risk is spread so that sound operations may partially be able to absorb or offset problems elsewhere.
- Larger companies are more likely to have manufacturing problems which trigger off a complex network of inter-related problems connected with quality, delivery, loss of customer credibility, etc.

Secondly, the nature of managerial weakness varies by size of company. In small companies the lack of managerial expertise of the founder(s) plays a major part in the demise of the company, even though the management team is committed and hard-working. In larger companies, the influence of the founder has often diminished somewhat as the result of the appointment of "professional" managers, and decline or crisis is the result of management's inability to establish priorities and "see the wood for the trees".

Thirdly, the nature of manufacturing problems varies by size of company. Small companies lack the capital, expertise and volumes to justify in-house manufacture. As a consequence, the companies develop relationships with key suppliers to manufacture and assemble products. These suppliers are also often small, resource-constrained companies because of their lack of bargaining power with larger subcontractors. Not surprisingly, the supplier lacks the required levels of manufacturing expertise, and quality and delivery problems quickly result. Far from easing problems for the small company, outsourcing can result in product and process engineering problems and a high level of customer dissatisfaction. In the larger companies manufacturing issues remain critical, but are of a different kind. Here, the company has built sufficient volumes to bring manufacturing in-house, but there is a tendency for them to try to participate at all levels in the value chain, manufacturing primary and secondary components, and assembling the final product. As a consequence, there is no back-up source of supply when problems occur.

Fourthly, lack of customer credibility is a real problem for the smaller companies. Many of those in the study had difficulty building credibility with their customers, and lack of credibility was undoubtedly a contributory cause of the company's eventual crisis. Credibility is also an issue in the medium-sized high-tech companies. The magnitude of the problem is not as large since by this time they had well-developed technologies, a diverse and usually loyal customer base, and a history of on-time quality deliveries. With larger companies, credibility issues were found to have resulted from the crisis rather than having been a basic cause.

Company Growth Rate

Both high- and low-growth companies tend to experience problems due to inadequate financial controls and unexpected changes in market demand. Both, of course, experience management problems with the faster growth companies experiencing the same management problems as the larger companies (and vice versa). The major differences occur in the areas of competition, diversification and manufacturing, although there are some interesting differences between the two groups of companies in the way in which financial and human resources contribute to crisis.

Competition. High-growth companies were generally less affected by product competition than smaller companies. With some notable exceptions in the personal computer industry, this was also true for price competition. Why? The answer is that high-growth companies tend to be somewhat insulated from competitive pressures in the early phase of market growth because their product is unique; and early success provides sufficient cash to reinvest in maintaining their product advantage.

Diversification. A feature of low-growth companies is that many (over half in the sample) experience a fall in profits due to a failed acquisition. There is some further evidence that the pressure for growth discussed above can be a root cause of crisis among small high-tech firms.

Manufacturing. Fast growing companies exhibit a number of manufacturing problems which are often central to their decline. Their internal dependence on in-house production often results in continued crisis and strain as the organization seeks to cope with necessary increases in production. Direct consequences of this include reduced quality standards and poor delivery achievement. Indirect effects include increases in product cost as lack of capacity hinders production efficiencies.

Finance. Volume growth generally leads to a significant increase in the demand for finance to fund investment in working capital and, maybe, fixed assets as well. However, the rapidly growing company's lack of cash does not directly contribute to its decline. Lack of cash is a consequence of the crisis rather than a causal factor. Instead, venture capitalists are only too willing to support the company's rapid growth, provided targets are being met. Availability of funds does not appear to be a constraint to growing companies. One venture capitalist commented: "... Providing funds [for high-tech companies] is easy. In the second or third round deals everyone climbs on, we all like success ...". In the slow-growth companies, financial constraints do provide some impetus for the crisis. Few slow-growth companies track to budget, and if venture capitalists are involved, they become increasingly wary of supporting further development expenditure before market success has been demonstrated.

Human resources. In the human resource area one would expect that high-growth companies would find difficulty in recruiting key executives of sufficient calibre. Such executives might experience problems in their integration with the rest of the management team and might be incapable of managing the company through continued growth and change. The study found no evidence to suggest that fast-growing companies are constrained in terms of their human resource policies. Companies with rapid growth rates were usually capable of attracting talented managers. High salaries and share options often provided high-level incentives to these managers. By way of contrast, lower-growth firms had more difficulty attracting top quality employees.

Rate of Technological Innovation

In those sectors where the rate of technological innovation is fast (i.e. where the product life cycle is less than three years), technology problems are usually central to the crisis. The causal factors are either insufficient product development or some form of product or process engineering failure. A high rate of technological innovation may also lead to low barriers to entry, since proprietary technology is of limited value to a company unless it can constantly keep ahead of competitors' technology.

Type of Business

There are several noticeable differences between manufacturing and service businesses. Both types of company are characterized by many causes of decline, but only poor management, inadequate financial controls and changes in market demand are frequent causes of crisis in both service and manufacturing businesses. For the manufacturing business, there are five significant causes of decline which are less likely to be found among service businesses. These are:

- product competition;
- price competition;
- manufacturing problems;
- diversification and acquisitions;
- cancellation of major contract.

As a general rule, small high-tech manufacturing companies are subject to greater competitive problems than service companies. It is easier to take apart and produce a monitor than learn to write a COBOL systems program. When the high-tech manufacturing companies first develop their products they are often unique and, therefore, can be produced and marketed by a small company. However, if the products become a success then they are quickly imitated, often by Far Eastern manufacturers, on a scale and at a price which undermines the smaller operation.

The problems affecting service companies tend to be more diverse, and include problems such as lack of staff training which, while not a frequent cause of crisis, was significant in a Chicago-based computer maintenance company. The one overwhelming characteristic of service businesses in trouble, in addition to those already mentioned, is high overheads— making profitability of such businesses very sensitive to small drops in volume.

THE SPIRAL OF DECLINE

Crisis situations evolve in small high-tech firms as a consequence of management's failure to deal with an escalating number of problems within the organization. The speed of decline can be quite dramatic, due to both external factors— changing market conditions, speed of technological innovation by competitors, new entrants to the market, etc.—and internal factors such as low quality, high returns, increasing inventory levels and plummeting morale. The net result is that the managers of small high-tech companies have less time to identify decline and act on it than their counterparts in conventional companies.

The study identified two patterns of problem escalation leading to crisis. The first is similar to that outlined in *Corporate Recovery* (Slatter, 1984—see note 2), whereby there is a variety of independent problems occurring simultaneously. All firms are characterized by two or three problems, but as new problems arise, the number and complexity of the situation overwhelms top management. Thus, for one company in the study, the need to develop a second generation product coincided with the decision to acquire another company. The management were unable to meet the challenges faced by declining performance of the acquisition and their inability to develop the new generation of product.

A variant of this pattern is where a company exhibits a number of causes of failure but, even when combined, the problems are offset by strong market demand for the company's product(s). However, it only needs some other problem to emerge—called here a "trigger" problem—for the whole company to be in an immediate crisis. For companies already weakened by a number of independent causes of decline, a relatively small downturn in the business cycle, a delay in receiving a contract from a customer, or a problem with a subcontractor can act as a trigger problem.

The second pattern of decline may be unique to high-tech companies. It starts with a single trigger cause of decline at an identifiable point in time which sets off a chain reaction of sequential causes and symptoms of decline. Here, there is interdependence between a variety of causes and symptoms of decline. One problem leads to another and a causal relationship can be identified. For example, product development difficulties lead to process engineering problems, which in turn result in lower quality products. A subsequent high level of returns then increases work in progress, with the result that manufacturing efficiencies decline further. Customer confidence declines, sales volume drops, finished goods inventories increase, and a cash crisis develops. The sequence is shown in Figure 8.1.

Taken individually, the problems might be readily manage-
able, but because they are interdependent there is often a complex web of problems difficult to disentangle. The big difference
between the two patterns of decline is in the position of the
trigger cause. Where the causes are largely independent, the
trigger comes at the end of the process, after the company has

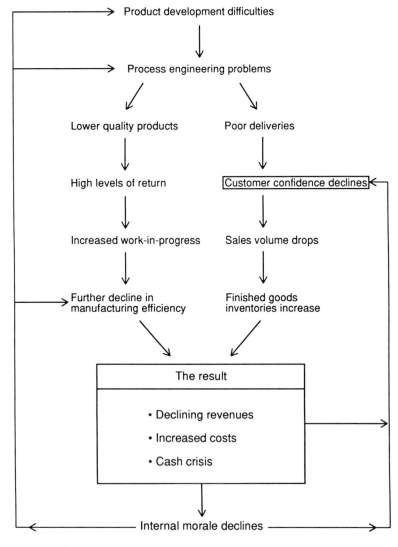

Figure 8.1 *Sequential causes of decline—an example*

already been weakened by a series of problems. Where they are sequential and interdependent, the trigger cause comes first. In the latter situation, the five principal *trigger* causes identified by the study are:

1 product competition due to failure to generate new generation of products on time, or product design weaknesses;
2 new entrants competing on basis of price competition;
3 manufacturing problems that affect product quality (including supplier and subcontracting problems);
4 changing market conditions, usually a drop in demand;
5 cancellation or delay of a major contract.

As the health of the company starts to deteriorate rapidly, there are two critical areas which act like cogs in accelerating the process of decline. Firstly, loss of customer confidence; unacceptable quality, late deliveries and declining financial performance (no customer wants to buy a high-tech product from a company it thinks might become insolvent) becomes self-reinforcing with a disastrous impact on sales volume. And, secondly, the internal morale of management and staff spirals downward at a rapid rate as they hear one piece of bad news after another. Poor internal morale means some key individuals start to look for employment elsewhere—before the axe falls—and efforts to solve the company's technical problems become more difficult. The small high-tech firm can go through the typical stages of crisis development (from crisis denial to organizational collapse) in just a few weeks. [12]

SUMMARY

This chapter has outlined the ten major causes of decline in small high-tech companies. The external pressure for growth on these companies undoubtedly influences management actions, and leads to more crises than would otherwise be the case. A limited attempt was made to show how causes of decline vary by the size and growth rate of the company, the rate of technological innovation and whether the company is a manufacturing or service business. Finally, two patterns of decline were discussed showing how the small high-tech firm can appear healthy and normal one day, but be in need of intensive care the next.

NOTES

(1) Slatter, S. St. P. "Success and Failure in High Tech Turnarounds". Paper presented at Strategic Management Society Conference, San Francisco, October (1989).
(2) Slatter, S. St. P. *Corporate Recovery: A Guide To Turnaround Management*. Penguin Books, London (1984).
(3) As does Slatter, S. St. P. (1984), ibid., note 2.
(4) "Once Bankrupt The Good Times Come Back to Lattice", *Electronic Business*, November 27, p. 38 (1989).
(5) Levin, R. C. "A New Look at the Patent System", *American Economic Review*, 76, 2, pp. 199–202 (1986).
(6) "What's Next For Lotus?", *Venture*, January (1986).
(7) Ibid., note 4.
(8) Ibid., note 4.
(9) MBS Case Study in Slatter, S. St. P. *Cases in Strategic Management for the Smaller Firm*. Basil Blackwell, Oxford (1988).
(10) Slatter, S. St. P. 1984, ibid., note 2.
(11) Welles, E. O. "The Company Money Almost Killed", *Inc.*, November (1988).
(12) Slatter, S. St P. "The Impact of Crisis on Managerial Behaviour", *Business Horizons*, May–June (1984).

9
Recovery Strategies

By the time the small high-tech firm has reached crisis point and the board of directors, the bank or the investors have triggered the start of a turnaround, there are likely to be four priority areas that require immediate action:

1 the appointment of new management;
2 the cash crisis;
3 low employee morale;
4 credibility with customers and suppliers.

There will be a whole range of other remedial actions that will be necessary which will mirror the range of problems that have either caused the crisis or resulted from it. The choice of strategies open to the turnaround manager—usually the new chief executive—are the same as for turnarounds of more conventional firms, although there are some significant differences in emphasis. [1]

The study of recovery strategies in 30 small high-tech firms in the USA and the UK showed that successful recovery strategies for small high-tech firms pay greater attention to product-market and organizational change, investment in new product development, and the re-establishment of customer credibility than do successful recovery strategies for conventional firms.

This chapter discusses the eight principal recovery strategies used by small technology-based firms in a crisis. They are:

1 appointment of new management;
2 tackling the cash crisis—including asset reduction, cost reduction, new financing and financial control strategies;
3 improving employee morale—including changing the organizational culture;
4 regaining credibility with customers and suppliers;
5 change of business focus;
6 improved marketing;
7 manufacturing changes;
8 investment in focused product development.

Finally, the financial characteristics of successful turnarounds are discussed, together with a discussion of the factors determining successful recovery of the small high-tech firm.

APPOINTMENT OF NEW MANAGEMENT

The appointment of a new chairman or chief executive normally (but not always) implies the removal of one of the original founders of the company. It is, therefore, a traumatic event not only for the individual (and/or the founding team), but also for the company as a whole. The main reason why a new chief executive officer (CEO) is appointed is because the previous CEO is regarded by other board members or outside investors and bankers as unable to turn around the company. The classic situation is the one where a technically brilliant founder lacks general management skills, particularly in the area of direction and control. Interestingly, though, this lack of skills is hardly ever regarded as a problem until the crisis begins. However, in a crisis one must always ask if the CEO who has presided over the decline phase is able to grasp the change in direction which is necessary to turn the company round. The answer, nine times out of ten, is no. The CEO survived the crisis in only two out of the thirty companies in the study's sample. Survival occurred where (a) the crisis was caused by rapidly changing market conditions and the CEO showed himself capable of dealing with the crisis, and (b) where the CEO was the majority stockholder and was a superb salesman with financial institutions. However, in both situations other new executives from outside the company were appointed to assist the existing CEO.

The replacement of founders can be quite difficult to engineer and can end up being very acrimonious. Founders are invariably principal shareholders, and may indeed have recruited the individual who the board believes should be the new chief executive, prior to the crisis. The story of the "battle" between Steven Jobs and the man he recruited, John Sculley, at Apple is a well-documented example, albeit from the perspective of the individual that won the battle.[2] However, unlike non-high-tech turnarounds where the CEO once removed nearly always leaves the company completely, it is not uncommon to find founders, once relieved of overall responsibility, take up alternative roles as non-executive chairmen, or be put in charge of new product development. This is most common in those sectors where the rate of technological innovation is fast. Whether this is possible depends on the personality of the founder. Steve Jobs clearly was unwilling to settle for such a role at Apple Computer and decided to resign to start up all over again. Bob Metcalfe, at 3-COM, took the opposite view and decided to stay and work with the professional manager he had recruited prior to the crisis.

Bob Metcalfe, the founder of 3-COM and the co-inventor of Ethernet, a local area network product, was prepared to move aside as CEO and take on the role of Vice President, Sales and Marketing. Metcalfe, when Chairman and Chief Executive, hired Bill Krause from Hewlett Packard in March 1981 to be President, just before the company found itself in a cash crisis due to over-expansion. In late 1981 the board decided that Krause should take over as CEO, but, knowing how difficult it would be for Metcalfe to give up power and that he could not dictate to Metcalfe, Krause looked for a way to avoid confrontation. He formed an executive committee made up of himself as Chairman, Metcalfe, and the four vice presidents. Howard Charney, Vice President of Manufacturing, commenting on this, said: "War would have ensued if he [Krause] had tried to exclude Bob, so he included him. That made it easier for Bob to give up power because he was able to participate in the decisions." Metcalfe, however, feels that in the end it was their equity stake in the business that kept him and Krause working together. Metcalfe was 3-COM's largest shareholder with just under 21%, while Krause had received 9% when he joined. "Equity does tend to hold people together during emergencies … More than once we were a sentence away from ending the company … we just didn't let it happen," says Metcalfe. [3]

Where do the new chief executives come from for small high-tech firms? In almost half the 30 companies participating in the research into small high-tech turnarounds, the replacement, surprisingly, came from *within* the organization—and was almost always an individual with a finance or sales and marketing background. One or two new chief executives were venture capitalists who wanted to try their hand but, with a few exceptions, they were not the "professional" turnaround manager who moves from one crisis to the next. Figure 9.1 shows the skills most needed by the successful turnaround manager of small high-tech companies.

At the level below that of chief executive there are usually some management changes, particularly in the USA where, in contrast to Europe, there is a tradition of clearing out a significant portion of the old management team, whether or not they were directly to blame for the current crisis. In contrast to the new chief executive, who is often an internal candidate, many of the second tier management positions are filled by individuals from outside the organization: hardly surprising perhaps, since the typical small firm lacks management depth, particularly if it has been growing rapidly before the crisis.

The appointment of a new vice president of finance and/or the strengthening of the finance team is common practice, due to the previous lack of adequate control systems and the need for investors to feel comfortable with the financial management of the company. However, due to the customer credibility problem discussed below, the marketing role is also seen as critical in the majority of small high-tech turnarounds. Thus, new chief executives often appoint new marketing staff; although it is interesting to note that in the case of very small companies some CEOs implement marketing remedies themselves because a new marketing vice president is thought to be too expensive, or because they believe that they are best equipped for the job. When it is necessary to rebuild credibility

CHARACTERISTICS OF SMALL HIGH-TECH TURNAROUND MANAGERS

1. **Professional management expertise**
   New CEOs appointed from outside have substantial management experience. Few are under 45 years of age. They include managers who have held senior positions in companies such as IBM and Hewlett Packard. The main reasons why professional management expertise is valued are:
   - a "professional manager" is able to implement systems to get control of cash, costs, production problems and inventory;
   - the turnaround manager, particularly in small companies, is required by the pressures of the turnaround and cash constraints to act in a number of functional roles: head up business and marketing strategy; act as VP, Finance; co-ordinate improved production. A strong management background gives a better grounding for individuals to act in a number of roles.

2. **Understanding of techology**
   An understanding of technology is thought desirable. However, technological skills—often the main strength of the founder—are treated with suspicion, especially among venture capitalists, since such skills are associated with lack of managerial skills.

3. **Personal motivation**
   Motivation is rated as a key success factor. Executives and venture capitalists comment alike that the turnaround manager has to be able to operate in a small company environment—and enjoy it. As one venture capitalist put it:

   > "... The critical issue is what motivates the managers. Can they live without their expense account, their Mercedes? Do they really want to get their hands dirty or do they believe the turnarounds a quick and easy way to make money ..?"

4. **Interpersonal skills**
   One of the major challenges for the turnaround manager is the need to rebuild morale internally; the need to appoint capable people to the team, and to motivate those people; the need to build customer confidence; the need to maintain the confidence of the venture capitalists. Those who successfully manage these challenges are usually considered to be particularly charismatic and dynamic individuals.

Source: Based on interviews with US venture capitalists and successful turnaround managers.

Figure 9.1

with customers, the CEO often thinks it is critical that customers should have direct contact with the individual at the top of the organization.

TACKLING THE CASH CRISIS

Once the new chief executive is installed, his or her priority is to tackle the cash crisis which has hit the company. There are four major strategies commonly used: (1) Immediate implementation of tight financial and other controls; (2) seek additional sources of finance; (3) cut costs to stop the haemorrhaging; (4) institute an asset-reduction programme, if at all possible.

Sometimes the cash situation is so bad that a financial rescue package has to be put in place either before, or concurrent with the appointment of a new chief executive. The investors in a Californian manufacturer of disk drives for use in computer back-up systems had to inject cash to fund the payroll the day before the new chief executive arrived. The new CEO took command with $6m cash infusion; and he reduced employee numbers by 30% within a few days. He commented: "... Whatever else is wrong, you have to sort out the cash position. It's either that or bankruptcy. Then you have to cut costs or else you'll face the same cash crisis."

The four strategies used for tackling the cash crisis are outlined below.

Implement Tight Financial Controls

Tight financial control covers budgets, cash flow forecasts, capital expenditure and knowledge of manufacturing and overhead costs. These are important in all turnarounds but existing controls are typically poor in small firms. New procedures and systems will have to be introduced extremely quickly, something which is obviously easier to do in a small firm than a large firm. Three types of new control system are commonly needed to control cash flow, costs and risk.

Cash flow systems. Emphasis on systems that monitor cash are

Implementing financial control: An example

When the new chief executive joined the company, there were fifteen people working in the finance function. They had been "treated like dirt" by the founders, whose philosophy revolved around getting everything done as cheaply as possible. Immediately, he got rid of all the poor quality people because the department was overmanned, and replaced any that needed replacing with high quality people. "I got rid of four and hired one." He claimed that he halved the staff and doubled the productivity. He did this by instilling some commercial awareness to the department and by making them enthusiastic about the company.

An example of the type and style of the things he did to instill commercial awareness and commitment to the objectives of the company can be illustrated by the cash balance chart that hangs in the Accounts Department. Every day the cash balance is reconciled and plotted on a large chart in the accounts office, where it is visible to everyone who walks in and everyone responsible for it. It is immediately obvious whether cash is being controlled effectively or not, and acts as a constant reminder to those responsible for collecting payments and paying creditors what the implications of their actions are.

The chief executive's openness with the staff allowed him to make public all kinds of information that might otherwise remain hidden in the company records. He could then use this information to educate and motivate the staff. He could explain why certain parameters are important to the success of the company, and used the information as the basis of rewards and competition between the staff. Three examples make the point more clearly:

1 Previously, the sales staff were paid on orders taken, which did not help the company cash flow or bad debt situation; now they only get paid their commission when the cash is received from the customer. This encourages them to follow up on orders taken and ensure that they are paid promptly; it also makes them think about who they are selling to because there is no point in them wasting their time on a call which might default on payment, as they will not receive any commission for the order placed.
2 The MD restructured the sales incentive scheme so that it became more and more attractive to sell higher volumes. There is no limit on the earnings the sales representatives can make, and the young representatives they now employ are earning very good salaries.
3 The company has arranged for the weekly sales figures to be available on Friday afternoons at 5.00 p.m. The representatives gather round and wait to find out who has made the highest sales figures for the week, and there is a great deal of good-natured competition surrounding this "event". Again, charts are in the sales office showing the star performers for the week, month, and year to date.

The whole motivation scheme revolves around the data that the Finance Department produces, and it has changed its role from being a staff function which produced the end of year results to being the centre of the company, providing information for all the other areas and helping them to understand the impact that they are having on the overall company performance.

Figure 9.2

necessary in all situations. Monthly cash flow forecasts are useless since there are likely to be huge weekly and daily fluctuations in both cash in-flow and out-flow. Effective systems require good financial people with a commercial awareness about the company and a commitment to its objectives. Figure 9.2 provides an interesting example of how one small high-tech firm gained financial control.

Costing systems. Small firms rarely have adequate cost information to know which products and which customers are profitable. In small high-tech firms where margins can be rapidly eroded, and volumes can change overnight, the profitability of the firm's various product-market sectors needs regular monitoring. Regular customer or market segment profitability analysis needs to be built in as part of such a system, with particular attention being paid to the way in which overheads are allocated to customers. Since gross margins ought to be quite high for small high-tech firms, allocation of overheads becomes critical in determining profitability.

Controlling risk. Since one of the major causes of crisis is the cancellation or delay of major contracts, it is appropriate for some firms to introduce simple risk control systems. Thus, one company had adequate financial control systems, but no real system for evaluating large contracts. As the result of being in crisis, they have now developed a "warts report" which is a system whereby each contract is evaluated on the basis of ten factors which have caused contracts to go wrong in the past. If a project has a high score out of ten, then it is rejected.

Seeking Additional Sources of Finance

Unlike conventional turnarounds where obtaining additional funds is difficult, new finance is often available to the small high-tech firm if they can convince financial backers—often venture capitalists—that the business still has potential. Venture capitalists rarely refinance in a crisis without substantially diluting existing equity holders or demanding major strategic and management changes. A venture capitalist with considerable experience of turnarounds said: "It takes some convincing to throw in financing when the company is on the point of collapse. And the only way bankers will be convinced is if they know the knife will go in."

That said, there are innumerable examples of venture capitalists giving extraordinary levels of support to small high-tech firms in crisis in the hope of very high returns. There appear to be three critical reasons why venture capitalists lend such support: (1) the loss-making company is developing a proprietary technology; (2) the market opportunity is perceived to be strong; and (3) the impact of the founder. One venture capitalist commented: "Well, it had a lot to do with the charisma of the founder. But underlying that was our conviction that if the company could get the product right, the rewards would be astronomical."

Debt financing is almost never available to small high-tech firms in crisis. The normal financing instrument is new equity or some type of convertible preference share.

Cost Reduction

The most common source of cuts is typically in staff, which is not surprising since high overheads tend to be one of the causes of crisis, but the exact nature of the overhead reduction depends on the intensity of the crisis. Immediate and drastic overhead cost reduction is a characteristic of the successful turnaround situation, with as much as 50% of the management staff being cut in some companies. The aim is to lower the firm's break-even point. At Apple Computer, the break-even point was lowered by almost $400m a year in 1985 on revenues of $1.9 billion through cost-reduction programmes.

As a general rule, staff cuts are in administrative areas rather than in research and development, since without maintaining (and maybe bolstering) product development activity, there is little likelihood of a sustainable turnaround. In addition, there are the usual cost-cutting measures of turning off unnecessary lights, making phone calls at cheaper times, no unnecessary travel, etc. Since small firms tend to have only one site, there is usually limited opportunity for significant rationalization. Where the firm has developed or grown with multiple sites, there may be the opportunity to integrate operations. One UK manufacturer of scientific equipment integrated its automatic test equipment business with its test instrument operations. This allowed increased utilization of manufacturing capacity and permitted some economies in sales and distribution.

Cost reduction by reducing manufacturing costs has a somewhat longer time horizon and is not a feasible strategy for specialist niche manufacturers who are price takers as far as raw material and equipment supplies are concerned. Some productivity improvement may be possible in the manufacturing area and these are discussed later in this chapter.

Cost reduction strategies do not of course generate cash, but, if implemented quickly and drastically enough, they can stop the company bleeding to death. The cash effect will vary by country, since in some European countries the severance pay required by law could actually worsen the short-term cash flow position. However, many small high-tech firms in crisis are young companies with relatively high staff turnover, which means that severance pay requirements are reduced, since the amount is usually calculated in part based on length of service.

Asset Reduction

Few small firms have much in the way of fixed assets that can be sold off either directly or on a sale and lease back basis, although two UK firms in the study did just that to solve their immediate cash needs. Divestment, which is the most common cash generating strategy adopted by large companies in a crisis, is, as might be expected, much less commonly used by smaller companies. However, where firms have diversified this is an important option.

The major emphasis on asset reduction in small high-tech companies is reduction of working capital. As shown in the previous chapter, companies lose control of working capital very rapidly leading up to the crisis point. Small high-tech firms in crisis tend to reduce working capital significantly during the year in which the crisis is at its peak, or during the following year. However, in most cases the reduction is only a return to previous levels, as witnessed by one company that doubled its working capital days to 308 days in the year prior to crisis, and then cut them back to 164 days as part of the recovery plan.

The personal computer companies provide the most dramatic examples of inventory reduction. Huge discounts are usually required to move surplus inventory quickly, particularly since news of the company's problems makes dealers and customers less willing to buy if they think there is a chance the firm will go bust. At Apple, inventory reduction was key. To quote John Sculley:

> "Del and Debi worked out a way to manage the inventory down, partly through a European deal in which we sold thousands of Apple IIs at steep discounts. More than anything else the deal bought us time. Our accounting policies required us to write off all inventories beyond six months. This barter agreement siphoned off inventories, lowering the size of our write off."[4]

IMPROVING EMPLOYEE MORALE

It is curious to think at one moment of drastic staff reductions and then in the next of building morale, but virtually all new chief executives in high-tech turnarounds say that rebuilding morale levels is an early priority. Most CEOs talk of the great lengths they will go to to encourage staff. They use a variety of methods to improve commitment to the ailing companies. For some, rebuilding morale is a matter of doing "small things". One CEO related:

> "In many ways it is the little things that count. I was met coming into the office this morning by three of the programmers, who casually suggested having breakfast. I never turn that sort of suggestion down. It gives me a chance to communicate my hopes for the company; to tell the staff that the management believes that the company has a future; to hear their problems; and to tell them the realities about the company. Everybody here knows how tight it is."

Rebuilding morale is about leadership, changing the organization culture and, above all, communications. The organizational characteristics of small high-tech firms (as described in Chapter 4) have a big influence on how this should be carried out. The tough, archetypal, no-nonsense turnaround manager described in *Corporate Recovery* (Slatter, 1984) is unlikely to be the right person to improve employee morale. High-tech employees are a different breed to employees in conventional companies, and need to be treated with a lighter touch. They need to be inspired and encouraged to meet tough targets rather than be subjected to constant criticism for failing to be the best. This is particularly true in a crisis when employees are feeling insecure, even if they are the survivors of a drastic cost and asset reduction exercise. If top management is not careful, the inherent mobility of the high-tech employee will see key technical resources leave the company. This would lead to an already fragile situation becoming even more fragile.

High-tech employees tend to be cynical of new management, particularly those coming in from outside who give the impression they know best. They do not readily accept new strategic directions and exhortations from top management. Their attitude tends to be to wait and see: to let the new chief executive prove him or herself. Thus, top management must work hard to get their message accepted. Although flat organization structures tend to facilitate good communications, emotional acceptance of the necessary changes is still hard to achieve. Changes in top management's technological outlook or philosophy are hard for middle managers and engineers to accept in small high-technology firms. The outward appearance of openness and flexibility to change can soon disappear when new ideas are introduced by top management. Thus, when Apple management decided it had to make Apple Computer into more of a "systems company", middle management rebelled and demanded a show-down meeting with John Sculley. They considered systems products dull and boring—a philosophy which did not fit with what they were trying to do at Apple! According to Sculley, a crisis was averted when he explained how the new moves were still consistent with the original Apple philosophy. [5] At the end of the day, nothing succeeds like success in turning the company around. Some cynics may remain, but the morale of the vast majority of employees will be improved as the company returns to profitability and, above all, begins to re-establish its reputation in the market-place and the local community.

REGAINING CREDIBILITY WITH CUSTOMERS AND SUPPLIERS

How to regain credibility in the market-place after a crisis is a key issue for those small high-tech firms that have been damaged by quality or delivery problems. However, all small high-tech firms that have been in a crisis have a job to do in restoring customer confidence. A venture capitalist suggested:

> "Often, high-tech companies are battling to persuade large customers, who depend in a critical function on the type of product, that their product should be trusted; that the benefits outweigh relying on trusted names like IBM. Often, because the product is proprietary, the company succeeds. But if things go wrong it is a much bigger battle to persuade companies to come back a second time. That's one reason why high-tech turnarounds can be so difficult."

To take one example, a company in Chicago began producing software for use by insurance companies which made the management of the "back room" functions much easier. The product was very effective, but even in the early days software projects ran over, and the company began to lose credibility with its customers. The new CEO commented:

> "Other than work on morale, I see my job as being Mr Nice Guy to the clients. I fend off irritated customers and build credibility with new ones. That job is getting easier as clients see that my company is now stable. It's taking a long time; it takes a lot of patience; but our clients are beginning to believe in us again."

Regaining credibility takes time. As a starting point, the new chief executive should contact all the company's customers, old and new, to introduce him or herself and explain what he or she is doing. Rumours will abound, often false rumours put about by competitors, and so it is critical that this is done immediately to arrest any further unnecessary loss of sales. Uncertainty in the minds of customers, be they dealers or end users, about the future of the company is a recipe for continued disaster. However, no firm that has lost credibility can expect to regain it completely overnight. Many of the remedial actions described in the following section on marketing and manufacturing must be implemented and seen to work before confidence will be fully restored. As with rebuilding internal morale, nothing breeds success like success: while a successful turnaround will restore customer confidence, customer confidence is needed to execute a successful turnaround.

While customer confidence is critical, supplier confidence and that of other third parties can also be crucially important if the suppliers' own success is intimately linked to the recovery of the crisis company. In many high-tech sectors, such as computers, success is dependent on a network of third-party companies creating products such as software and peripherals to expand the use of the firm's products. In a crisis situation, many of these firms—which themselves are fragile and may be overdependent on the fortunes of the crisis company—will quickly switch business focus, and abandon the crisis company. Quick management action is necessary to avoid the damage that this can have on the prospects of recovery.

Frequent and clear communication with the different customer, supplier and third-party constituencies is critical throughout the turnaround phase.

CHANGE OF BUSINESS FOCUS

The turnaround manager in a small high-tech firm—usually the new chief executive—does not have the luxury of taking a few months to decide on the appropriate business strategy the firm should adopt. Apart from the four actions already discussed, which nearly all small high-tech firms in crisis need if they are to recover successfully, change of business focus through product-market reorientation is the most widely used recovery strategy.[6] This should not be surprising, bearing in mind that four of the major causes of decline were product and price competition, changing market conditions and diversification.

The principal product-market strategies employed to reposition the company's business are:

- focus on specific product-market segments;
- withdrawal from market segments;
- introduction of value-added products;
- shift of position in the value-added chain.

Focus on Specific Product-Market Segments

Choice of *what* product-market segments to compete in is always the critical question—only then can firms decide *how* they are going to compete in their chosen segments. The decision to compete in any segment, however, has to be based on: (1) the inherent attractiveness of the segment; (2) the extent to which the firm can develop a competitive advantage in that segment; and (3) the firm's capability to implement its chosen strategy. Focus on a limited number of product-market segments is nearly always the strategy recommendation for small firms, since the resource base is narrow and the natural management tendency is to try to compete in too many segments simultaneously.

While product-market focus is important in nearly all small high-tech turnarounds, management must balance the need for focus against the danger of being overreliant on just a few customers. Chapter 8 showed how firms frequently get into trouble through the cancellation or delay of a major contract. The two objectives of focus and reducing reliance on a few customers need not be in conflict if the market segmentation issues are carefully thought through. What is required is to maximize product-market focus while at the same time ensuring as wide a customer base as possible. At Lattice Semiconductor, for example, Cyrus Tsui focused the business on the firm's proprietary product line—generic array logic devices—at the same time as rebuilding the customer base so that no single customer provides more than 10% of the company's revenues. [7]

Withdrawal from Market Segments

Withdrawal from one or more markets can take place either by divestment or by stopping all activities relating to a particular product-market segment. Where part of the business is a loss maker with little chance of developing a viable competitive position, it is clearly a drain on the small company's fragile resource base. Assuming the rest of the company's activities are profitable, divestment or closure are the only alternatives if the corporate entity is to survive. Divestment will always be the preferred option, even if for a nominal amount, due to the costs of closure. [8] In some instances, organizational restructuring is advisable prior to the disposal, so that the company can sell a "division" instead of just part of its business, or a product line. Such restructuring is purely "cosmetic" but sometimes makes the sale easier. The decision to close or divest a product line or business is typically based on a strategic assessment of the company's competitive position after taking into account both competitive forces and the company's capabilities. An analysis of competitive forces often shows that small high-tech firms, with their limited resources, are unable to compete with the "big names" as markets begin to globalize, in which case early divestment would be preferable. A realistic self-assessment of the company's capabilities can, however, be more difficult to obtain. Only rarely can a firm be found that knows its limitations. One firm that did, diversified into CAD software through acquisition, but eventually divested the acquisition because the management realized that they "only understood businesses with a sizeable hardware component, but not those that were totally dependent on software".

Not all divestment is due to pulling out of loss-making businesses. In some instances the reason for divestment is given as the "lack of fit" with existing businesses, or lack of fit with the company's long-term strategy. In both cases though, the underlying logic for divestment still rests on top management's assessment of market attractiveness and the company's limited capabilities.

Introduction of Value Added Products

Where one of the principal causes of crisis for the small high-tech company is product or price competition one common approach is to develop value-added products, either by enhancing the capabilities of existing products, or by bundling parts of the existing product range together. Adding value to products may mean adding services to enhance the total product offering, or may mean adding additional services to an existing service business. The most commonly used approach is when product manufacturers start to sell systems as their core basic products start to behave like commodity products. A systems approach involves a greater degree of differentiation and more customization. It therefore plays to the strength of the smaller company, although it no longer guarantees success as it might have done ten years ago. Today, many of the largest high-tech companies have had to move to a predominantly systems approach in order to maintain margins as whole sectors of the electronics industry have become virtual commodity markets.

Shift of Position in the Value Chain

Michael Porter's book, *Competitive Advantage*, places considerable emphasis on the need to analyze a firm's value chain in order to understand the sources of the firm's competitive advantage or disadvantage. [9] The value chain disaggregates a firm into its strategically relevant activities in order to understand the behaviour of costs and the existing and potential sources of competitive advantage. (A detailed account of such analysis is beyond the scope of this book; see Porter's (1985) *Competitive Advantage*.) However, the concept is useful in explaining one of the common strategies used by small high-tech firms to achieve business focus in a crisis—a shift in the focus of the firm's activities in the value chain. Typical shifts include: turning the firm from being a manufacturer into a distributor; greater use of subcontracting (particularly in the area of manufacturing); and greater emphasis on selling services rather than products.

The shift in position is invariably towards emphasizing those parts of the value chain where the firm has a cost or differentiation advantage; and pulling out of those areas where this is not the case. Using the terminology employed in Chapter 2 to discuss risk, the shift is virtually always from "hard" to "soft"—the opposite direction from the successful growing firm, which often takes on more risk and "hardens" as it develops. In a crisis the firm seeks to reduce risk as its resource base is eroded.

IMPROVED MARKETING

The installation of new marketing management is a prerequisite for improved marketing unless the chief executive is particularly inclined in this direction. Rebuilding credibility with customers is at the top of the priority list, but it is not marketing actions alone that will do this. Improved product development efforts and improved operations are often more important. What then, are the typical marketing improvements that must take place? There are four areas where changes are often needed: (1) redefining the product proposition, (2) increasing prices, (3) improving salesforce management, (4) changing distribution channels. In seeking correct decisions in these areas, there are no simple rules that can be applied. The only right way is to start by thoroughly analyzing customer and (where appropriate) dealer buying behaviour. The elements of the marketing mix flow logically from such an analysis. [10]

Redefining the Product Proposition

A manufacturer of computer-aided communication systems for use in specific customer applications (e.g. telephone customer service departments in credit card companies) was meeting significant sales resistance. The company had confidence in the product since it undoubtedly made the users' task much easier and improved efficiency. However, the marketing strategy had been to sell products direct to management information systems executives, who were reluctant to try an unproven technology. As the new CEO put it: "We are selling benefits, not systems. The company must sell to the users, people who can see the benefits of our products." The company persuaded customers to use the systems on a trial basis. Once the users themselves had enjoyed the benefits, sales increased.

This example provides a classic example of how the company had failed to analyze the needs of the end users and the buying process within the customer's own organization. As a result, they were unable to *position* their product correctly within the chosen product-market segment. The manufacturer of in-flight navigational equipment, referred to in Chapters 2 and 8, had a similar problem. Through "gimmicky" promotional efforts like giving away cheap watches, the company was positioning its product at the opposite end of the safety spectrum from where it ought to have been. New management overcame this problem by giving the product an enhanced image by using testimonials from its most prestigious customers.

Increasing Prices

Since underpricing is one of the causes of failure, where that has happened, increasing prices is the logical answer. The new CEO of a Silicon Valley company designing and manufacturing integrated circuits for use as semiconductors commented: "The company had no clear strategy and Sales and Marketing had no clear understanding of the pricing issues or of the technology ... it was often selling the product for less than the cost of manufacture ... in some cases prices were raised over 250%."

A second company, which manufactured tape drives, suffered from the same problem. On arrival, the new CEO found that money was being lost on every unit of production—material costs were higher than prices. The marketing department insisted that prices could not be raised. The new CEO raised prices across the board by 50% and no orders were lost.

Improving Salesforce Management

There are two issues which are critical to the small high-tech firm: (1) very careful targeting of the salesforce's efforts on the existing and potential customers, and (2) the recruitment, training and motivation of good, technically qualified salespeople. The issues are not unique and are faced by all companies using direct selling. However, implementation of changes in product-market focus and the importance of regaining customer credibility make both these issues particularly important for the small high-tech company.[11]

Changing Distribution Channels

Inappropriate marketing can sometimes mean the wrong channels of distribution are being used. The manufacturer of the in-flight navigational equipment mentioned earlier was, in addition to positioning this product wrongly, using an independent distributor. Independent distributors rarely provide enough push for a company's products. They are only rarely good at understanding and, hence, selling advanced technological products—they are merely order takers. The navigational equipment manufacturer ended up by establishing its own salesforce which concentrated on face-to-face selling to pilots so that the product benefits could be stressed.

Unfortunately for some small high-tech firms whose products need direct selling, the costs of establishing one's own sales force are too great, because the customer base is too fragmented and the dollar contribution for the typical order size fails to cover the cost of the salesman's visit. In such circumstances the company has to continue to rely on distributors, but its chances of success are considerably reduced.

MANUFACTURING CHANGES

In all the manufacturing companies in the study, the new CEO needed to institute dramatic changes to reduce costs, and/or improve quality. Changes most commonly took place in four areas: process engineering, delivery, sourcing and plant capacity.

Changes in Process Engineering

One cause of quality problems is poor process engineering, i.e. bad design of the manufacturing process. For one company, the process technology problems were so great that the new CEO was forced to shut down the production line twice—the second closure lasting for three weeks. Task forces were set up to solve the technical problems. The CEO commented: "... there was little point shipping product unless quality was good. Previously, people had felt that the company would go under unless product was shipped."

The appointment of a new technical expert to improve the production process is the usual starting point of the manufacturing turnaround. Existing technical people will typically have had their chance of solving the problem. Beyond a certain point—and certainly not too far into the crisis—management must call on outside technical expertise to help solve their process engineering problems. This may well upset existing staff, but any delay is likely to have a significant negative impact on cash flow.

Establish Targets to Meet Delivery Dates

This is a necessary step where the ailing company has missed delivery dates. There is little chance of regaining lost customer confidence if delivery promises continue to be missed. [12]

Sourcing

In those product-markets where severe price competition develops—typically high-volume, micro-electronic based products—it is essential for the ailing companies' survival to lower costs drastically. Off-shore sourcing is often the preferred route to do this. In one example, following the appointment of a new VP, Operations, the company set about establishing an external manufacturing base. While they were identifying sources in Hong Kong and Taiwan, they used value engineering to reduce costs by 25%. Improved processes cut a further 10%, but moving off-shore brought the total reduction in costs to 63%.

Where overseas sourcing is not feasible and the turnaround involves significant improvements in manufacturing to lower the cost base, as was necessary for example at Apple in 1984/85, improved sourcing is still one of the key manufacturing issues. At Apple, the number of vendors was reduced from 1500 to under 250. [13]

Reduce Manufacturing Capacity

Where the firm has been through a period of substantial growth prior to hitting a crisis and has developed multi-plant manufacturing facilities, a sudden drop in volume may mean plant closures are necessary to bring capacity in line with volume. Taking the example of Apple again, management closed three of their six factories in 1984, cutting 1200 jobs out of a total workforce of 5800 (60% of whom were manufacturing employees).[14]

INVESTMENT IN FOCUSED PRODUCT DEVELOPMENT

The one area which top management tries to avoid cutting back in small high-tech firms is the new product development function. Once a small firm gets behind in product development, it is very difficult to catch up. In theory, a firm can skip a generation of products and leap-frog straight into the following generation. While this may be feasible for a large company with large financial resources, it is rarely feasible for the small firm since their technical people tend to develop new products incrementally.

The challenges facing the new turnaround manager in this area are threefold: understanding the technology; deciding on what projects to focus; deciding how to speed up the process. Decisions in this area may involve the turnaround manager taking some significant risks. Expenditure on product development may have to increase significantly if the company has any chance of survival. Once again, Apple provides a good example. In John Sculley's words:

> When many people weren't sure we would even be profitable the following year, we also *accelerated product development expenses by 70 percent*. Not only did we have to gain control of the company, we had to prepare for a successful future. That also led to our $15 million investment in a Cray supercomputer in January of 1986, at a time when the public wasn't yet convinced that we had turned the company around. We bought the Cray to do simulations of future products to speed up the design of software development tools—to eliminate one of the reasons for the initial failure of the Macintosh.[15]

Seeq Technology tells a similar story. Even in the bad times of 1986, 20% of revenues went into research and development—an investment which started to pay off in 1987 as a new 256K CMOS E^2 chip was successfully introduced. [16] The future of high-tech companies is critically dependent on product development—and usually plays a lead role in any high-tech manufacturing turnaround.

Concomitant with such investment must be increased focus of the development effort—cutting out projects where both the combined market and technological risk of success is too great. Care must be taken not to throw out important core technologies, but in most high-tech development departments there are a number of "pet" projects which need eliminating on a regular basis. Some such projects may be true skunk works of the type favoured by writers on excellence and intrapreneurship, but the small firm cannot afford such luxuries in a crisis. What is needed is to harness the ingenuity of the development team to solve the critical problems of the hour.

Speeding up the product development process is likely to be critical to turnaround success if the technology is not to leap ahead of the firm's capabilities, and the firm's fragile and probably tentative market position is not to disappear altogether. Thus, one of Cyrus Tsui's turnaround strategies at Lattice Computer concentrated on reducing design cycle times. A 35–40% reduction was achieved in a matter of months.

FINANCIAL CHARACTERISTICS OF SUCCESSFUL TURNAROUNDS

Although based on an analysis of only 20 small high-tech firms, it is interesting to compare the financial performance of those companies that appear to have undertaken a successful turnaround, and those that have not. By comparing accounting data for three years before and two years after the crisis year, the following characteristics emerge for successful turnarounds:

- Dramatic sales growth occurs within two years of the crisis point. Sales growth usually stops or declines slightly in the year prior to the crisis for all companies, but those that recover experience rapid sales growth after the turnaround. The sales growth is particularly strong in the second year after the crisis. In the failed recovery situations sales, perhaps not unexpectedly, continue to decline sharply (see Figure 9.3a).

- Profits bounce back immediately. Successful turnarounds are characterized by a severe drop in profits in the year prior to the crisis, but the turnaround is quick. The failed turnarounds tend to take longer to get into the real crisis and, by definition, do not regain their profitability (see Figure 9.3b).

- Debt levels are sharply reduced in the first year of the turnaround. Although small high-tech firms generally have relatively low borrowing levels due to the risks involved, debt levels do rise in the run-up to a crisis. What is noticeable, however, is that the successful recovery situations are those where the debt levels have been held steady in the year prior to the crisis, whereas in the failed situations, debt has continued to increase (see Figure 9.3c).

- The fixed asset base is expanded quickly. In the year prior to the crisis, fixed asset investment has usually stopped. After the crisis, the recovered firms are able to expand on the back of their return to profitability, while those firms that continue in a crisis reduce their fixed asset base (see Figure 9.3d).

- Inventory levels are reduced sharply before the end of the crisis year. Firms which failed to recover continued to increase stocks up to one year after the crisis before making very rapid adjustments (see Figure 9.3e).

- Receivables (debtor days) are reduced during the crisis year to normal levels, and controlled thereafter. Failed turnarounds, however, show a different pattern. Receivables are reduced to normal levels during the crisis year, but then control disappears and receivables jump sharply. In the study's sample, receivable days outstanding increased 80% in the year following the crisis year for failed turnarounds (see Figure 9.3f). It seems that customers are reluctant to pay their supplier once it becomes widely known that the firm is in deep trouble.

- Payables (creditor days) are also reduced to normal levels during the crisis year. It is noticeable that the successful recovery situations tend not to extend their payables

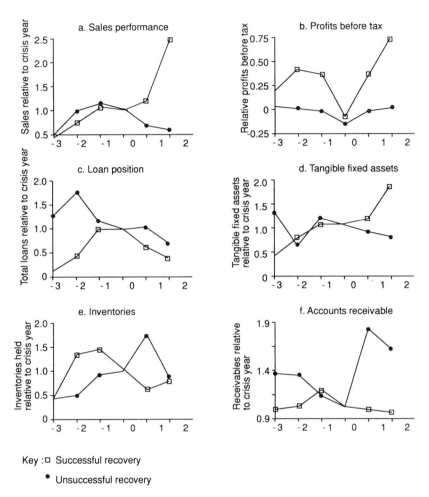

Key : □ Successful recovery

• Unsuccessful recovery

Figure 9.3 *Comparison of financial performance of successful and unsuccessful turnarounds of small high-tech firms**

dramatically in the two years prior to the crisis year, whereas the failed turnarounds have doubled the length of time they take to pay their suppliers in the two years prior to the crisis, and are forced to extend payables even further as they fail to recover.

---

*Based on averaged accounting data for 20 firms for three years before and two years after crisis. All averages for years prior to and after the crisis year (year zero) expressed as a percentage of the average in the crisis year.

Chapter 8 discussed the various reasons why small high-tech firms get into crisis so quickly. However, what is interesting is the speed with which some of them can get out of trouble. At Seeq Technology, for example, the company lost $24m on sales of $30.5m in the year ending September 20, 1986, but in the following year made a profit of $2m on sales of $44.6m. The speed of turnaround is helped by the fact that most serious attempts at turning around small high-tech companies are accompanied by an injection of additional finance which allows loans to be reduced, the situation regarding payables and receivables to be rectified, and further investment in fixed assets where appropriate. However, refinancing is obviously insufficient by itself.

FACTORS DETERMINING SUCCESSFUL RECOVERY

Five factors determine the likelihood of implementing a successful turnaround of a small high-tech firm:

1 the use of many strategies simultaneously;
2 the causes of decline;
3 industry characteristics;
4 the core technological competence within the firm;
5 the speed and vigour of implementation.

The Use of Many Strategies Simultaneously

Successful turnarounds need simultaneously to use most of the eight strategies discussed earlier in this chapter. Figures 9.4 and 9.5 show in summary form the nature of the strategies adopted at Lattice Semiconductor and Seeq Technology. While the details of the strategies differ, the overall approach is similar in each situation—the simultaneous implementation of seven or eight basic strategies. The turnaround of Apple Computer shows a similar mix of strategies was used.

There is little difference between the basic strategies used by different types of small high-tech firms; any differences tend to be ones of emphasis. In service firms, for example, senior

Crisis and recovery at Lattice Semiconductor

Founded in 1983, Oregon-based Lattice Semiconductor Corp. was in serious trouble by December 1986. Rahul Sud, its principal founder and CEO, had resigned under protest. Sud added to the multiple lawsuits pending against Lattice by suing the company and certain officers for libel when he left. There was no money in the bank—for two and a half months, no one had been paid. Forty per cent of the workforce had left or been laid off since September.

"We weren't running the company as a business," recalls Jan Johannessen, in *Electronic Business* (27 November, 1989), Vice President for Finance and Administration, who was in marketing at the time. "We didn't pay attention to revenue levels compared with expense levels. Sales were always going to take off next quarter." [3]

For the year ending March 30, 1987 Lattice reported revenue of $11.7m with net losses of $8.5m. Things were so bad that Lattice could not afford a janitor; employees took turns cleaning out the restrooms. In July, Lattice filed a petition for reorganization under Chapter 11 of the US Bankruptcy Code.

Two months later, the company emerged with a new business plan, plans for new management, and an increased focus on their proprietary product line—generic array logic (GAL) devices—which they believed could be a profitable niche market.

Over the next two years, Lattice was successful in raising almost $10m in operating funds, due mostly to the efforts of Chairman Norman Winningstead. But Winningstead had no interest in running the company on a day-to-day basis, so in September 1988 he hired Cyrus Y. Tsui, former Vice President and General Manager of the Programmable Logic Division at Advanced Micro Devices, who showed investors that Lattice was serious about turning the company around.

After joining Lattice, Tsui concentrated on improving the product development area. Within a year, design-cycle times were cut by 35% to 40%, and new products started to appear. Tsui believed that this was crucial to the success of the company. In addition, Tsui worked to rebuild the customer base, flatten the management structure, and institutionalize service, making it something company employees offer one another. The strategy appeared to pay off. In fiscal year 1989, Lattice made $2.2m on sales of $21.5m.

Sources:
(1) Anderson, M. A. "Semiconductors: Just When Lattice Thought It Was Safe ...", *Business Week*, 17 November, p. 158 (1986).
(2) Rice, V. "Comeback Kids: How Seeq and Lattice Got Out of Trouble", *Electronic Business*, 1 November, pp. 86–88, (1988).
(3) Rice, V. "Once Bankrupt, the Good Times Come Back to Lattice", *Electronic Business*, 27 November, pp. 38–41 (1989).
(4) Weigner, K. K. "How Lattice Almost Went Under", *Forbes*, 12 December, pp. 238–241 (1988).
(5) Buck, R. "Going for Broke", *Venture*, November, pp. 31–32 (1988).

Figure 9.4

Crisis and recovery at Seeq Technology

Seeq Technology came into being in 1981. The founders, led by Gordon Campbell, were all former Intel employees. They planned to make memory chips known as EEPROMS (electrically erasable programmable read only memories), or E-squares; it was believed that these superior chips would take over the $600m market held by the older PROMS.

Seeq raised $50m in venture capital, and a further $18m in 1983 in a public stock offering. Dataquest, a leading Silicon Valley research house, predicted that the E^2 market would grow to $1 billion by 1987. Seeq built up the company to support that market size.

Problems began early on: Seeq was a year late in shipping their first product. Intel filed a lawsuit against them, claiming that the founders had taken valuable technology with them when they left. By 1983, Seeq's salesforce realized that selling the E^2 was going to be more difficult than they had anticipated. Seeq had built its manufacturing facility to serve a $600m market, but it was turning out to be only around $60m.

The biggest buyers of chips, the data processing companies, just weren't interested. "In interviews," said McCranie in *Forbes* (19 April, 1988), "[Seeq] management would give all these occult reasons why the E-square market wasn't growing. Like the lack of standardization. That was baloney. The reason the market wasn't growing was that E-squares were, on average, five times more expensive than EPROMS. It was felt that innovation would occur, and the next thing you know E-squares would cost no more than EPROMS. That didn't happen."

Seeq management knew they had to produce some revenue, so in 1984 they decided to begin making the older EPROMS in addition to the E-squares. Seeq's revenues increased dramatically, from $9m in 1983 to $43m in 1984. But the good times were short-lived. Japan began flooding the market with chips, and between the last quarter of 1984 and the third quarter of 1985, the price of a standard 128K EPROM fell from $15 to $2. Seeq, which relied on EPROMS for 75% of sales, was making them for $5.

Campbell had left the company in the fall of 1984. His successor lasted less than a year, and was followed by a three-man "office of the president". In March 1986, J. Daniel McCranie took over as CEO. McCranie inherited a company in trouble. By May of that year, Seeq was down to $13 000 in the bank, and in the year ending September 1986, they lost $24m on sales of $30.5m. Drastic action was needed to save the company.

The workforce had shrunk from a peak of 700 employees down to 400, but McCranie felt it needed to be reduced further. Returning from the July 4th holiday weekend, he told managers to lay off a further 130 people, and to do it that afternoon, not the following week. This cut the weekly payroll from $310 000 to less than $200 000. They were able to keep the best people, but morale was low. Experienced R & D technicians were assigned to rote work in wafer fabrication, resulting in a jump in productivity. McCranie told these employees that their sacrifice was necessary to keep the firm alive.

McCranie next moved to cut back on other expenses. He rene-
gotiated all of the plant and equipment leases, effectively reducing payments by 50%; in return, he offered warrants to the lessors, allowing
them to buy stock in the company. Excess building space was released.
Almost every segment of the company was sliced, except R & D. They
got out of the EPROM market, except for a small profitable segment.

To raise needed cash, McCranie sold 14% of Seeq to Monolithic
Memories for S4m, and agreed to a four-year joint-technology pro-
gramme. A further $2m was brought in by a joint-development deal with
Motorola.

McCranie knew that the future of the company depended on product
development. Even in the bad times of 1986, 20% of revenues went to
R & D. In 1987, that development began to pay off. A new 256K CMOS
E^2 chip began to sell briskly. Flash E^2 chips also went into production,
costing one-quarter of what the full featured chips cost.

Seeq began to make money again in the first quarter of 1987. For the
year, they netted $2m on sales of $44.6m. At the end of the year, they
had $13m in the bank.

Sources:
(1) Rice, V. "Comeback Kids: How Seeq and Lattice Got Out of
    Trouble", *Electronic Business*, 1 November, pp. 86–88 (1988).
(2) Weigner, K. K. "You Can't Keep a Good Technology Down",
    Forbes, 19 April, pp. 51–53 (1988).
(3) Welles, E. O. "The Company Money Almost Killed", *Inc.*,
    November, pp. 46–61 (1988).

Figure 9.5

management is more likely to be bolstered rather than removed
in a crisis because the original founder is less likely to have
given up majority control to outside investors, as service businesses are less asset-intensive. Perhaps the most noticeable difference in emphasis is between the recovery of fast-growth and
slower-growth companies. In fast-growth situations, there is
usually a more fundamental shift in organization structures,
systems and culture as new management takes the opportunity
of dealing with the inevitable strains on the organizational
systems which are characteristic of fast-growth situations.

The Causes of Decline

In the earlier research into the turnaround of non-high-tech
companies it was found, perhaps not unexpectedly, that there

was an inverse relationship between the number of causes of decline and the chance of success: the fewer the causes the more likely the chance of success. For small high-tech firms this relationship does not appear to hold true. As was pointed out at the end of Chapter 8, a single cause of decline can just as easily lead to crisis as multiple causes of decline. It appears that, on average, there is little difference between the number of causes of decline between firms that recover and those that do not. In trying to look at the influence of causes of decline on the success of recovery strategies, the single most important issue that stands out is the influence of severe product competition on the firm's likely chance of recovery. Most common is competition with the firm's second generation product. If one of the firm's basic problems is failure to generate a robust second generation product, there is usually little that can be done to salvage the company.

The Market Sector Characteristics

Within the broad definition of high-technology industries used in this book there are many different industry sectors with distinctive competitive market and technological characteristics. These many and varied characteristics determine both the likelihood of success and the speed at which it can be achieved. The principal characteristics to be considered include:

- *Market growth rate.* The faster the growth rate of the firm's markets the easier the turnaround. Turnarounds are difficult in emerging markets.
- *Degree of market segmentation.* A more fragmented industry or more segmented market provides more opportunity for refocusing the business.
- *Competitive situation.* The absence of large, powerful competitors makes turnaround easier for the small company, although low barriers to entry may make developing a competitive advantage difficult.
- *The nature of the product.* A firm with more differentiated, less price-sensitive products is easier to turn around than one whose products are rapidly moving towards commodity status.

- *Powerful customers.* The absence of powerful customers makes price increases easier to implement.
- *Substitute technologies.* Firms competing against cost effective, substitute technologies find turnarounds more difficult.
- *Lead times.* Firms manufacturing capital goods face long lead times to win orders and sometimes long manufacturing lead times as well. Such a situation is extremely difficult to turn around since a prolonged period of negative cash flow is inevitable.
- *The business cycle.* Economic downswings are always a problem for firms making and servicing capital goods. The effect on other firms will vary, depending on the rate of growth of the market at the time the downswing occurs.

The Core Technological Competences

Since technology is at the root of the small high-tech firm, even if it is a service business, the firm's future is intimately connected to its technological competence. The need to invest in new product development is an integral part of most recovery strategies, and is sometimes central to recovery (as it was, for example, at Seeq Technology). Not surprisingly, therefore, product development is often the only area not cut back in a crisis. In theory, firms can buy in new competence if it is lacking, but two problems make this difficult. Firstly, good product development people are difficult to recruit if the firm is in a crisis. Bad news travels fast and nobody wants to join an obviously risky situation. Secondly, it takes too long to recruit a new team and bring it "up to speed" with the particular product technology. Speed of new product development is critical, hence the need to build as far as possible on the existing in-house competences.

Firms that rely on third-party technology often provide little added value. While the market is growing fast they can be profitable but as soon as a more competitive situation emerges, crisis rapidly ensues. These companies are near impossible to turn around as there is no core capability on which to build.

The Speed and Vigour of Implementation

Turnaround management always requires quick decisions and vigorous implementation, but nowhere is this more true than with a small high-tech firm. The firm typically has few assets apart from the skills and expertise of its people, who will leave the sinking ship fast if given half a chance. Profits can turn into horrendously large losses in a matter of weeks with the company moving into a negative net worth situation at astonishing speed. Failure to implement quickly will make recovery extremely unlikely unless yet another round of finance can be found. This becomes extremely difficult as the firm's technology and market positions erode to the point at which there is nothing left to salvage in the company.

IMPLEMENTING RECOVERY STRATEGIES

Action plans need to be developed for each of the eight turn-around strategies identified in this chapter. As with virtually all turnarounds, new management needs to take action on many fronts simultaneously and to implement its recovery plan in a determined and sometimes drastic way. As with conventional, non-high-tech turnarounds, there is a need to be almost ruthless in the implementation of the strategies. A slight adjustment to existing strategies is almost never adequate—drastic action is required to pull the company out of crisis. Thus, when implementing a cost reduction strategy, for example, it is almost always necessary to take more costs out than may seem practicable at first glance. Thus, when J. Daniel McCranie took over as CEO of Seeq, he had to reduce head count by an additional 130 people on top of the 300 that had already been laid off out of a total work force of 700. Turnaround managers should not be afraid to shrink drastically the already small size of firms in an effort to save the business from insolvency.

Speed of action is even more essential than in conventional turnaround situations, due to the extreme fragility of the typical small to medium-sized, technology-based firm. Chapter 8 showed how firms can get into trouble extremely quickly and lose a phenomenal amount of money very rapidly. There is, therefore, little time for analysis before "life and death" decisions concerning the future of the company have to be made. A rapid assessment of the situation is necessary, and since most small firms are relatively simple businesses this need not be a problem for an experienced manager. The small high-tech firm just does not have the luxury of going through the implementation phases of analysis, emergency actions and refocusing in a sequential order. In conventional turnarounds, emergency actions—asset reduction, refinancing, cost reduction and tighter financial controls—are usually necessary before a complete turnaround plan has been produced, and may indeed be implemented before any detailed analysis of the situation has taken place. Experienced turnaround managers often know what action they are going to take prior to their arrival at the crisis company.

Strategies which involve product-market refocusing, investment and organization building typically come after the emergency phase in the implementation time scale. This *cannot* be the case for the small high-tech firm. The turnaround manager has to implement new strategies in these areas simultaneously with the traditional emergency strategies. The reason for this is that the nature of the crisis facing small high-tech firms is different from that facing conventional firms, even small ones, in four ways:

1 they lose credibility with their customers at a phenomenal rate;
2 they suffer from product competition;
3 product quality problems are often a principal cause of decline;
4 employee morale declines extremely fast.

Some or all of these problems are present in every crisis, with the result that immediate action is necessary if the company is to have any long-term future. Finding and implementing the appropriate strategies to rectify these problems is more difficult. Strategies such as cost and asset reduction are relatively straightforward to formulate and implement, but strategies that involve new product-market directions and revitalizing the organization are more difficult. It is not always obvious, particularly in the absence of adequate market and competitor information, to know what segments to focus on, yet the organization needs a vision of the future from the chief executive if morale is to be re-established. It is the so-called "soft" issues—changing employee attitudes, changing the corporate culture and the nature of the communications that take place between management and employees—which appear to be more important in the small high-tech company. Perhaps this should not be surprising given the characteristics of these organizations described in Chapter 4. The successful implementation of recovery requires many actions, co-ordinated and mutually supportive, to maximize the effectiveness of the individual strategies.

SUMMARY

This chapter has discussed the eight recovery strategies commonly used by small high-tech firms in a crisis situation. They are: (1) appointment of new management; (2) strategies to tackle the cash crisis—tight financial controls, additional financing, cash and asset reduction programmes; (3) improve employee morale; (4) regain customer credibility; (5) change business focus; (6) improve marketing; (7) manufacturing changes; and (8) investment in focused product development.

The speed and magnitude of small high-tech turnarounds can be quite staggering. Fragility may mean fast decline into a crisis, but can equally mean rapid growth in sales and a dramatic turnaround in profitability. Successful turnarounds are characterized by the implementation of seven or eight of the basic strategies simultaneously.

Four factors appear to influence the likelihood of implementing a successful turnaround—the causes of decline, the market sector characteristics, the firm's core technological competence and, above all, the speed and vigour of the implementation effort.

NOTES

(1) Slatter, S. St. P. *Corporate Recovery: A Guide to Turnaround Management*. Penguin Books, London (1984).

(2) Sculley, J. and Byrne, J. *Odyssey ... a Journey of Adventure. Ideas and the Future*, Chapter 10. Harper & Row, New York (1987).

(3) Richman, T. "Who's in Charge Here?" *Inc.*, June, pp. 36–46 (1989).

(4) Sculley, J. *Odyssey*, ibid. p. 308.

(5) Sculley, J. *Odyssey*, ibid. p. 379.

(6) This result is similar to that found in Schendel, D., Patton, R. and Riggs, J. "Corporate Turnaround Strategies: A Study of Profit Decline and Recovery", *Journal of General Management*, Vol. 3, No. 3, Spring (1976).

(7) Rice, V. "Once Bankrupt the Good Times Come Back to Lattice", *Electronic Business*, November 27 (1989).

(8) Porter, M. "Please Note Location of Nearest Exit: Exit Barriers and Planning", *California Managmenet Review*, Vol. XIX, Winter (1976).

(9) Porter, M. *Competitive Advantage*. Free Press, New York, pp. 21–33 (1985).

(10) For a good discussion of high-tech marketing, see, for example, Davidow, W. *High Technology Marketing*. Free Press, New York (1986).

(11) For details on how to implement these strategies, see, for example, Davis, R. T. and Gordon Smith, F. *Marketing in Emerging Companies*. Addison-Wesley, New York (1984).

(12) The practical manufacturing systems needed to ensure delivery dates are met are covered in standard manufacturing texts. See, for example, Hill, T. *Manufacturing Strategy: The Strategic Management of the Manufacturing Function*. Macmillan, Basingstoke, Hampshire (1985).

(13) Sculley, J. *Odyssey*, ibid. p. 309.

(14) Sculley, J. *Odyssey*, ibid. p. 293.

(15) Sculley, J. *Odyssey*, ibid. p. 265.

(16) Rice, V. "Comeback Kids: How Seeq and Lattice got out of Trouble", *Electronic Business*, November 1 (1988).

Appendix:
Research Approach

The ideas on which this book is based arose out of a series of research projects undertaken when I was Director of the Institute of Small Business Management at the London Business School. Small high-tech firms were very much in favour in 1983/1984, and Coopers & Lybrand agreed to fund a research unit within the Institute of Small Business to look specifically at the management problems of small technology-based firms. The aim was to explore the management problems these firms face with the intention of generating concepts and models rather than to test any formal propositions. The objective was to provide some pragmatic advice for those running, advising and investing in small high-tech firms on what factors lead to superior performance. The methodology was varied and open-ended, but it may be useful to some readers to describe how the data was collected and analysed.

The project was launched with a pilot study in 1984 to identify the problems and issues facing small high-tech firms. Specific studies were then undertaken into the new product development process, diversification, problems of managing growth, the internationalization process, the causes of decline and subsequent turnaround strategies, the motivation of technical employees, and the relationships of small firms to larger competitors.

SAMPLE FIRMS

The initial sample for the pilot study was chosen almost entirely as a result of the existing management contacts of the Institute of Small Business and was heavily biased to firms which already had venture

capitalists as investors. The sample was not scientifically representative but I am confident that it included a broad range of manufacturing and service businesses that met the broad criteria set out in
Chapter 1 for a small high-tech firm. Biotechnology companies were
specifically excluded from the pilot sample, since we planned to look
at biotechnologies as a separate set of firms with unique
characteristics.

From the pilot study a series of separate projects was undertaken
on the issues we identified. Some of the firms used in the pilot study
were revisited and included in the subsequent projects, while in other
projects, a new set of companies was interviewed. Two of the projects
involved interviewing US-based firms—the study of turnaround
strategies, and the study of the internationalization process. In total
25 interviews were undertaken in North America including ten interviews with the US subsidiaries of UK firms. Two projects required
samples in specific industry sectors—the project on the motivation of
technical employees and the project on new product development
processes. In these situations the sample sizes were 11 and 12 firms
respectively but all the other projects used sample sizes of between
20 and 30 firms. The project on the motivation of technical employees
undertaken by Dr Garden focused on only 11 firms in the software
industry, but it used a different methodology from the other projects
(see below). The CAD/CAM industry was chosen as a sector for
studying new product development processes because it was a young
industry where we could identify all the players easily. Our sample
covered virtually all the players in the emerging CAD/CAM market
of the early 1980s in the UK.

Altogether over 100 firms participated in the research during the
period 1984 to 1990. Access to firms was not a problem: most firms
that were approached agreed to be interviewed.

DATA COLLECTION

Interviews with the chief executive and/or some of the functional
directors was the main process for gathering data. Typically the interview process began with the history of the firm, its strategy and
organization, and then focused on a set of questions that had been
designed to collect data about the specific issues relevant to the
research topic. Individual interviews normally lasted between $1\frac{1}{2}$ and
2 hours. Interviews were purposely open ended in an attempt to
learn as much as we could about the nuances of the small firm.

Almost half the interviews were taped and transcribed while in the

other interviews detailed notes were taken and written up as company profiles. Interviewees were assured of the confidentiality of the
meetings. All of the quotes that are attributed in the book to particular
companies or individuals are from public sources. The few quotes
used from the interviews have not been identified with specific
individuals or specific sample companies. In the work undertaken by
the High Tech Unit on the motivation of technical employees, interviewing was supplemented by questionnaires distributed to all the
technical employees to ascertain various behavioural characteristics.
The details of this research are to be found in Dr Garden's articles and
working papers which have been footnoted in the text.

In addition to interview data, we collected, where available, annual
reports, press clippings, product literature, other relevant articles
about the company and its market. In some instances companies gave
us access to unpublished in-company reports. Nevertheless, interviews remained the prime source of data, since apart from those firms
that had had a public flotation, the amount of extra information available on small firms is strictly limited.

PROGRESS TOWARDS CONCLUSIONS

As each project was completed, the results were presented in work-
shop sessions attended by the participating companies and professionals involved with small technology-based firms (venture
capitalists, accountants and bankers). A series of open presentations
were also made to high-tech firms not participating in the research.
All these sessions provided valuable feedback and ensured that the
conclusions were practically oriented. Papers were also presented at
various academic conferences, including two at the Strategic Management Society Conference in Boston in 1987 and San Francisco in
1989.

During the time that the various projects were undertaken in the
High Tech Unit at London Business School, interest by the academic
community in entrepreneurship, and in particular in the unique management problems of high-tech firms, has rapidly developed in North
America. Some of the interest on small high-tech firms has included
more scientific testing of some of the propositions put forward in this
book. Most of this new academic research corroborates the general
findings and conclusions put forward and, where appropriate, the
findings of such research have been incorporated in the book.

Although the study of small high-tech firms is still in its infancy, there are enough similar findings emerging from different research studies for me to feel confident that the ideas put forward in this book are generalizable assertions, which if followed sensibly, will improve the performance of small high-tech firms.

Index

Index compiled by Annette J. Musker